P9-ELI-218

The
Kwangju
Uprising

A Pacific Basin Institute Book

The Pacific Basin Institute at Pomona College

Now entering its twentieth year of service, the Pacific Basin Institute at Pomona College remains dedicated to its original goal of furthering intelligent communication between the nations of the Pacific Basin and increasing knowledge among Americans of the cultures, politics and economics of the Asia/Pacific countries.

Since moving to Pomona College in 1997, PBI has greatly extended the scope of its activities. Our Pacific Basin Archive of film, video and documentary material, based on the footage used for *The Pacific Century* TV series, has expanded to include more documentary and feature films. PBI's on-going Library of Japan, the first in a planned program of translations from Asian languages.

Pacific Basin Institute Books published By M. E. Sharpe

The Kwangju Uprising
Eyewitness Press Accounts of Korea's Tiananmen
Henry Scott-Stokes and Lee Jai Eui, editors

The Vietnamese War
Revolution and Social Change in the Mekong Delta
David Elliott

The Nanjing Massacre
A Japanese Novelist Confronts Japan's National Shame
by Honda Katsuichi
Frank B. Gibney, editor
Karen Sandness, translator

Silk and Insight: A Novel
by Mishima Yukio
Frank B. Gibney, editor
Hiroaki Sato, translator

SENSŌ: The Japanese Remember the Pacific War
Letters to the Editor of Asahi Shimbun
Frank B. Gibney, editor
Beth Cary, translator

The Kwangju Uprising

Eyewitness Press Accounts of Korea's Tiananmen

Foreword by President Kim Dae Jung

Henry Scott-Stokes and Lee Jai Eui, Editors

An East Gate Book

M.E.Sharpe
Armonk, New York
London, England

An East Gate Book

Copyright © 2000 by Kwangju Citizens' Solidarity

All rights reserved. No part of this book may be reproduced in any form
without written permission from the publisher, M. E. Sharpe, Inc.,
80 Business Park Drive, Armonk, New York 10504.

www.mesharpe. com

Library of Congress Cataloging-in-Publication Data

The Kwangju uprising : Eyewitness Press accounts of Korea's Tiananmen / edited by
Henry Scott-Stokes and Lee Jai Eui.
    p. cm. — (Pacific Basin Institute book)
"An East gate book."
ISBN 0-7656-0636-4 (alk. paper) — ISBN 0-7656-0637-2 (pbk. : alk. paper)
    1. Kwangju Uprising, Kwangju-si, Korea, 1980. 2. Korea (South)—Politics and
government—1960–1988. I. Scott-Stokes, Henry, 1938– II. Lee, Jai-eui. III. Series.

DS922.445.K86 2000
951.904′3—dc21   00-021813
                                                  CIP

Printed in the United States of America

The paper used in this publication meets the minimum requirements of
American National Standard for Information Sciences
Permanence of Paper for Printed Library Materials,
ANSI Z 39.48-1984.

BM (c) 10   9   8   7   6   5   4   3   2   1
BM (p) 10   9   8   7   6   5   4   3   2   1

To the memory of Yun Sang Won and hundreds of others
who died in Kwangju during May 1980 or thereafter
from injuries received in the uprising; to the memory of others
who took up the struggle in the years that followed
and died often solitary deaths; and for those who survived
but could not lead fruitful lives.

To some among us comes that implacable day...

—C.P. Cavafy, *Che Fece . . . Il Gran Rifutio*, tr. Lawrence Durrell.

CONTENTS

Part One: Two Korean Voices

Part Two: The Foreign Press

Part Three: The Korean Press

WORKS OF ART, PHOTOS, AND MAPS

The woodblocks featured in this book are the work of Hong Sung Dam. They were lent by the artist. Hong, a witness of the Kwangju uprising, created these works when he was twenty-five years old. The posthumous photo of Yun Sang Won was taken in the Provincial Hall on the morning of May 27, 1980, by Norman Thorpe, who lent the work for this publication. Other photos derive from sources contacted by Kwangju Citizens' Solidarity. The maps of Kwangju during the uprising were prepared by Lee Jai Eui and Cho Yang Hoon.

FOREWORD

Kim Dae Jung, President of the Republic of Korea

The events that took place in Kwangju in May 1980 still trouble me. Yes, I feel guilt over the deaths of those young people who were killed by troops in broad daylight on the city's main thoroughfares—Chungjang-ro and Gumnam-ro—and at the Provincial Hall. There was nothing I could do to save them.

How shall I put it? The city was invaded by ghouls on the morning of May 18, twenty years ago. On the previous day, Saturday, May 17, 1980, I was dragged from my home in Seoul by armed soldiers. I was held and interrogated at the headquarters of the Korean Central Intelligence Agency (KCIA). My ordeal lasted for forty days. Finally, I received a visitor. This person held ultimate power in the nation, which was under martial law at the time. The man in question—a Martial Law Command officer—made me an offer: "Cooperate with us, and we will give you anything you ask." He added: "Should you decline, we will have to mete out capital punishment." Seeing me grope for an answer, that man departed. He left a pile of newspapers for me to read. He also left a note requesting a positive response to his proposal.

I read the newspapers. This was how I learned, for the first time, that a series of demonstrations had broken out in Kwangju on May 18. The demonstrators had demanded my release and called for an end to martial law. A ten-day struggle that followed had finally been crushed by the army. Many were killed (there were 200 or more victims, I heard later). Thus I learned about the "Kwangju Democratization Movement," as we called it later, from newspapers that carried only incomplete, warped reports of what had happened.

The shock was huge. I lost consciousness on the spot. After a prison doctor revived me. I had to face reality. It was the worst form of torture. Obliged to accept the fact of my powerlessness in the face of events, I was weighed down with shame.

That night I wept in my cell at the KCIA. I had been weakened physically and emotionally in the course of my forty days of imprisonment. However, the example of the victims of this outrage in Kwangju gave me the strength to refuse the generals' enticing offer of mercy in return for my cooperation. I preferred to die in the name of democracy and for the sake of the Korean people. Thus it came about that I was accused of being the chief instigator of the Kwangju "rebellion"—of plotting the violent overthrow of the government. I was tried on a charge of treason, found guilty, and sentenced to death.

Three years later—my sentence had been commuted to life in prison in early 1981, and I was later freed—I was shown a video of what happened at Kwangju. Watching it was again my worst torture ever. I witnessed, over and over again, the cruelty of the soldiers. Yet I watched the whole thing. What spirit the people showed! I was overwhelmed by that video—by the active principles as I see them, of the Kwangju Democratization Movement:

1. Human rights is a first principle. Freedom, democracy, and human rights are the values. This was the banner under which Kwangju rose up against armed suppression. The unarmed people resisted the guns of our then military rulers.
2. Nonviolence is a second principle. The citizens of Kwangju fought bare-handed for human rights under the banner of freedom, democracy, and nonviolence. When they resisted, they were shot down with guns. Only then, for self-protection, did they take up weapons.
3. A mature citizenry is third. After the military and the police were driven out—they left the city in disorder—there was no robbery or looting in Kwangju. There was, however, camaraderie; and concern for the weak.
4. A peaceful attitude is another principle. Despite the fact that the fabric of society had been torn apart, there were no incidents of revenge during the five days when the city was under self-rule.

The people of Kwangju carried on, convinced that justice would prevail. There is an international aspect to this. The spirit of Kwangju is not a monopoly of Koreans, something we keep to ourselves. That spirit is cherished by mankind at large—wherever democracy and human rights are respected.

Let us remember that back in 1980 the Kwangju Movement was portrayed by the martial-law authorities as "rioting." The citizens were condemned as rioters, rebels, and pro-communists. They deserved capital punishment by massacre, the generals in Seoul decided. The people of Kwangju were depicted by the press, under army censorship, as "hooligans." Nothing was said of the actual motivation—to resist injustice. The truth was distorted by manipulation and censorship.

Yet justice was done eventually. The outcome was a victory for democracy. The name of Kwangju stands as a symbol of justice for the oppressed. Kwangju became a holy spot. Meanwhile, "traitor" that I once was, I now serve as President of the Republic of Korea—an honor I would like to share with the citizens of Kwangju.

This book is a work of history. It records what foreign correspondents and Korean journalists saw in Kwangju in May 1980. The journalists had a duty to record what they saw, brushing aside an official cover-up. In other words they had to furnish objective accounts and let the world know the facts (unavailable to Koreans due to military censorship). Still, one also finds here elements of the subjective. These reporters were compelled to describe what they saw—thereby letting those who died before their eyes live on. Here are confessions, accounts of personal conflicts, and instances of introspection, as well as reporting. I pay my respects to the contributors, to the Korean Press Club, and to Kwangju Citizens' Solidarity.

Seoul, November 30, 1999

INTRODUCTION AND ACKNOWLEDGMENTS

Henry Scott-Stokes and Lee Jai Eui

The aim of this book is to unveil—using journalists' eyewitness accounts published in the West for the first time here—the course of events during a ten-day period in the provincial city of Kwangju, South Korea, starting on Sunday, May 18, 1980. Some of the contributions raise the thorny topic of U.S. accountability for an imbroglio often compared to the Tiananmen Square Incident of 1989. On both occasions soldiers were unleashed on unarmed students and citizens. But the record is not in every way comparable. Thus far the outcome has been a lot more favorable in Korea than in China. We can now see that the Kwangju uprising was a turning point in Korean history—toward freedom and away from tyranny—thanks to the courage of hundreds of young people who were killed at Kwangju. These days human rights are prized as highly in South Korea as anywhere in Asia. South Korea wholly surpasses China in terms of respect for human rights. Meanwhile, Koreans have become accustomed to wider horizons, as found in Kim Dae Jung's 1999 proposal, put forward in a speech to the Japanese parliament, for a "tripartite" effort at regional cooperation by China, Japan, and Korea. The idealism found in Korea, which is once again engaged in rapid economic growth, has its origin, or at least gained strength following on the Kwangju uprising. Yesterday's student activists in Kwangju—many survived—are today's Rotarians in the city, as Bradley Martin notes in his contribution.

We would like to thank the following for their help. First, the journalists, both Korea and Western, who gladly offered their contributions to us; second, the artist Hong Sung Dam, who lent his woodblock prints, created shortly after the Kwangju uprising, when he was twenty-five years old—Mr. Hong did a cover design for an earlier English-language version of this work published in Korea in 1997 under the title *Kwangju in the Eyes of the World,* and he allowed use of one of his woodblock prints for the cover of this volume; third, those many, often unknown photographers whose work we have used, including Na Kyung Taek of Yonhap Press; fourth, Cho Yang Hoon for his map design for the original *Kwangju in the Eyes of the World*—his efforts helped Lee Jai Eui to produce the maps found in this work.

Special thanks to Norman Thorpe, for permission to use his photograph of Yun Sang Won taken after Yun was killed at the Provincial Hall on May 27, 1980. We also thank the family of Yun Sang Won, who loaned photographs of that outstanding man; his younger brother Yun Tae Won brought us the photos on behalf of his father Yun Sok Dong. In addition we would like to thank those who selected and translated the Korean language manuscripts. They are Professor Gyonggu Shin of Chonnam National University, who took overall responsibility for translations, including the selection of pieces, and Seung Jin Han (their names are written here in Western style at their request with the given name first).

We would like to make special mention of those who pioneered this project, starting with the publication of *Kwangju in the Eyes of the World* three years ago, using works by foreign journalists alone. They are Dr. Yun Jang Hyun, who lead the project, both conceptually and financially; Eugene Soh, who coordinated efforts to find foreign correspondents; and also Kim Sung, who contacted Korean reporters who covered the uprising. Amalie Weber, an American graduate student who then resided in Kwangju, edited *Kwangju in the Eyes of the World,* which contained most of the contributions by foreign correspondents reprinted here. She also coordinated initial efforts to find a publisher in New York.

Our thanks are due to President Kim Dae Jung, who furnished a foreword, and to Kim Hyun Sup of his staff, who dealt with our request for a foreword and checked the translation.

Support for this project came in part through Kwangju Citizens'

Solidarity, a public interest group based in the city. Na Gan Chae, as co-chair of KCS, was instrumental in furthering the work. The Journalists' Association of Korea and the newspaper *Moo-Deung Ilbo* also helped with the project for *Kwangju in the Eyes of the World*. We also wish to recognize individuals who supported the original *Kwangju in the Eyes of the World*—published by Pulbit Publishing Co. They were Kang Jung Mi, Kim Sung Hae, Kim Young Jibb, Park Jae Man, and Park Yong Soo. We thank the Justice and Peace Committee of the Kwangju Archdiocese for its gracious support.

We would like to identify our contributors by the media organizations they represented at the time of the Kwangju uprising and to thank those organizations. Our contributors are: Kim Chung Keun of *Dong-A Ilbo*, Terry Anderson of the Associated Press, Ghebhard Hielscher of *Suddeutsche Zeitung*, Jurgen Hinzpeter of ARD-NDR German TV, Sam Jameson of the *Los Angeles Times,* Bradley Martin of the *Baltimore Sun,* Shim Jae Hoon of the *New York Times,* Philippe Pons of *Le Monde*, Norman Thorpe of the *Asian Wall Street Journal,* Kim Dae Jung of Chosun Ilbo, Cho Sung Ho of *Hankook Ilbo*, Suh Chung Won of *Chosun Ilbo*, Chang Jae Yol of *Joongang Ilbo*, Hwang Jong Gon of *Dong-A Ilbo*, Ryu Jong Hwan of *Pusan Ilbo*, Oh Hyo Jin of Munhwa Broadcasting Company and Kim Yang Woo of *Kukje Shinmun*.

We coordinated all decisions regarding the book with Doug Merwin and Patricia Loo of M.E. Sharpe. Many thanks to Doug and Patty for moving so energetically to publish in time for the twentieth anniversary of the Kwangju uprising in May 2000. We thank Angela Piliouras, senior production editor at M.E. Sharpe and Angela Doescher who cleaned up a messy text. We are grateful to Ambassador Don Gregg, the president of the Korea Society in New York, who suggested that we contact M.E. Sharpe as our publishers.

In his contribution Lee Jai Eui quotes passages from his work *Kwangju Diary,* translated by Kap Su Seol and Nick Mamatas and published in 1999 in the UCLA Asian Pacific Monograph Series. He offers his grateful thanks for this renewed opportunity to acknowledge their support and hard work on *Kwangju Diary,* which included annotation and corrections, as well as actual translation. We have used material from the introduction to *Kwangju Diary* by Professor Bruce Cumings of the University of Chicago and we have benefited from reading Tim Shorrock's concluding essay in the same work. We thank them both.

Meanwhile we note that many local Kwangju journalists were on the spot during the uprising. We would like, ideally, to have included their work. However, our intention was to show the Kwangju uprising as perceived by outsiders. A separate volume is needed, perhaps, to contain the huge documentation, much of it yet to be organized, on the ten-day period in 1980. Many of us from outside the city were helped by local media people, as noted by some of our contributors in the text that follows.

The epilogue, also written by us, mainly focuses on our colleagues' contributions and on one or two gaps found in their and our own pieces. We have not had time—to our regret—to consider their two recent books by the two highest-ranking U.S. officials in South Korea at the time of the Kwangju uprising, Ambassador William H. Gleysteen and General John A. Wickham. Their books came out just as we were concluding our work, and going to press. Their titles are *Massive Entanglement, Marginal Influence: Carter and Korea in Crisis* by William H. Gleysteen and *Korea on the Brink: From the '12/12' Incident to the Kwangju Uprising, 1979–1980* by John Adams Wickham.

KOREA

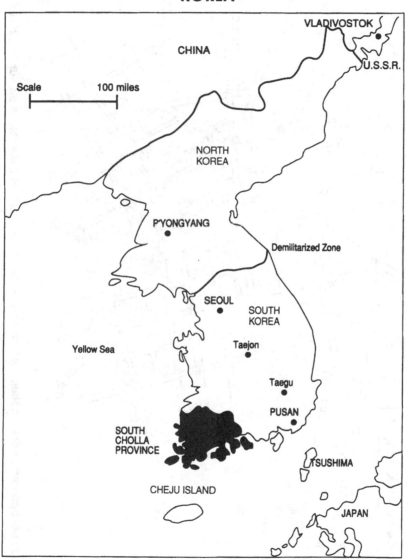

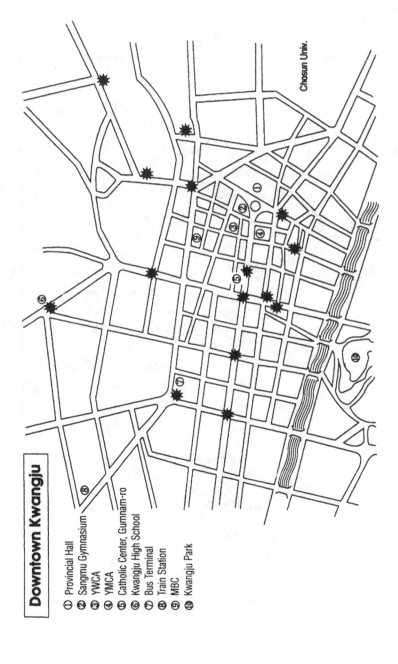

Downtown Kwangju

① Provincial Hall
② Sangmu Gymnasium
③ YWCA
④ YMCA
⑤ Catholic Center, Gumnam-ro
⑥ Kwangju High School
⑦ Bus Terminal
⑧ Train Station
⑨ MBC
⑩ Kwangju Park

Chosun Univ.

The clashpoints between Chonnam National University students and martial army forces on Sunday, May 18, 1980.

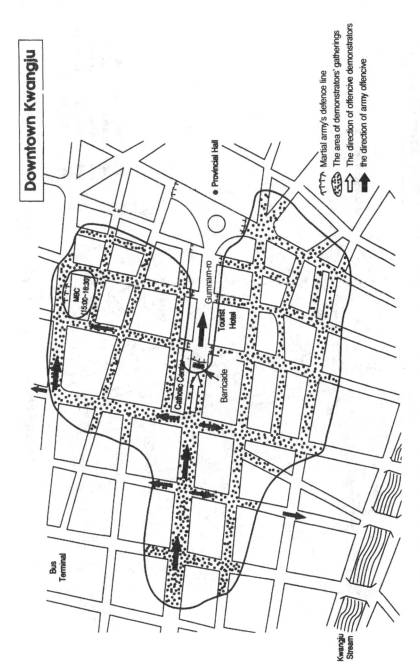

Downtown Kwangju

MBC (15:00–16:30)

Bus Terminal

Catholic Centre

Gumnam-ro

Barricade

Tourist Hotel

• Provincial Hall

Kwangju Stream

Martial army's defence line
The area of demonstrators' gatherings
The direction of offencive demonstrators
the direction of army offencive

The site of clashes between demonstrators and martial army forces on May 19, 1980.

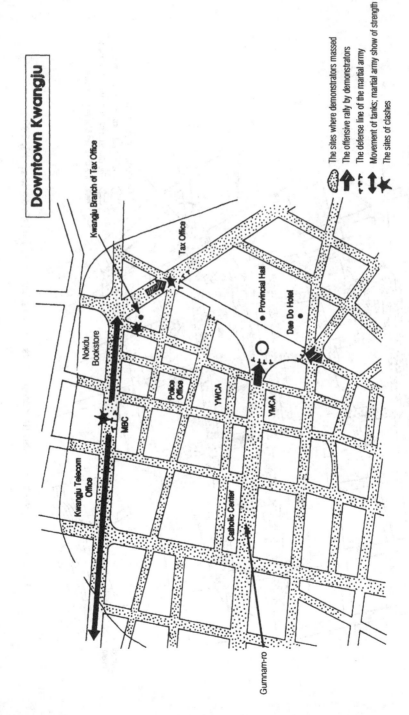

Downtown Kwangju

Kwangju Branch of Tax Office

Tax Office

Noktu Bookstore

Provincial Hall

Dae Do Hotel

Police Office

YWCA

YWCA

MBC

Kwangju Telecom Office

Catholic Center

Gumnam-ro

The sites where demonstrators massed
The offensive rally by demonstrators
The defense line of the martial army
Movement of tanks; martial army show of strength
The sites of clashes

The situation on the night of May 20, 1980.

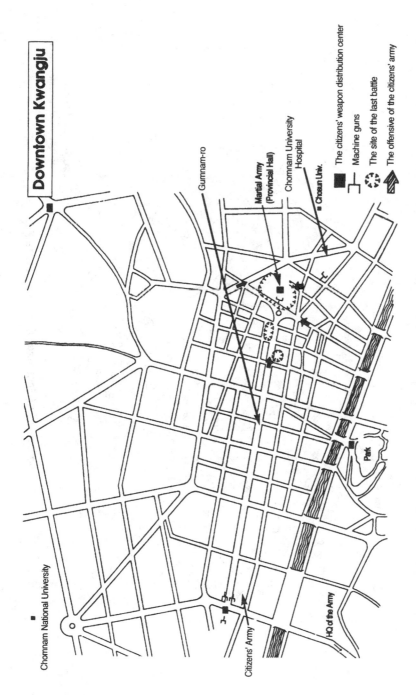

The site of the last battle before the withdrawal of the army, May 21, 1980.

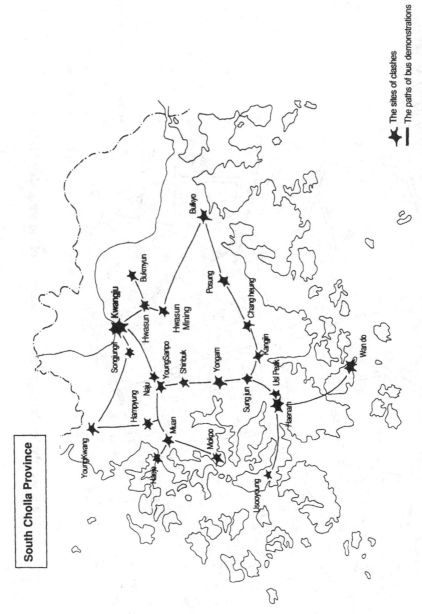

The spread of demonstrations, May 21, 1980.

South Cholla Province

The sites of clashes
The paths of bus demonstrations

Kwangju
Bukmyun
Hwasun
Hwasun Mining
Songjungri
YoungSanpo
Shinbuk
Naju
Hampyung
Muan
YoungKwang
Haepe
Mokpo
Usooyung
Sung jun
Yongam
Ushi Peak
Haenam
Kangin
Chang heung
Posung
Bukyo
Wando

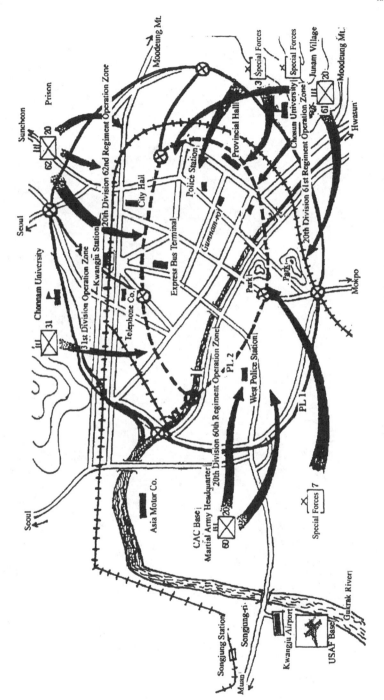

The recapture of Kwangju by martial army forces, early morning of May 27, 1980.

PART ONE

TWO KOREAN VOICES

Introduction

Major news stories have a way of drawing the most competitive journalists in any country. Kim Chung Keun of *Dong-A Ilbo*, a leading Korean daily, was one of the first Seoul-based reporters to arrive in Kwangju. In his account he discloses how his editors in Seoul sent him into action as early as the afternoon of May 17, 1980, hours before South Korea's new military ruler, General Chun Doo Hwan, declared full martial law. Either Mr. Kim's editors had been tipped off that the military intended to crack down on Kwangju, the home base of Kim Dae Jung, South Korea's chief opposition politician—then blame "DJ" for any riots and try him for treason; or the *Dong-A Ilbo* editors had an uncanny premonition of what would happen. In any event, the newspaper packed off its streetwise reporter to Kwangju.

The eventual result, though the newspaper could not publish one line of Kim's reporting at the time because of military censorship, is perhaps the most vivid piece ever written on the Kwangju uprising in terms of what it was like to be on the streets of the city then, day and night, in the thick of the action. Kim, then just thirty, was close to the age of Kwangju's student leaders. He saw instantly what the military were up to. Chun's paratroop commanders had developed a new form of bloodsport, which the Korean press dubbed "hunting for humans"—i.e., beating the daylights out of anything that moved on the street, male or female, young or old. After seven days and nights of watching this degradation, which culminated in soldiers' opening fire on citizens at the end of a gathering held on Buddha's birthday on Wednesday, May 21, Kim quit the city and returned to Seoul. He left before the denouement—the military's triumphal reentry into Kwangju in the early hours of Tuesday, May 27. Kim's terse description of his departure from Kwangju, with the disembodied voice of a powerless president (Choi Gyu Ha, a puppet of General Chun) floating from a helicopter above his head, is the culminating touch of his piece.

A second writer featured in this section is Lee Jai Eui, a coeditor of this book. Lee, then a third-year student at Chonnam National University, Kwangju's premier university, was just twenty-five at the time of the uprising. He is the best-known Korean writer on the Kwangju uprising, as the author of *Kwangju Diary* (UCLA Asian Pacific Monograph Series, 1999, published by the University of California, Los Angeles). This short book, originally published in Korean as a clandestine work of record, was compiled by Lee and others at great personal risk in the mid-1980s, when Chun was still president of South Korea. In a newly prepared text Lee looks at two matters that play little part in other Korean reporters' writings here. These two topics are U.S. responsibility for the atrocities at Kwangju, whether indirect or direct, moral or military, perceived or not; and the student leadership in Kwangju during May 18–27, in particular the role played by Yun Sang Won, a born leader.

Lee was in the thick of events. A sensitive and inexperienced youth, he was confronted by violent death. He saw horrific incidents—a soldier stabbing a civilian to death with a bayonet; a young woman, caught in an alley and stripped and attacked by two young soldiers, who grinned as they finished their work and lugged the woman's unconscious body toward a waiting truck. Lee was moving, meanwhile, toward a turning point in his life; close to the end of the uprising, he "sneaked" out of Kwangju, abandoning his comrades in the Provincial Hall, the symbolic center of the province of South Cholla. Lee's confession of how he fled is followed by a description of a city battered by an insane violence that was all the more frightening because it was indiscriminate. The bizarre code name chosen for this operation by the Korean armed forces' leaders was "Fascinating Vacations."

CHAPTER ONE
DAYS AND NIGHTS ON THE STREET

Kim Chung Keun

Blood and Tears 3

It was about 4 P.M. on Saturday, May 17, 1980. National politics were at fever pitch in Seoul. Everyone on the city desk was on duty that day, even though it was a weekend.

I was outside the office. I had been assigned to cover a student leaders' gathering at Ewha Womans University in central Seoul. The meeting was going on, interminably, in the student-union hall. The presidents of student councils of universities from all over the country, the top student leaders in South Korea, had gathered that weekend to debate strategy. The government, meanwhile, was insisting on continuing martial law despite the fact that North Korea, a perennial concern, was not stirring things up. For the time being, in Seoul the student leaders had taken a decision just the day before to refrain from further demonstrations to avoid provoking the South Korean military.

(On that same evening, unknown to us, martial law was to be suddenly expanded. From then on, South Korea was covered by martial-law prohibitions—the universities were closed, the National Assembly was dissolved, and military censorship was asserted. At one stroke, the original intention of the military—to crack down under full martial law—was made manifest. This was in the cards by late that afternoon. Outside the university gates, police and military intelligence were poised to arrest the students in one fell swoop.)

Just then, when I was concentrating on events at Ewha, I got a call from my office. It was from Lee Sang Ha, the head of the provincial news desk.

"Something's happening in Kwangju! Please go down there straightaway."

Kwangju: Saturday, May 17 (9 P.M.)

The entire city was under curfew. You had to be indoors unless you had a pass.

There were checkpoints on the streets. No matter, I had accreditation. I headed for the police department of South Cholla province, having arrived in Kwangju, the provincial capital. I found the detectives standing around or sitting at their desks drinking *soju* (cheap spirits).

"It's all over, f—— hell. That was the army plot all along!"

"Why couldn't the three Kims and the students have predicted this!"

(The reference was to Kim Jong Pil, Kim Young Sam, and Kim Dae Jung, the three prospective candidates in planned forthcoming direct presidential elections—planned until that point.)

"So? And what could they have done even if they had smelled a rat?"

"The whole thing was planned in advance from the word go! S——. Now what are we going to do? There's a rumor that everyone will gather on Gumnam-ro and spread all over."

The street he referred to, Gumnam-ro, is the traditional rallying spot for demonstrators in Kwangju.

"Then what do we do?"

"God! Kwangju of all places! S——!"

These guys knew. There were plans for a heavy crackdown on and in the city. They'd got wind of something—violent suppression. Something bad, if not ghastly, was coming up, I sensed.

I read their faces. Self-contempt, sadness and lamentation, reproaches of the hostile variety, resentment and anger, despair—the whole gamut of emotion was there to read in their faces as they talked on.

Kwangju: Sunday, May 18 (early morning)

The next morning, I was up and about near the Provincial Hall, the traditional and symbolic center of the city as well as the actual administrative center of the province of South Cholla. I was uncomfortable just going into the restaurants, even without hearing a word. People were uneasy. Some customers saw that we—I, a cameraman, and our driver from Seoul—were press from *Dong-A Ilbo* newspaper, a big paper. They started needling us at once.

"How come they stepped up martial law, even when the student demonstrations had stopped, eh?"

"What's this about beating up students at Chonnam University last night?"

Word of some unwonted violence up there at the main university in Kwangju just the night before had spread like wildfire in the city.

"If we had foreseen this situation . . . ," they said, they would have risen in support of demonstrations at Pusan and Masan six months earlier—just before the assassination of President Park Chung Hee by his KCIA (Korean Central Intelligence Agency) chief in Seoul on October 26, 1979.

"What a situation! The Park military dictatorship finally collapses . . .

finally after 18 years . . . and out come the soldiers with their guns and bayonets at the ready! What kind of f—— logic is that?"

Then the punchline: "So Chun Doo Hwan is planning to swallow the whole government for breakfast . . . Yep, yep."

More and more people gathered. Soon, there were twenty, including the owner of the restaurant. Customers were there, plus the storekeeper from next door, plus some passersby.

They were primed, alerted: "Gumnam-ro, 10 A.M."

The word had gone round. People were learning of the gathering by word of mouth.

"Something is happening" all right, I thought, recalling the words of my city editor. Holy Christ.

Kwangju: Sunday, May 18 (10 A.M.)

It was a Sunday. All the same, people were gathering in groups on Gumnam-ro. Looking into their eyes I saw tension, resolve, and determination, and of these three tension was the strongest. Someone shouted.

"End martial law!"

It was like a gunshot.

People poured out of shops, side streets and buildings. They had been waiting for the word, and a demonstration was forming. Leaders shouted slogans.

"Let the prisoners go. Let them go."

"Let Kim Dae Jung go!"

"Announce the nation's political timetable. ANNOUNCE!"

That was not all. The people demanded to know who was responsible for the violence at Chonnam University the day before (when the military had broken in on students studying for their exams and beaten them indiscriminately).

"Apologize, Apologize!"

That was how the demonstrations began in downtown Kwangju that morning. Out came the riot police, of course. They chased after the demonstrators, doing their best to catch them, but still numbers were limited. It was close on lunchtime when the whole streetview changed. People in business suits came out for lunch and mingled with the demonstrators as they came. The riot police got pushed back, lacking numbers. Steadily and then suddenly, the whole of Gumnam-ro was inundated with people. A sit-down demonstration commenced.

What followed is all but impossible to describe: an army attack—a pincer attack on civilians. Military trucks crammed with heavily armed paratroopers with fixed bayonets lurched into sight at both ends of Gumnam-ro simultaneously. The paras jumped out and waded into the crowd from both ends of the street, working toward the middle—striking out with heavy-duty clubs, left, right, left, right . . . with no regard to who was there, male or female, young or old. The soldiers went for headshots with their big clubs. Gumnam-ro—moments before the scene of a peaceful sitdown demo—was transformed in a matter of seconds into a hell on earth.

It was terribly one-sided. Some bold spirits threw stones. Others had bottles full of petrol—Molotov cocktails—prepared. But the soldiers reacted quickly. They chased after anyone young, beat them with their rifle butts and kicked them with their heavy army boots. If they caught them . . .

The outcome? The Kwangju citizens' idea—to demonstrate peacefully against martial law and to protest violence—was blown away. The exorbitant violence of the troops was what did it. The reaction was: "What the hell is the military up to?" "How could a (Korean) national army do this to fellow Koreans?" Rank incomprehension was overtaken by a sense of outrage.

Hunting Humans

Covering the Kwangju uprising—and writing of it in the aftermath—I was stuck for words. A reporter is supposed to be able to write. I couldn't get down on paper, for myself even, what I had seen.

Some events, some actions resist words: they beggar description.

The original outrages by the troops, remember, took place in broad daylight, with thousands of people present. Afterward? "Massacre" is the word, the only word to begin to describe what followed.

More than that I cannot say. Here and there in the city, in different spots, I encountered situations that boggled the mind and left me numb, left me without the faculty of cognition, over on the other side of the mind.

Typically—in other places, in other situations—the authorities put down demos following a standard pattern that I was deeply familiar with. The way to quell a demo, usually, was to threaten the crowd of demostrators or to make a limited, controlled attack on that crowd. The military used a totally different quelling model at Kwangju, not at all like the usual one I had seen at other times.

At Kwangju, once the soldiers showed up on Gumnam-ro, they ran headlong into the demonstrators. The boundary that had existed between the soldiers and the crowd was eliminated. It vanished in the midst of a melee, a free-for-all with no holds barred and no rules. The soldiers smashed out with their clubs at all and sundry, regardless of age, sex or anything else. Worst of all were the attacks on young women and office workers—identifiable by their regulation dark suits. If a soldier found himself facing a young male, he lit into that man, got him down and kicked the shit out of the guy. The soldiers had a trampling routine that they enjoyed. Suddenly lives were at risk. But if one of those young civilians tried to flee, the soldier chased him, hit him with everything he had, and did his utmost to trap him and reduce him to an immobile heap.

One time I witnessed this sequence of events: A young man who had been caught and was being beaten by a soldier took flight, escaping into a side street and taking refuge in the Moodeung Examination Institute, a cram school to prepare students for exams. The soldier suddenly tired of chasing his target. He snatched the bayonet off his rifle and flung it after the retreating boy, but that was not the end of the incident. A moment later a group of soldiers appeared, rushed into the institute, and beat up anyone they could lay their hands on.

That was not all. Women and young girls were choice targets. The martial-army men stripped them, cutting up their blouses or their skirts using their bayonets, and more or less leaving them naked, whereupon they set about pounding the most delicate parts of the body, using their clubs, their booted feet, anything. All without reason. Why were they picking on these young girls?

On the street, anyone who fought back, anyone who threw stones was in for it. They became number-one targets. The soldiers chased them everywhere and anywhere. They ran into people's shops and private homes and brutalized anyone present. Words fail me in seeking to describe what I saw. "Brutality." "Outrage." "Indiscriminate assault." The words fall short, way short, of the reality. I came up with this expression: "hunting humans" or "Human hunting." I had seen this expression written down somewhere, though it never appeared in a newspaper, given the strict censorship under the Martial Law Command.

How can we describe violence of this type, violence that mounts in proportion to a girl's looks? The more well-dressed she was, the prettier she was, the more certain she was to have her clothes torn off. Look, this was taking place in broad daylight, with witnesses on all sides, this sexually perverse armed suppression. OK, but these words too fail to convey the reality.

My frustration with my own inability to cover what was going on in Kwangju at the time peaked when I made my daily call to my boss, Lee Sang Ha, back in Seoul at the head office. How could I get it across to him? There was no system to follow for a reporter, no police record of events, no documentation to consult. My only resort was to write down what I saw, to move about and witness events as best I could.

But still it was not enough. Very well, the situation was wholly without precedent, not just in my experience, but in history as we knew it. Naturally, I could not convey that at one go, especially when the situation was changing, swinging back and forth every hour, heartbreakingly and urgently.

Once, talking on the phone to Lee, my director, I suddenly hit on this way of summing up what was happening by making a comparison with other violent events I covered: "Suppose the original Masan uprising of October 1979—I am from Masan myself—corresponded to 40 degrees of a maximum 100 degrees on a seismograph. Then the Sabuk coalmine strike of March–April this year hit 45 degrees. The turmoil at Pusan and Masan in October 1979, just before President Park got killed, hit 60 degrees. But here in Kwangju the needle on the seismograph hit 100 and broke."

Arirang and *Our Wishes*—Traditional Korean Songs

To describe the uprising, to invoke its spirit, the best way is those two songs—*Arirang* and *Our Wishes*. The uprising involved people from all walks of life, male and female, young and old. It was *not* led by ideologically inclined students or by some political organization or social body—no, it was broader than that.

There in the city, as the days' events unfolded and the demonstrations grew more furious, the crowds shouted out slogans and said what they liked, criticizing whomever and whatever. Somehow they needed a song to unify their purpose, to make their minds as one, to inspire them to go forward to their goal of victory. Sometimes students would strike up with one of the songs they used at rallies in their own towns, but the crowds didn't warm to that too much.

The people sang *Aekukga*, the national anthem, from the very beginning, from the time of the earliest clashes with the military. The crowds would dissolve away and then re-form, building up numbers, and they would sing the anthem to recharge their wills and pledge loyalty to one other.

Aekukga alone wasn't enough, though, not for demonstrations that went on and on, day after day. So people tried traditional songs and folk songs. Of these, *Arirang* and *Our Wishes* went best. That was because, no matter who was doing the singing—men wearing neckties, hucksters from the stalls in the street markets, laborers, farmers, students, women—they all knew those two songs.

In Kwangju then, I realized for the first time that *Arirang* has a blood-chilling quality, a hold on you, a way of touching you.

At night, with everything blacked out, it was pitch dark. The power was suspended, as was the water supply. The TV broadcasting stations stood in burned ruins. Police boxes were torched. Dark smoke added to the blackness of it all. So when I saw how people flocked into central Kwangju from the suburbs, how they gathered in front of the Provincial Hall, joined hands and sang *Arirang*, waving the *Taekukki,* the national flag, I felt stirred to my being. How I wept.

This was how I came to see that *Arirang* pulses with intense desires and with resentments too. It expresses an ardent fighting spirit, it is martial not lyrical. Pathos is there too, but gives way to something else, more positive, stronger, more vital. So, yes, I would say the symbols of the Kwangju uprising—if traditional tunes can be symbols—were those two songs that people sang all day.

How so, symbols? I have to say it again. They brought together all types of beings, of whatever background—welded them as one to fight against unimaginable acts of violence by the army. And so those ordinary citizens rose as one. Let us be clear. The uprising, such as it was, was not based on any one political group or party or political faction—that is important—or on ideology of a leftist or crypto-communist variety. No, the uprising sprang to life in response to grassroots-type, basic, simple questions such as what is the nation, and what should the national army be to us?

Chun Ok Ju, the Woman of That Time

I met and interviewed many in Kwangju who led demonstrations. But Chun Ok Ju was the most startling of those leaders, the least forgettable. Her career and her actions have been made known by others. But Chun, the person I met and saw in demonstrations, was special.

She was resolute, logical, enthusiastic, and incendiary. I saw her all the

time at demonstrations. I interviewed her on the spot at three different demos.
I think I was the only reporter who met her under those conditions.

It started off like this. There was a lull in a round of bloody street fighting. I asked her for an interview. She was wary, and no wonder. The locals would not and did not trust reporters, especially locally based ones. That's how it was. Communications with the outside were completely blocked. No news was getting through. The citizens distrusted reporters.

I was an object of suspicion. I moved about among the demonstrators, martial-army men, and the police. I alone wore a big helmet with big red letters saying *Dong-A Ilbo*, the name of my newspaper. I had a press armband on, and I carried a gasmask. In short, I wore heavy-duty reporting gear. When I asked Chun for an interview, she responded by asking to see my credentials, my ID, and my identification as a reporter. Only after I produced these did she speak.

"I graduated from the school of dance at Chosun University. Now I run a dance school at Masan in Kyongnam. I came up on holiday to Jangsung Lake with my boyfriend, to do some fishing. Then I heard the news. Soldiers were beating and killing people in Kwangju. I hurried here at once. I have no interest in politics, but how could the nation's army kill its citizens? That was my question.

"If there is violent distrust between the armed forces and the citizens of a country, that entire country risks collapse. It's high time that someone in a position of responsibility apologized for the army's behavior, for their provocation. When that happens, I'll go back to Masan."

As the interview continued, I saw how threatened she felt, how she was seized with fear and anxiety. She ate, slept, and even relieved herself in her clothes, she said. She was worried that an army spy—she had one in mind—might creep in among the demonstrators. If she separated herself from the citizens, she felt, she might be shot by a sniper or arrested—she was afraid. Chun wore jeans, held up by suspenders. She told me to touch them at the back. I grasped her jeans there. They were damp. A mass of excrement, semi-solid by that time, was stuck inside. Her mouth and her hair gave off a dank smell. She hadn't bathed or brushed her teeth for days.

Later, she was arrested on suspicion of being a spy. The martial-law authorities took her in. They tortured her and finally released her. From time to time, word of her appeared in the press. I had known nothing of her beforehand, nor did I learn more of her later.

Chun Ok Ju, to sum up, did not plunge into those demonstrations, risking her life, with a purpose in mind. She just could not stand injustice, so she pushed herself to the front in demos. There are citizens everywhere, anywhere, like that. The course of history can be dictated or shaped by such intrinsically small individuals, who use their hands and their voices, I learned.

Sleeping with Corpses

While covering the uprising, I often went hungry. I witnessed many deaths. Privation was my lot as it was for others. I saw how make-or-break situations—starvation and death—push people into manifestations of unwonted pluck, gallantry, and, at the limit, transcendental experience.

At one point I was covering a strategic spot outside Kwangju High School. An army tank had broken down there. Citizens had surrounded it, and there was a standoff. In the midst of this we drove by in our car and were promptly attacked with Molotov cocktails. As if this were not enough, the lieutenant in command of the tank ordered me to come close. I was obliged to obey. He told me: "Let the HQ at Sangmu gymnasium know that we've broken down here!"

I was compromised. As I was about to take off, still in the car, the bystanders and militants there launched an attack on us. Our car was enveloped in flames. The driver didn't know what to do. Seeking an escape route he flung the car to the right, and suddenly we were heading into a crowd bunched in a narrow market lane. I saw it all. If one person was run down, we were dead. My obituary would be: "He died a spy for the martial army in Kwangju." I flung myself at the wheel, steering the car in an opposite direction, the car still spouting flames. Suddenly a high-school student sprang forward from the crowd, to help us by opening the way. We tumbled out of the car, escaping with our lives. But at that moment guns barked behind us and the high-school kid tumbled to the ground, blood spurting from his body. That innocent boy, I thought, sacrificed his life for us "neutral observers"—in fact the boy, Kim Young Chan, survived his injuries.

I had another narrow escape when four riot policemen I was with—men from Hampyung police station—were run into by accident in the dark in front of the Provincial Hall by a speeding bus driven by a demonstrator during a night demo.

The point had come when both sides—riot police and demonstrators alike—were exhausted and had collapsed into heaps to rest. I took off my helmet, squatted on it, and fell fast asleep perched on it. The helmet was uncomfortable, and I woke up, moved from the road where I was, and positioned myself half on the sidewalk close by, still half asleep and half awake. I was settling down once more, to squat on the curb when something popped, sounding like a bursting tire. A bus had rushed over the very spot where I had dozed. Several policemen were run over and killed in the twinkling of an eye. That was when I learned that an exploding human stomach sounds like a tire getting punctured.

Night brought the lowest points. Outside the Provincial Hall, unknown to me then, there was an air-raid shelter. One night, I went to crouch there. I was worn out, having covered demos all day and on into the evening. I hadn't eaten. How long I slept I do not know. In any event, I felt iciness across my knees and something weighing down on my shoulders. I opened my eyes. The dim light of dawn peeped through a slit window in the shelter. The cold things leaning on me were corpses, not one but two. Their faces were crushed in. Someone had stashed the bodies in the shelter overnight, without knowing I was there.

I was shaken, but at the same time I felt overcome by extreme drowsiness and fatigue. Some part of me said to move, another barely conscious part of me resisted getting up. I pushed the corpses aside and slumbered on for a while. Working had become totally impossible by that point, the demos were getting so violent. Still, to this day, I remember the night I shared my shelter outside the Kwangju Provincial Hall with two smashed-up dead men.

Pusan-Masan and Kwangju

At the time of the uprising, I was already branded by my colleagues as a troubleshooting reporter. I was the one assigned to cover the big historical turning points. The Pusan-Masan disturbances of early October 1979, which preceded the murder of President Park Chung Hee; the Sabuk affair, where a coalminers' strike suddenly threatened the established order; the assassination of Park on October 26, 1979; the military coup of December 12, 1979, the coup inside the army that brought Chun Doo Hwan to prominence—I covered them all.

That was why I was selected by my boss Lee Sang Ha to go down to Kwangju. He wanted to send someone who knew from his own experience what had happened in Pusan and Masan—not so far away in southern South Korea—only months before. Lee told me later that he wanted a man in Kwangju who could make dispassionate judgments on the events, having a basis of comparison through having seen violent suppression of demos elsewhere, for example in the Youngnam area—Masan is there—where I was born.

Well, what did I find? Basically that the Kwangju uprising was one of a kind, unique in one respect. It was something new, somewhat different from the mayhem that had come before. To be sure, the troops were menacing and wild enough out on the streets of Pusan and Masan in autumn 1979. They were rough. They had a simple and plausible objective though: to break up demos, to push people back off the streets and at the same time, to keep the city functioning. At that time the so-called *Yushin* ("Restoration") philosophy of state was the official doctrine. President Park Chung Hee was established and in power, with eighteen years as president behind him. The government strategy at Pusan and Masan was to maintain the status quo, not to rock the boat, not to subvert.

Kwangju was different. When the martial-law army showed up in the heart of the city for the first time—I was there—they paraded in front of the Provincial Hall in a very official way. They formed up in ranks, and when they marched, they marched in columns. They did their exercises as if on the parade ground, doing their bayonet drills, marking each move with shouts, letting their voices sound out to defy the demonstrators massed before their eyes.

It was done in a very orderly way. The soldiers formed up in lines, spacing themselves out as the drillbooks require. Then, off they went, marching toward the heart of the demonstration. Stones struck them. Molotov cocktails set their sleeves on fire. Paying no attention, they kept formation and marched ahead. The demonstrators stepped aside to let them pass, and the soldiers went on toward the core of the demo in the heart of Gumnam-ro. As the column passed through them, the demonstrators closed up behind them.

Then an order was shouted. The soldiers broke ranks, dashing into the demonstrators around them, beating them mercilessly with their heavy sticks—those especially heavy sticks. This was not a strategy for nudging a crowd or demo off a street from one side—as at Pusan and Masan the previous year—to get the streets back to normal and open and functioning. It was a strategy of terror, a blitzkrieg.

Here, I should mention the uniforms the men wore at Kwangju, as compared with the kit they had on the previous year. At Pusan and Masan the men wore uniforms showing what regiments they were from. Not so at Kwangju. The soldiers' names were hidden, as were their regimental insignia. They were unidentified soldiers, unidentifiable. Only their ranks were shown, only that much. That was all. There was no way to know the units of these men.

That is not all. There was something truly astounding. As the men marched in column into the demonstration, they were led by lieutenants at the front. Behind the officers came the privates. Behind them came MPs with armbands, carrying rifles. The MPs pointed their barrels at the columns ahead. To recap: The officers led the way, at the rear came those MPs. A private who broke ranks without receiving a direct order to do so was to be shot by one of the MPs.

I think back. Park had been assassinated seven months earlier. The father of the nation was gone after so many, many years. Suddenly it was not clear who was in charge. There was a regime of sorts, there were politicians, but what was going on at the center was veiled in mist. The martial-law army men, however, the new set of officers in charge were bent on showing who was top dog. They made their intentions clear.

Kwangju, Wednesday, May 21 (2 P.M.)

I stood on the third floor of a building overlooking the square in front of Provincial Hall. I was looking down on the heart of Kwangju. The square was on my right, Gumnam-ro was on my left.

It was Buddha's Birthday, a day of celebrations and of gathering to give thanks. On this day, a huge crowd had gathered below me, facing toward the Provincial Hall that serves as the central rallying point and focus of the city. The ceremony was coming to an end with a rendering of the Korean national anthem. The anthem came to an end, and those gathered below—they were seated on the ground—stood up. As they did so—I was watching—some of those in front lurched suddenly and fell, blood spurting from their backs. Then—the sound was delayed, the bullets struck before the sound reached me—came a volley of shots.

I swung round to the right. Soldiers were lined up before the Provincial Hall. Those in line in front were seated. They were firing. Behind them was a second line of standing soldiers. They too were firing. At a given point those seated moved back and made off by truck.

If I had not been there, I could not have written this. Who would imagine such a sight? The end of the national anthem used as a signal to open fire on a crowd? On Buddha's Birthday?

A celebratory, temporary ornamental arch stood over Gumnam-ro to mark the day. Beneath that arch lay the victims of the massacre that had just been perpetrated in front of me.

I Left the City Finally

Three days later, on May 24, I left Kwangju. I could no longer keep up communications with my head office in Seoul. I left Kwangju riding on a bicycle accompanied by a press photographer. We two bicyclists had just left Kwangju—looking like the ruined remains of a battlefield— behind us, when we were stopped in a village called Songjung-ri by local people and asked who we were.

When we identified ourselves, the people gripped our arms and sleeves. "Do the authorities in Seoul know what has been going on in Kwangju?" they wanted to know. "Do the newspapers and the broadcasters know the situation or not?"

I have a broad Kyongsang accent. One of the men shouted out: "It is good that a reporter from Kyongsang came and saw this. When you arrive in Seoul, please report that soldiers are killing everyone in Kwangju."

If we were to continue on our bicycles, they insisted, we would need to take plenty of food with us. Out they came with boiled eggs, bread, and soda pop . . . and fastened the goodies to the backs of our bicycles.

Just as the victualing operation was ending, an army helicopter came whirring over our heads, broadcasting a message, a recorded speech, high up in the air.

"I am the president of this country, Choi Gyu Ha," boomed the announcement. "I remember that not long ago I attended a ceremony in Kwangju to lay the foundation of a water plant for citizens suffering from lack of drinking water . . . I feel sorry for you in your misfortune."

"This country"?

"President Choi Gyu Ha"?

What on earth could these concepts—a nation, a president—mean when presented in that particular way at that particular time? I asked myself that question, again and again.

CHAPTER TWO

OPERATION "FASCINATING VACATIONS"

Lee Jai Eui

Daybreak

I would like here to recount memories of four quite distinct topics: a visit by two foreign correspondents to Kwangju, and how, as an impromptu spokesman for student militants, I reacted to their questions about the origins of the violence there; the student leadership —how it worked, who was there, and what my role in it was, however briefly; the conduct of the martial-law troops in the city, as I saw it, during the early days of the uprising; and, finally, my own pitiful behavior as I saw the way things were going—and faced a choice between (a) staying on in the Provincial Hall, the seat of government in the province in normal times, where the student leadership was to be found during the last five days of the uprising (May 21–27) and where many of them died, or (b) making my escape.

Let me address the last topic first. I sneaked out of the city on May 24, abandoning my post in the militant student group running, or attempting to run, the city—I had been put in charge of an operations room on the first floor of the building on May 22. My reasoning was that if I died there, nothing would remain. Everything I had stored up in my head would be lost forever. Naturally, I was under pressure from my family, who wished me to make my escape. But the central fact was fear. On the first evening at my post, on the evening of May 22, I sat in that operations room, smoking a cigarette and summing up on paper, or trying to, what we students were doing for the citizens. As I sat there, struggling with the text, a still, small voice tempted me, saying "Leave all this, if you want to achieve anything, should you want anything to remain. You are so isolated, you are so alone. Kwangju is cut off from the outside world. No one will ever know what happened."

I will not belabor this topic, but, the time came, years later, when I was strongly motivated to work on a detailed account of the Kwangju uprising—the opportunity arose in 1985, shortly after I got married. A small team of us worked in secret to produce a work that was published in clandestine fashion as *Kwangju Diary*, based upon many interviews. This publication achieved huge notoriety in Korea at the time and helped, I believe, to propel my country back onto the path of democracy. Everything stemmed, however, from the sacrifices of my colleagues and friends at Kwangju and elsewhere, notably at the end of the uprising, and also later, in the following years, when many of us including me (I was jailed from October 10, 1980 to August 15, 1981) were imprisoned and tortured; some of us died in detention, either from physical abuse or from hunger strikes.

I shall not forget those with whom I served. Foremost among them was Yun Sang Won, twenty-nine. He acted as spokesman for the students and was in fact our leader, though he used a modest title. A labor activist—a star student from the Kwangju region, who left a secure job in a bank in Seoul to serve workers in factories—Yun was the outstanding personality around us, as people saw immediately when they met him. An example comes to mind. Many years after the uprising, in 1997, I contacted Norman Thorpe, who was serving as *The Asian Wall Street Journal* Seoul bureau chief at the time of the events and came down to Kwangju to report. This was in connection with publication of a first edition of this book in Korea (*Kwangju in the Eyes of the World*, Kwangju Citizens' Solidarity, 1997). When I re-met Norm—we had previously met just once in the operations room in the Provincial Hall on May 22, 1980—he showed me a photograph he had taken in the hall on the morning of May 27 after the military came back into the city. The photo showed a man sprawled on his back, with one eye open. This was Yun Sang Won. A shock went through me. That photo portrays to me the way the uprising ended, namely in the deaths of Yun and a score of others. Norman himself wanted to know who the person was. That was why he showed me a picture that he had kept for many years, always wondering about the man's identity.

I remember my first and only previous conversation with Norm and one other reporter from *The Asian Wall Street Journal*—they were the only foreign correspondents I met in May 1980. They asked me: "How come you have turned to violence?" Or words to that effect. Why the uprising? I exploded.

"Massacre! There was an army massacre of unarmed civilians, what would you do yourselves under such circumstances?"

An Army Massacre

I need to convey what came before the army's irruption into Kwangju. Life was going on at an even pace. Spring is very much a season for students in Korea. It is a time when young people come out on the streets and stroll about. At the same time Kwangju was far, far from being a center of national attention in mid-May. All eyes were on Seoul. That was where the student demonstrations were taking place. Following one such demonstration—on May 13—we in Kwangju picked up the thread.

"The students of Chonnam and Chosun universities demonstrated, attempting to take over the streets," I noted in my *Kwangju Diary* (p. 37).

Still, Seoul was the center of everything for most people. Down in Kwangju, relations between the police and the student leaders were, oddly, fairly close. No one knew it at the time but the main student-organized event that month—a torch-lit parade on the night of May 16—was made possible by Park Gwan Hyun, the president of the Chonnam University student union (someone I knew personally), having a chat with the chief of South Cholla police, Ahn Byung Ha. I confirmed this with Ahn in a conversation at his home in 1987.

Both Park, I must add, and Ahn were taken into custody by the military after the uprising ended. Both suffered hideous treatment in prison, being subjected to tremendous torture. Park went on a hunger strike and died in jail in 1982. Ahn ended his days in 1988, a terribly weakened man. He suffered at home for years before succumbing to injuries inflicted on him in prison.

The military did not forget when they had a score to settle. How could they forget, in particular, the fact that Ahn, I believe for the first time in police history in Korea, disobeyed an order to stop demonstrations. His arrest followed on May 27, the moment the army re-entered Kwangju (see part 3 for an eyewitness account by Kim Yang Woo of the *Kukje Shinmu*).

"My husband died in 1988," Ahn's widow Chun Im Soon told me when I met her in Seoul in 1989. "Before his death he used to say that he decided to protect the citizens of Kwangju from the brutal martial-law army. He declined to obey an order from the army to suppress demonstrations in Kwangju. His action embarrassed the Martial Law Command. That was why they immediately arrested him. He was ferociously tortured and quit his career. He was sick in bed for years."

Those of us who were student activists in Kwangju could have no idea of what was going on at that level in the city in police-student relations at the time—it took me years to find out. As *Kwangju Diary* (hereafter *KD*) shows, we were, however, conscious of things gradually growing wrong.

The night of May 15, students on a sit-in saw military reconnaissance

squads lurking about the campus. None of the foreign lecturers at Chonnam
University showed up to teach their classes the next morning. (*KD*, p. 39)

Even though student rallies were peaceful in Kwangju up to that time,
tension had gradually increased between those in the student movement
and the authorities.

As the movement gained momentum, we student leaders, began to worry
about the possibility of the government shutting down the campus. The
Chonnam University student union decided to gather students at the main
gate at 10 A.M. if at any time a shutdown was imposed. If the police stopped
(us) at the gate, the students would gather at Provincial Hall Square at
noon. The student union spread the word throughout the student body.
(*KD*, p. 38)

Nobody, including me, knew that in making this arrangement we had in
fact installed a fuse that could blast off a full-blown uprising at any time.

On May 16, the student leadership in Seoul ended their street demonstrations . . . to watch for new political developments. But in the Cholla provinces of south-west Korea—notably in Kwangju—the students organized
a night-time "march of torches" that would unite students and the rest of
the urban population. May 16 was the anniversary of Park Chung Hee's
1961 military coup, which had trampled on the first fruits of a democratic
movement. Kwangju's student leaders believed that an upsurge in energy
was needed to show our will to resist government repression. They wanted
to raise massive numbers of torches to light up the darkness after eighteen years of Park Chung Hee's military dictatorship. (*KD*, p. 38)

This is a crucial point to distinguish Kwangju from other regions of
South Korea. We, the Kwangju student leadership, had somewhat different ideas to those of students in Seoul. There, the leadership suspended demonstrations, to wait and see.

With tension increasing, I played a role as an intermediary. Thus, I
kept Park Gwan Hyun, the president of the student union at Chonnam
University, in contact with Kim Sang Yun and Yun Han Bong, two older
activists. The former owned a bookstore called Nokdu, a key gathering
point for students; the latter, who managed the Modern Cultural Institute, was a notable activist outside the university world. To keep information flowing, I secretly organized a group of students to publish
samizdat-style literature under the title of *The Voice of the University*, to

let citizens know what we thought. Both Kim Sang Yun and Yun Han Bong had been leaders of the student movement in the early 1970s; they tried to expand student activism into other spheres—for example, trade unions, the peasant movement, and the urban poor in Kwangju. They analyzed the political situation and helped me to understand it (Kim was arrested by the police on May 17, 1971, the day full martial law was announced; Yun sneaked out of Kwangju just before the May uprising and found a ship to take him to the United States after the events). Another person involved in our activities was Chun Yong Ho, who helped us editorially and also functioned as a member of Clown, a theatrical activist group.

Most of the hardline student leadership that was to emerge in May 22–27 were connected with this world centered on the bookshop Nokdu and the Modern Cultural Institute. The key figures, all members of what we called the Citizens' Fighting Committee—a body created on May 25—are listed below:

Kim Chong Bae, 27	chair, junior at Chosun University
Huh Kyu Jung, 27	vice chair, sophomore at Chosun University
Yun Sang Won, 29	spokesperson, labor activist
Park Nam Sun, 26	transport worker
Kim Young Chul, 30	planning director, urban poor activist
Chung Sang Yong, 30	vice chair and external secretary, activist
Lee Yang Hyun, 30	assistant planning director, labor activist
Yun Kang Ok, 28	planning director, senior at Chonnam University
Park Hyo Sun, 28	publicity bureau director, teacher and theatrical activist
Chung Hae Jik, 29	civil affairs bureau director
Kim Jun Bong, 21	investigation bureau and militia member, clerical worker
Ku Sung Ju, 25	distribution secretary, worker

One can see, looking at their names and ages, that they were a relatively experienced core group of "eternal student" activists. They were idealists, who had held on to the aspirations of their student days. Without this group—older and more experienced in the ways of the world than the generation of students I belonged to—the Kwangju uprising could, most likely, not have ended, as it did in an organized, sustained confrontation under martial law. This is the group that stayed to the last in the Provincial Hall. Had they not been there, everyone would have scattered, I believe. The list names a number of key people, who were not part of the Nokdu group and got included by Yun Sang Won; these were people who joined in during the uprising and were included in the leadership by Yun. These were Kim Chong Bae, Huh Kyu Jung, Park Nam Sun, Kim Jun Bong, and Ku Sung Ju. Miraculously, none of these key members were killed on May 27, 1980, with the exception of Yun Sang Won. Of the others, Kim Young Chul and Park Hyo Sun were seriously injured.

Up to May 18 we spent a lot of time in discussions. We attempted, of course, to analyze the political situation. The aim was to arrive at an objective conclusion and to base the next line of action on it. One of our main concerns, naturally, was to try to understand in advance how the United States and the military—we thought of them in one breath—would react to the protest movement. Once again I would like to quote from *Kwangju Diary* (p. 39):

> The United States and the (South Korean) military were seen as the only players that could bring about change. . . . Seoul's student leadership suspended their demonstrations, believing that the military was subordinate to the United States but was still independent of the domestic government. Everybody expected a military reaction as the movement peaked. The question was, if the military used force to end the pro-democracy movement, what would the United States do? It was a tough question that nobody could answer, but the students struggled with it. The dominant opinion held that in principle, the United States was the world leader of neoimperalism and was responsible for holding back the national reunification of Korea. Nevertheless, at this phase, democratic reforms in South Korea were in Washington's interest. The United States would not want radicals to incite anti-American feelings as part of the resistance against military rule. The students imagined that the United States would welcome reforms as long those reforms did not run counter to its interests in the region. If the pro-democracy movement intensified, the United States, to avoid another Iran-style fiasco, would cooperate in transferring political power from the military to a civilian parliament. For the activists, the most important task was leading the movement to the point where the United States would intervene on the side of democracy.

The activists concerned, I included, could not imagine that our forecast of a likely U.S. response would be disproved within a short period of time. We continued blithely on our way. On May 16, a Friday, the end of the working week, we held our great torch rally in the evening, a splendid occasion. A weekend, May 17–18, lay ahead, and, honestly, we were tired. We had been rallying and demonstrating since the beginning of the month. We decided to hold another rally on the Monday, but basically we agreed to take the weekend off. As our torch gathering came to an end at about 10 P.M., we agreed that we would gather immediately at the main gate of the university if there was a clampdown. That night I went home and fell into a deep sleep. We all had reason to relax, or so we thought.

> The government announced that the National Assembly would convene on May 17 to settle the political problems caused by student protests and the other dissident movements. The government claimed that the Assembly would discuss lifting martial law and propose the introduction of a new timetable for political reforms. (*KD*, p. 40)

I read this news in the morning newspaper on Saturday, May 17. So all is well, I thought. Here was a solution at hand for a complicated political situation. This was the start of a real change. A step forward could be anticipated. All day long, I relaxed. I took a long hot bath. My spirits recovered, thanks to the rest. It was great to go outside, where a warm spring breeze blew.

The real situation, of course, was that we were at a turning point in South Korea. Things were headed in exactly the opposite direction to that announced in the paper. Everything came to a head, all of a sudden, with a call from Seoul. The caller was a female student up there. She made the call to the student union at Chonnam University. All of the student leaders in Seoul had been arrested, she announced. The arrests had been made under martial law. At the same time, there were reports of paratroopers heading down the expressway from the north by truck. Everything that followed was done under the seal of military secrecy. We had no idea what exactly what happened until many years later. The facts are: The crack paratroop forces sent into Kwangju came from Kumma in North Cholla, 80 kilometers north of Kwangju. They arrived during the night of May 17–18. Nine years later, in 1989, I came across this record of movements by the 31st Division, made public by South Korean Army Headquarters:

> May 18, 2:26 A.M.: arrival of 7th Special Forces Brigade, 33rd and 35th Battalions, with 96th Regiment on assignment (Chungjung Operation Order No. I).

On taking over universities, the 33rd Battalion (38 officers, 294 men) arrested 69 Chonnam University students and 43 Chosun University students who had remained on the premises. The 96th Regiment took over Honam and Daegun Theological Colleges, Dongshin College, Seogang College, Sungin College, Songwon College, and Christian Nursing School. Five officers and 80 men took over four broadcasting stations in Kwangju.

Everything had been prepared in advance, we were to confirm many years later. Chung Ung, a commander of the 31st Division located in Kwangju, who later entered politics, testified at a 1988 hearing that he "received an order to prepare barracks for the arrival of paratroops on May 15, two days before the extension of martial law." Another former officer, Kim Il Ok, who was commander of the 35th Battalion of the 7th Special Forces Brigade and took control of Chosun University, early on the morning of May 18, testified that "all the facilities—barracks, radios, etc.—had been set up when I arrived at Chosun University."

Other sources showed that paratroop elements had been sent in advance to every major city throughout the nation except Pusan during the period May 3–18, in secret, to familiarize themselves with the terrain. By the time the actual announcement of full martial law came at 11:40 P.M. on May 17, everything was ready. The announcement contained the usual type of remarks reserved for such occasions: "With the suspicious movements of the North Korean armed forces and the nationwide unrest, we have declared a state of emergency." Within two hours of that announcement, troops had occupied the two main universities in Kwangju, Chonnam and Chosun universities. At the same time Kim Dae Jung and other opposition politicians were pulled in and arrested in Seoul on trumped-up charges of engineering unrest among students and workers.

The First Clash

I arrived at the main gate of Chonnam University at about 9 A.M. on Sunday, May 18. I immediately saw what martial law meant in practice. Six or eight paratroopers were there, armed for combat in war. They carried M-16 rifles and grenades and had fixed their bayonets. Students began to gather, as we had agreed in advance. My body shook with anger. I picked up a stone and then stopped myself. How could I influence the course of events with one small stone? I clutched the stone pathetically. What a lousy situation. My brother had a store close by. At

9:50 A.M. I decided to go over there on my bike. Ten minutes later, the first clash erupted. I was not there. This is how I described the events in my book:

> By 10 A.M. nearly 100 students were assembled and taunting the soldiers, their confidence increasing with their numbers. Almost by reflex, fifty people began a sit-in on a nearby bridge. As they sang and chanted anti-government slogans, others joined in. Nearly 300 students began to shout, "End martial law!" "Chun Doo Hwan, a plague on you!" "Martial law troops go away!" and "End the shutdown!" The squad leader announced that he would use force to remove the students, but was drowned out by the chanting. Suddenly, the soldiers raised a battle cry of their own and charged the students. They waded into the crowd, swinging their batons. The soldiers looked ready to kill. Several students writhed on the ground, and the concrete ran red with their blood. Others were run off into a side street and cornered by half a dozen troopers. The students managed to regroup and threw stones at the squad of soldiers. The soldiers began a bold assault. They rushed the students, not bothering to dodge the rocks, and each soldier picked his target. Each soldier rushed in, incapacitated his target with one quick blow to the head, and dragged the body away. The battle lasted half an hour. The troops were a special force, trained in antiriot tactics and urban warfare. Bare hands and hope were not enough. (*KD*, p. 42)

I stayed in the center of the city at my brother's shop. At 11 A.M. a bunch of students passed directly in front of the shop. They were chanting "Free Kim Dae Jung!" Among that group were some students I knew. One was Park Mong Ku, twenty-four, a junior at Chonnam University; another was Lee Don Kyu, twenty-one, a sophomore at Chonnam University. They were leading the demonstrators. I was taken aback. I had no idea they would react so strongly. I joined them at once and set off with them.

We began a sit-down demo downtown on Gumnam-ro, near the Catholic Center, a well-known rendezvous point. The group swelled and grew in size. Finally, we were about 500. Traffic ground to a halt. We shouted out loudly and urged people to join us. Mostly, the onlookers hesitated. It was still only the afternoon of May 18. They had seen nothing.

Ten minutes later, the police moved. They came firing tear gas grenades. I was damned nigh suffocated by that gas. I ran off into a narrow alley to one side, as fast and as far as I could. Thus I escaped the jaws of death. Some of the others were caught and beaten. The police were suddenly brutal and swift. Their behavior had totally changed, compared with that of the previous day. The students scattered at first, then tried to re-form into a group again. So it went on. I tried to join up again. This went on for three or four hours—our group was scattered, and then built up again. We tried to persuade others to join in—the citizens and onlookers around. They didn't do so yet. Meanwhile, the number of students swelled dramatically. The demo was getting better organized and more aggressive. Many who saw us—shopkeepers and stallkeepers—gave us food and drinks. At the same time some choppers showed up. There were two or three of them, circling over our heads, making a tremendous racket. Finally, my clothes were totally soaked through with sweat. But I enjoyed myself. It seemed we could win a victory, and soon.

Not that I saw more than a small portion of the city around Gumnam-ro. Elsewhere, as I was to learn in 1984, when doing interviews for my book, there was all kinds of action. Over near the Sansu-dong junction on the east side of the city, demonstrators managed to disarm forty-five police. They then tried to swap the police, as hostages, for students whom the police had arrested earlier. Around 4:40 P.M. the police were released. Soon after that, there was a sudden, dramatic upward shift of gears. Troops appeared. They made direct attacks on the demonstrators. They worked with the police, of course. They broke up the crowds, picking on individual students, running them down, beating them to the ground. They had a technique: crack open a student's head; next stomp on his back as he went down; then kick the face with a boot—putting the boot in. The victim lost consciousness. The paratroopers grabbed him by the neck, dragged him to police vans nearby, and tossed him casually one on top of others, like so many animal carcasses.

It was shocking to behold. I shuddered. By around 4:30 P.M. I had moved back a bit toward my brother's shop again. I found myself in a spot where I could watch the paratroopers from a safe distance. This was near the bus station. I saw a squad stop all the buses and check the passengers. Any young person they found got pulled off. When some kids who did not look like students, by their dress, made a fuss, half a dozen soldiers shouted back: "We'll kill every bastard in Kwangju!"

One guy I was watching escaped. He ran into an old woman's house. A group of soldiers entered. I watched them, to see what would happen. They demanded that the old lady hand over the boy. She hesitated. In a flash one of the paratroopers landed a tremendous blow on her temple.

"Bitch, I'll take care of you!"

She fell to the ground, unconscious.

The men entered the house, wrenched open a cabinet and pulled out the boy, dragging him with them and beating him. It looked as if they were killing him.

Close by stood an old man. "How did this happen?" he cried. "I saw many brutal Japanese cops during the colonial period. I saw communists during the Korean War. I have never seen cruelty like this before!"

A middle-aged man ground his teeth. "I am a veteran of the Vietnam War. I killed Vietcong. But we were never this brutal. These kids were beaten to death. It would have been kinder to shoot them. We should kill all those bastards!"

A terrible silence fell over the city. The roads and sidewalks were soaked with blood. To resist seemed to me inconceivable. Frankly, I could hardly move my legs. I could see nothing anymore. Of course, I was crying.

Whenever I think of that scene, it comes to mind as clearly as a nightmare movie.

It won't go away.

This was "Fascinating Vacations," to use the military code name for the operation.

Later, on the last day of the uprising, the last operation of all was to go under the code name "Loyalty." That was to be the day for killing dissidents.

The 7th Special Forces Brigade was the key unit we saw. It acted as Chun Doo Hwan's private army, we thought. From the very start of the operations that day, the soldiers acted as if they had licenses to kill.

That night, the Martial Law Command local HQ announced a curfew, to take effect from 9 P.M. Everyone had to stay inside. No one could go out. But the people did not sleep. Horror and rage hung over the city like a fog. The telephone lines buzzed with rumors of the crackdown—a wildfire of whispers.

I couldn't get a wink of sleep.

May 19, Dawn

As dawn broke I rode my bicycle to my brother's shop. I laid a package of cloth on my bike, to make it look as if I was working. I needed some kind of disguise, not to appear as a student.

By 10 A.M. about 4,000 people, I estimated, had gathered at Gumnam-ro. The numbers kept going up. Most people watched silently while the soldiers set up cordons and checkpoints. Some part of Gumnam-ro had already been sealed off at dawn. The soldiers stopped the buses and checked people's IDs, always the young kids. Most stores around there stayed shut.

But around the usual street markets it was different. The hawkers were there. They exchanged stories of what they had seen before. The brutality had made its mark on these people.

The heart of the city pounded. Anger grew. Sorrow bubbled from beneath the surface. More and more people gathered. About 10:40 A.M. people's anger was ready to burst. They swore and shook their fists at the helicopters overhead.

Suddenly the police attacked, again using tear gas. They went for the crowds in Gumnam-ro once more. But it was not a day like the previous day. Most of those on the street were not students. They were street vendors, store clerks, and housewives. The populace had turned out for the first time. They grew violent. They threw bits of broken flowerpots and bricks. They barricaded the streets, using rails they tore off and broken telephone booths that they had torn down with their hands.

I was astounded. I'd never expected anything like this. It was unbelievable. The day before no one had joined in, no ordinary citizens. All of a sudden they were acting in unison with the students.

I joined them. We threw stones. We snatched up steel pipes from a nearby construction site. The resisters became more and more militant, as they armed themselves, even with staves or pipes. Suddenly I recognized one of my school seniors in the mob. He gave me a huge grin and emptied out his pockets, giving me money. "Even if I cannot strike fully," he said, "I share this struggle with you." My eyes blinded with tears.

We all began to find ways to engage ourselves more fully. I issued orders to those with me to gather bottles and petrol for firebombs. One or two hours later we brought back two or three boxes full of these Molotov cocktails. The battle was picking up.

But how the paratroops counterattacked. They didn't duck the stones we threw at them. They simply ignored the firebombs. They tore through the crowd, swinging their bayonets, rifle butts, and heavy sticks.

Just near me, a soldier had grabbed a young man. He kept beating his chest as though trying to cave it in. Then he drew back his rifle, with bayonet fixed, and made two, three hits into the boy's back. The youth twisted his whole body, screaming and writhing with pain. In a moment the soldier's camouflage uniform was splashed with blood. It was all over in a flash. Nobody, I included, had been able to prevent this.

I was horrified by this display. Surely, that soldier did it for show. He wanted to terrify us. People scattered, leaving the injured on the streets.

Elsewhere, not far away, I saw that in an alley at the back of Suchang Elementary School two soldiers had caught a young woman.

The paratroopers stripped her, then they kicked her in the stomach, and they kicked her breasts. Finally, they slammed her up against the wall, beating her head against the wall, time and again. Their hands grew slick with blood. They wiped them on their uniforms and grinned. This done, they hauled the unconscious woman over to a truck and threw her into the back, like an old piece of sacking.

The paratroopers, I saw, really enjoyed their "Fascinating Vacation."

U.S. Responsibility for Kwangju

It goes without saying that, all during the months leading up to the Chun crackdown of May 17—during the entire half year between the murder of President Park and the accession of his fellow soldier from North Kyongsang province, Chun Doo Hwan—one of the key questions on the minds of students such as I was the attitude of the United States. We always believed this was primary. To the small group of "hardline" students and young workers I have named above—led by Yun Sang Won—there was no more important matter than what America would do.

We were, in a word, far too hopeful, if not pie-eyed in our optimism. We believed that the United States was the ultimate fount of "neoimperialism" in the world, as indicated in the long quotation from my *Kwangju Diary* cited earlier, that is to say we analyzed matters from a left-wing viewpoint of the type very common among students all over the world during and after the Vietnam War. At the same time, more pragmatically, we believed that the United States was far from indifferent to the reputation it had built up for itself as an aggressor in Vietnam; we noted that a "dove-ish" president, Jimmy Carter, was winner of the U.S. presidential elections in 1976. We thought, again as indicated earlier, that on balance Americans wanted democracy to prevail in Korea, for strategic reasons. A democratic South Korea would be a stronger ally in the longer run than one run by a military dictator. We noted the "human rights" element in Carter's thinking.

We never took very seriously Carter's assertions that he would withdraw from South Korea—a vital part of his 1976 campaign, when it came to foreign affairs. Or, putting it differently, we never spoke much of that. As soon as he was elected, Carter started to back away from his original position, which had been to call for the withdrawal of most U.S. forces in Korea. It took him three years to un-make his mind and visit South Korea, but in the end he did and met Park. Our belief in the primacy of the United States in our lives was based, among other things, on the fact that there were close to 50,000 U.S. soldiers in South Korea at any given time. The Korean peninsula, we knew, was considered one of the two or three most highly strategic spots in the world—along with the Middle East and Berlin. If anything major happened in Korea it was printed on page one of the *New York Times* and the *Washington Post* the next morning, all those thousands of miles away. Yun Sang Won was extremely alert to this fact of American interest in Korea, as seen through the press.

I note in my *Kwangju Diary* that Yun gave a press conference in the Provincial Hall on May 26—the day before he died along with so many comrades. For that press conference he made fairly exhaustive preparations as the spokesman for the "hardline" or, I should say, actual leadership:

> The spokesperson, Yun Sang Won, worked with the press to win public trust in the new leadership. In a bid to publicize the uprising, Yun held a press conference for many foreign correspondents and some domestic reporters (on May 26, as soon as the new leadership was installed). . . . Correspondents for America's *Asian Wall Street Journal* and *Baltimore Sun*, NBC, CBS, UPI, AP, Britain's *Sunday Times*, Japan's *Asahi*, NHK, and several other foreign correspondents attended the conference. Three South Korean papers, *Dong-A Ilbo*, *Kyonghyang Shinmun* and *Chonnam Ilbo*, also participated. A Korean employee of NHK, the Japanese public broadcasting station, translated the conference into English. With a set of flip charts, Yun Sang Won explained the new leadership's plan and overall situation and answered questions. (*KD*, p. 133)

In addition, Yun met that day with reporters from *Le Monde* and the *New York Times*—Phillippe Pons and Henry Scott-Stokes—for their own exclusive session. At these meetings his basic line was that the students in Kwangju looked to the United States to involve itself. He asked the American reporters not only to report to their newspapers but to contact

American officials in Seoul—he mentioned U.S. Ambassador Gleysteen—and urge them to intervene, to halt the bloodshed in Kwangju, and to bring medical supplies to save the lives of those in critical condition in Kwangju's hospitals. He purported to believe that America certainly would involve itself in a positive manner in Kwangju to settle things peacefully, rather than simply endorse Chun Doo Hwan for security reasons. Our analysis was that this would be best for the United States. For selfish reasons America would not want to see instability in South Korea.

I am not sure how much the student leadership in Kwangju knew of actual American movements in the region. In *Kwangju Diary* I recorded that Americans in the vicinity were suddenly withdrawn, as were U.S. warplanes:

> On May 21, two hundred Americans in Kwangju (mainly military) were evacuated. They were transported to Seoul by airplane from a nearby U.S. airbase in Songjung-ri. Between 9:00 P.M. and 12:00 A.M. all U.S. aircraft in Songjung-ri were redeployed to other U.S. airbases in Osan and Kunsan. (*KD*, p. 80)

But the student leaders were aware of bigger U.S. military steps. We knew, for example, that a carrier task force centering on the U.S. carrier *Coral Sea* had sailed into the waters off Korea, as events unrolled in Kwangju following the declaration of martial law by Chun. We saw hope in this development. Surely, the Americans would want to restrain Chun from cracking down with further bloodshed, thereby giving the United States a bad name. It was a slim hope, perhaps, but it was all that we had going for us. Yun Sang Won was quick to utilize any opportunities that arose. When the *New York Times* interviewed him, he made sure that posters went up in the square outside the Provincial Hall stating that the *Times* had come to report the situation. He announced the names of the reporters in question (Henry Scott-Stokes and Shim Jae Hoon) to the people in the square outside through posters. The intention was to boost their morale.

What was going on in Yun Sang Won's mind? Did he really believe that the United States would intervene? This was the very subject of a last conversation I had with him. It was a crucial topic, actually it was *the* crucial topic. I remember this conversation as if it had taken place half an hour ago, instead of two decades ago ... I met Yun at the YWCA hall on May 23, in the evening at 5 P.M., with about fifteen other men. They included Chun Yong Ho and five or six others I knew, for example Lee Yang Hyun, a labor activist who became planning director under the "hardline" leadership. Another person there was Park Hyo Sun, who became the publicity bureau chief of that new leadership—he was originally a teacher and a member of Clown, the theater activist group. We gathered to assess the outcome of a big rally just ending in the square in front of the Provincial Hall.

Initially, we exchanged information on other matters than the U.S. role. I reported what was happening, seen from my angle. First, I said, we needed to pay attention to the Settlement Committee run by older citizens. Local government officials and well-known citizens on that committee, I said, had increasing opportunities to distort the whole thrust of what the people wanted. I urged a strong line. I was in favor of holding citywide rallies to change the leadership of the Settlement Committee, thereby preserving solidarity with the citizens and securing unity in action. Second, I said, we were completely isolated by the martial-law army and besieged by them. To survive, we had to strengthen our defenses, with the possibility of an attack in mind; it could come at any time. Third, I maintained, we had to economize on the use of scarce gasoline supplies in the city. Cars and trucks had to stop dashing about and using up fuel. We had to keep an eye on food supplies and emerging shortages. Finally, we were short of ammunition, and we should consider how to use the dynamite we had seized along with other supplies and kept stored in the Provincial Hall. Yun Sang Won completely agreed with what I said.

The conversation turned toward the position of the United States . . . I clearly remember one part of that exchange.

"What do you expect of the United States? Do you really believe that the United States will help us, as someone just said at the rally?" I asked. It had been announced at the rally that the carrier *Coral Sea* was on its way into South Korean waters:

> The United States dispatched two airborne command-post planes and the aircraft carrier *Coral Sea* to South Korean waters. The carrier was headed home from duty in the Indian Ocean when it was diverted as a show of force when the Kwangju uprising erupted. It was reported that Washington placed the protection of South Korea against the North as a top priority. Its second priority was to work through South Korea's domestic problems. When they heard that a U.S. aircraft carrier would

enter the port city of Pusan, the insurgents were naively hopeful. "The U.S. is coming to help us," people thought. "If it knows about the massacre, the U.S. Government will not forgive Chun Doo Hwan and his clique." (*KD*, p. 110)

I asked Yun, "Do you really believe the U.S. will help us?"

He looked at me steadily and then said, "No, I don't, but possibly I should say 'yes.'"

"What do you mean by that?" I asked immediately.

"I'm not sure that the United States will truly help us, but there is no way to avoid saying what we say now. If I say 'no' in front of people, how could we mobilize the masses? We need to give people hope, to let them believe that there can be a peaceful outcome to this cruel incident. I am eager to believe that the United States will help us."

I nodded, acquiescing in what he said. I asked no more. I went home, thoroughly exhausted. This was the last time I saw Yun Sang Won. I left Kwangju on the following day, May 24, heading for Seoul, leaving my colleagues to cope as best they could.

The Gleysteen Position

Meanwhile, up in Seoul, on that same day

> . . . William Gleysteen, the U.S. ambassador to Seoul, had a luncheon meeting with eight members of the National Assembly. The Assembly had already been dissolved by the military. A National Assembly member expressed appreciation for America's role in maintaining South Korean national security, and explained his concerns over the unrest in Kwangju. The ambassador said that the Carter administration held South Korea's political situation at a higher priority than the problems in Iran (the U.S. hostage crisis in Teheran) and Afghanistan (invaded by the Soviet Union in 1979). He also said his government through certain diplomatic channels had delivered a clear message to North Korea about the U.S. commitment to South Korea. (*KD*, p. 119)

Gleysteen's views focused, then, on North Korea, not on how to end the Kwangju incident peacefully. My experience was that Yun Sang Won was the only person who had thought through what was involved in this regard. When I was shown his photo by Norman Thorpe, as mentioned earlier, after the passage of sixteen years, this is the thought that came to me. Really, only Yun knew.

In Conclusion?

It might be useful to step back and consider history. The Cholla provinces, going back at least to the ninth century A.D., somehow fostered a radical tradition. Zen Buddhism, imported from China, took on a radical hue in the Cholla regions of that era. This did not happen elsewhere in Korea, but it is a commonplace that Cholla danced to a different drummer . . . Pressing the fast-forward button and coming to the present century: the discrimination practiced against Cholla under Park Chung Hee after he seized power in 1961—his refusal to treat the region on a basis of equality—was obvious to all at the time; coveted appointments went to officials from other regions, as did the people's tax money. The Cholla provinces' under-weighting in national budgeting was pronounced throughout the modern period in Korea, dating back to Park's coup d'état and climb to power in the early 1960s. That bias was based in turn on centuries of tension between the different provinces of Korea, notably Kyongsang—from which both Park and Chun came—and Cholla. The radical streak in the Cholla tradition surfaced in an agrarian uprising—the Donghak Peasants' Revolution of 1894 and again after World War II, when the Cholla area was more left-wing in the early post-1945 years than most of what became North Korea.

Without a knowledge of these events—without this background—it is not easy perhaps for a non-Korean to see how the Korean military could have hit any part of their own nation as hard as they hit Kwangju in May 1980. Their error—a basic error of analysis—was to confuse a long-standing tradition of rugged independence and radicalism in Cholla with communist sympathies. The way people in Kwangju sang the national anthem at rallies—and waved the national flag at every opportunity—was a reflection, simple and uncalculated, of the very strong patriotism that exists in Kwangju and in Cholla at large.

How could the Korean military not see this? In part, it was a lack of education. Chun himself had essentially no education other than military-academy training. He mixed only with academy classmates. His friendship with Roh Tae Woo, the number two in the junta that shot its way to power in Seoul in December 1979, was a friendship between intellectual non-equals: Chun, the rough, tough leader type; Roh, the much softer, more thoughtful, more subtle personality. Chun, many years later, still did not—could not—understand what he had done at Kwangju.

As head of military intelligence in Seoul he believed in a basic assessment that Kwangju was a Kim Dae Jung stronghold, shot through with pro-communist sympathies. Such a view had been encouraged by the KCIA for years, if not decades. Unfortunately, lacking a free press, South Korea was subject to Red scares of a type encouraged by the United States once the Cold War set in after World War II. There is no evidence that Chun's mind ever enlarged to the point where he understood the larger issues. Look at the film clips of Chun and Roh at their joint trial in Seoul in 1996. Roh, to judge by his expression and demeanor, understands everything. He has been cornered. He lowers his head. Chun is supremely unaware and confident, even uninterested. He never got it.

Thus, the question of U.S. responsibility resurfaces. Could Americans in Seoul not *see* who they were dealing with in Chun? Strictly speaking, Gleysteen, as the senior American in Seoul, representing the president, was the person who was supposed to deal with Chun and other Korean leaders. They had almost no interest in him. The person they took seriously was General John A. Wickham, the senior U.S. officer in Korea. Under a joint-command structure set up with the U.N. during the Korean War, Wickham was the general in command of most of South Korea's 600,000 soldiers. Nominally, a U.N. commander, he was, like others who hold the post, first and foremost an American general. It was to him that Korean military people looked, to give them a lead. Meanwhile, Wickham, for his part, needed someone to deal with, it really didn't terribly matter who that person was, he had to be there. Chun was there. When he walked into a room, heads turned. He had a certain physical magnetism. Other Korean soldiers looked to him . . . Wickham responded to that. Once the Kwangju uprising had receded—in the summer of 1980—Wickham let it be known that he expected Chun to step up into the presidency, displacing his puppet acting president (Choi Gyu Ha). He let his views come out through the American press—at an interview he gave to two of the contributors to this book, Terry Anderson of the Associated Press and Sam Jameson of the *Los Angeles Times*. Wickham gave that interview on condition that it was sourced only to a senior U.S. official, not himself by name. However, on the following day, Chun, meeting with Henry Scott-Stokes and Shim Jae Hoon of the *New York Times*, let it be known that he appreciated Wickham's endorsement. Weeks later Chun made himself president, an office he was to hold for seven years—a period during which anti-American feeling rose to a pitch never before seen in South Korea.

Professor Bruce Cumings, in an introduction to *Kwangju Diary*, described the situation in these terms:

> Kwangju convinced a new generation of young (Koreans) that the democratic movement had developed not with the support of Washington, as an older generation of more conservative Koreans thought, but in the face of daily American support for any dictator who could quell the democratic aspirations of the Korean people. The result was an anti-American movement in the 1980s that threatened to bring down the whole structure of American support for the ROK. American cultural centers were burned to the ground (more than once in Kwangju); students immolated themselves in protest of Reagan's support for Chun . . . (*KD*, p. 27)

Such were the fruits of the massacres in Kwangju . . . Yet Yun Sang Won had fostered an attitude, that took root, that in the longer run the United States was an indispensable support for democracy in Korea. And so it turned out.

> At the end of 1986 American policy shifted, however, as Washington began to worry about a popular revolution in South Korea and as U.S. policy shifted on a world scale toward support for limited forms of democracy . . . the Philippines was a test case for the Reagan Administration after the murder of Benigno Aquino in 1983. A secret NSC directive approved in November 1984 called for American intervention in Philippine politics—"we are urging revitalization of democratic institutions, dismantling 'crony' monopoly capitalism and allowing the economy to respond to free market forces." . . . Washington vastly augmented the Manila embassy's political staff. The same thing happened in late 1986 in Korea, as long-time CIA official James R. Lilley became ambassador to Seoul and began meeting with opposition forces for the first time since 1980. (*KD*, p. 28).

Thus came the first overt signs of a sea change in U.S. policy toward South Korea, a shift that involved, among other things, a reassessment of what had happened in Kwangju in 1980. Foreign reporters who had been on the spot in Kwangju surely helped to turn the tide by their objective reporting of the most violent scenes to have taken place in Korea since the Civil War (1950–53).

Yun Sang Won in 1980.

Children at a grave.

A captured jeep.

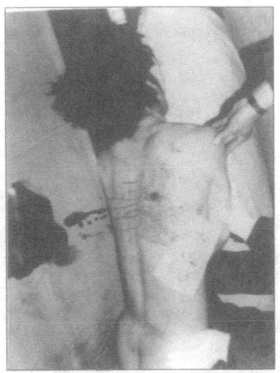

A victim.

A grieving relative.

Arrest of a protestor.

Troops beating protestors in the street.

Protestors being herded into waiting trucks.

The world press at work.

The Citizens' Army.

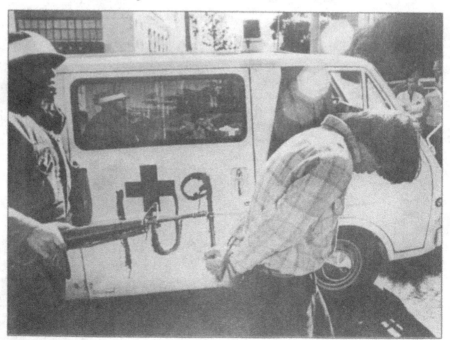

Soldier with captive.

Hysterical captive.

Government soldiers' packs in front of Provincial Hall.

photo by Na Kyung Taek

Action on Gumnam-ro.

Troops wearing riot gear.

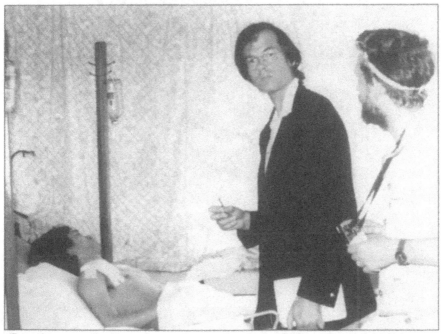

Foreign correspondents interviewing victim. Donald Kirk, center.

©1980 by Norman Thorpe

Yun Sang Won in death.

PART TWO

THE FOREIGN PRESS

Introduction

The idea of a bunch of foreign correspondents sitting down years after an event and writing about it once again might seem odd. It is in fact rare for foreign correspondents to retrace their steps like this. One may trace the genesis of this effort to one man—namely Bradley Martin of the *Baltimore Sun*—or rather to two men, to Brad and to the leader of the hard-line student militants in Kwangju, Yun Sang Won. Brad interviewed Yun with others on May 26, 1980. He could not forget Yun, even though he did not know and was unable to ascertain the student leader's name at the time. He eventually learned the name, as he states in his piece, many years later, from a Kwangju-born human rights activist, Eugene Soh. Brad's moving piece traces Yun's life, dwelling on how this then quite unheralded twenty-nine-year-old turned the potential fiasco of the Kwangju uprising into a triumph of the human spirit. It is thanks to Yun that Kwangju now ranks, in the words of President Kim Dae Jung, as a "holy place."

CHAPTER THREE

REMEMBERING KWANGJU

Terry Anderson

Devil Unmasked

Covering the Kwangju rebellion in 1980 was one of the most difficult, exhausting, and emotionally demanding assignments I have ever had. Though a professional triumph for the Associated Press (AP) and for me personally, it left me with emotional and psychological scars that took years to heal.

I had been writing about South Korea for several years before Kwangju. I was assigned to Tokyo in 1976 after two years in the AP's domestic service and jobs in both radio/television and newspaper journalism. I had lived in Japan before—during a six-year stint in the U.S. Marine Corps, including a tour in Vietnam. Despite being married to a Japanese and having some knowledge of the language, the country—with its closed social structure and psychology and the ever-present tinge of xenophobia—was difficult for a foreigner to live in. I welcomed my frequent trips to South Korea, which I found much more open and congenial to an American.

My main assignment in South Korea was to take the heat off our local correspondent, K.C. Hwang, one of the finest journalists I have had the pleasure of working with. Under the dictatorial regime of Park Chung Hee, in spite of his skill and courage, there were many stories that were just too dangerous for "K.C." to cover himself. The threat of arrest and imprisonment was always present for him. (In fact, at one point, he was abducted by South Korean intelligence agents and held for five days before being forced to agree not to speak of his imprisonment and released.) Therefore, I would often fly to Seoul and, using K.C.'s encyclopedic knowledge and extensive sources, write about the labor unrest or political issues that he could not safely cover. Like all journalists, I was followed and my telephone conversations were listened to by the Korean Central Intelligence Agency (KCIA), but I was never interfered with. At that time, the most an American correspondent had to fear was temporary or permanent expulsion from the country.

I came to like and admire many people, including opposition leaders who risked their freedom and even their lives, but most especially K.C. and the many other first-class journalists I worked with. I looked forward to every trip.

The Assassination of Park Chung Hee

In October of 1979, I had been in Seoul for a week or so on several stories. There were few foreign correspondents there at the time. In fact, on the night of October 26, there was only one other, a Reuters man. Deep asleep at the Chosun Hotel, I was wakened by a predawn telephone call from K.C.

"I'm not sure what's going on, but something bad has happened," he told me. "I think the president (Park Chung Hee) has been shot, and there are tanks on the street. Can you get to the office?"

I lurched out of bed, regretting the evening spent in the Chosun's bar, dressed hurriedly, and headed down the street for the AP office. While I saw some police and military activity, it did not seem unusual, and nobody stopped me. At the AP, K.C., his assistant Simon Kim, and the third local AP staffer, Mr. Ahn, filled me in. There had been an abrupt and taciturn announcement on the radio: the prime minister, Choi Gyu Ha, had assumed the duties of president in accordance with the constitution. There was no explanation, no word on what had happened to President Park (after eighteen years of rule, including seven years as president under his Yushin Constitution of 1972, a charter that made Park, a former army general, president for life).

K.C. hit the phones, tapping all his sources. I began writing. Slowly, in dribs and drabs, the official information expanded. Park had been wounded in a shooting accident. Several others had also been hurt. Park was seriously wounded. Several were dead. Park was dead.

As each government communiqué was issued, K.C.'s sources filled in the story. That night and over the succeeding days, we gradually learned and printed the truth. The president was at a small, private party with a famous actress and several officials. The head of the KCIA, Kim Jae Kyu, had invited Park to dinner. Then he and his aides shot him and five bodyguards to death. Kim was in league with several other top civilian and military officials, and, although Choi was nominally acting president, they had taken over the country.

Their rule lasted only a few weeks. What Kim Jae Kyu and the generals with him had forgotten was that they actually directly commanded no troops other than those that manned their headquarter offices. A number of younger South Korean army officers loyal to Park Chung Hee were very unhappy with the coup, and they *did* have troops. On December 12, 1979, a former colonel (soon to be lieutenant general) named Chun Doo Hwan ordered his men into action. Kim Jae Kyu and the others were arrested. A new group of military officers was in charge.

Chun quickly earned support from the United States, which was far more interested in stability on the Korean peninsula than in who was in charge. For the next five months, the newly minted military chief consolidated his power under the martial law originally imposed by the men he had jailed. But he was not without opposition, especially from South Korea's ever politically active students.

Chun's Grievous Error

I was in Seoul yet again in May, following that consolidation, when news came of serious student riots in the southern provincial capital of Kwangju—the power base of Korea's most prominent political dissident, Kim Dae Jung. On May 1 several hundred students had marched in Kwangju to protest martial law and demand an end to Chun's hard-fisted rule. The protests continued for the next two weeks, spreading to Seoul and other cities. Then Chun made a grievous error. On May 17 he extended the already wide rule of martial law, began arresting opposition figures (including Kim Dae Jung) and sent into Kwangju units of paratroopers from elsewhere—highly trained, hard men who already had a regional antipathy to the southerners.

The paratroopers launched a virtual army riot, chasing demonstrators through the streets, clubbing, gassing, and even shooting many in front of the astonished and increasingly outraged citizens of Kwangju. Soldiers chased young men into stores and even onto city buses to catch them and drag them away. The riots spread. Clashes with police and soldiers grew more vicious. In Seoul we dispatched young Simon Kim to Kwangju. On the night of May 20 the telephoned dispatch was grim. Some 100,000 demonstrators, no longer just students, had besieged the provincial capital building, the Provincial Hall, always the great rallying point in the city, a symbolic center.

The army opened fire, killing many. The city rose in rage. By the next day the townspeople had destroyed the Korean Broadcasting Service office and many tax offices, raided local armories, and were battling the army. Chun ordered both police and army units out of the city, hoping the situation would calm.

By then, I was on my way to Kwangju, accompanied by *Time* magazine photographer Robin Moyer, who happened to be in the AP office in

Seoul as I was leaving. We flew to a nearby city, hired a reluctant taxi driver, and headed for Kwangju. At dusk we were ten or fifteen kilometers from the city when we began to run into refugees streaming back down the road. They warned that the road ahead was very dangerous, with small firefights between protestors and soldiers breaking out without warning. The taxi driver stopped the cab and made it clear that he intended to go no further. Robin and I got out and began walking down the road.

A few kilometers later, we came across the first sign of violence—a burning city bus blocking the road. We continued into the darkness. By now, there was absolutely no one to be seen on the road or in the houses we infrequently passed. Finally, some time after midnight, we entered the edge of Kwangju. The signs of fighting were frequent now, with cars and buses lying on their sides, burned out or with all the glass destroyed.

As we came to the first two- and three-story buildings, we saw a barricade of vehicles ahead. A shot was fired, and we ducked against a wrecked bus. Neither Robin nor I understood or spoke more than one or two words of Korean. Mustering my courage, I shouted out "*Kija! Kija!*" meaning "reporter." Raising my hands, I stepped carefully away from the bus and walked toward the barricade. We could hear the snap of rifles being cocked from the tops of the buildings on either side. A shadowy figure stepped out to me and spoke in Korean. I slowly offered my Korean press card, making no quick movement that might alarm the other person. Finally, someone spoke in English, offering to take us to the rebel headquarters. We quickly agreed.

By dawn, we had identified ourselves satisfactorily to the leaders of the rebellion, located Simon Kim, and were traveling through the city trying to assess the situation. As a reporter for the AP, which provides first basic and accurate information to all the world's media, I was most immediately concerned with gathering accounts of the previous two days and finding out exactly how many people had been killed. That proved impossible. No one could tell me how many people had been arrested and taken away by the paratroopers, but many accounts were given of soldiers loading bodies onto trucks before pulling out of the city. I did my best, moving from temporary morgue to temporary morgue around Kwangju. By afternoon I had counted more than 100 bodies, some shot, some bludgeoned, some crushed by vehicles. The sight of those victims and the sickly-sweet, overpowering smell of bodies decomposing were burned into my mind.

Getting the Story Out

My next task was to find some way to tell the story. The South Korean army had already surrounded the city and cut off all telephone and telegraph service. A kind Korean minister, who had provided much of our transportation during the day, offered an alternative. He knew where there were some bicycles we could borrow and could guide us to a possible route—down small lanes and across rice paddy dikes—out of the city to the nearest known operating telephone in a post office fifteen to twenty kilometers away. I eagerly accepted the offer.

That began a week of exhausting, sometimes grimly funny efforts to get my dispatches to AP's Seoul office. After the first couple of days, the minister kindly offered us use of his own car—which we plastered with "Press" signs and proceeded to beat nearly to death on bad roads and tracks, slipping through the army's lines and back again. The post office was our most frequent destination. We made one attempt to use the telephone at a nearby U.S. army post. The officers there allowed us to file once, but, listening in on my report, decided the whole thing was far too controversial for them and banned us from the base.

Those days were filled with both action and a horrible suspense. We talked to the newly formed citizens' committee that was trying to negotiate a compromise between the hard-line students and the harder-line army. We talked to students on the barricades hastily erected on major streets. We even tried to interview (without success) the soldiers on the other side. Several times we were detained for hours by the army, which strongly opposed our presence in the town. Over everyone hung the knowledge that compromise was unlikely, that sooner or later the battle would be joined, and that the rebels had no chance. Their few rifles (around 4,000 weapons taken from the local armories) were less than a snowflake against tanks and armored personnel carriers and heavy machine-guns.

On one occasion, after the student leaders had begun to organize themselves, we had an hour-long session with a young student leader, designated as press liaison, who issued crude press cards to the fewer than a dozen foreign correspondents who had made their way into Kwangju. That interview remains clear in my mind, both for the passion and the convincing arguments of the young man, and because of the circumstances in which I next saw him. His name was Yun Sang Won [Ed: see contribution by Bradley Martin].

The foreign press had all gathered in a small hotel just behind the Provincial Hall, now the rebels' main office. There were of course few businesses or restaurants open, and even food was becoming increasingly scarce. At one small restaurant opened just for the evening to feed the press corps, the proprietor gently observed at the end of the meal that we had consumed his entire stock of meat and nearly all his vegetables. Another businessman heard me complaining that I had entirely worn out the soles of my brand-new, light, Italian-made loafers. He found the owner of a shoe store, who rolled up the iron screen on his shop and searched his stock for extra-large shoes. The best he could find was a pair of sneakers, one size too small, which I happily paid for, ignoring the pinching of my toes.

By then it was clear that more than 300 people (a conservative estimate) had died in that first burst of battle between the townspeople and the soldiers. It was feared that many more would follow them before the end. The army had tightened its ring around the city, frightening many and causing urgent, but false, press reports of an attack by moving its dozens of tanks closer to the center of Kwangju.

The people of the city were scared, but determined. Many ordinary citizens had joined the students and manned makeshift barricades on the main roads. They stared over light rifles at the tanks and armored vehicles of the army, just seventy-five yards or so away. The heaviest weapon I saw among the rebels was a Korean War–vintage antitank gun, unlikely to cause any damage to the modern tanks it was pointed at.

By now a dozen or more foreign journalists had slipped into the city. They were eagerly welcomed by the students, who wanted the world to know what was happening in Kwangju. As we drove around the city in our car bedecked with "Press" and "AP" signs, we were cheered by every crowd.

The Final Assault

Finally, at 2 A.M. on May 27, the army issued its ultimatum. Surrender in two hours, or face attack.

At the Provincial Hall, students handed out M-1 rifles. Others drove through the center of the city, calling on the citizens to help them. But few responded to the call. We could hear the tanks grinding down the avenues toward the center square and the beginnings of rifle fire. It was obvious that anyone in the open when the final attack came risked death.

The correspondents, by agreement, withdrew to the small hotel behind the Provincial Hall, where we watched from darkened windows. The firefights grew heavier, and we could hear heavier weapons being used.

Just before dawn, I watched paratroopers filter quietly around the hotel, then begin their assault on the Provincial Hall. Using classic urban warfare tactics, one unit swarmed up the outside of the building to the top, then began working its way down, floor by floor. The soldiers threw stun grenades into each room and shot at anything that moved.

As the light grew, I saw two paratroopers on top of the building, just fifteen or twenty yards away. Taking my camera, I cautiously crouched at the window, trying to take a picture. Both men spotted me, then opened up with their M-16s. The first bullet struck inches from my ear, and I threw myself into a corner where Ahn and another correspondent were already crouched. When the soldiers began shooting through the thin lath-and-plaster wall, we dived frantically out of the room into the hallway. We had believed the government knew this hotel was occupied by foreign press, but either no one had told the soldiers or they didn't care.

The attack on the Provincial Hall was the end of the battle, though occasional gunfire continued for an hour or so. As the foreign press—including one television crew—emerged from the hotel, we encountered a senior army sergeant seated and trembling from adrenaline. He pointed his rifle at us and shouted in Korean. We waved our press cards, but he refused to allow us to pass. Just then, a colonel drove up in a jeep. We pushed past the sergeant and called out to him.

"Colonel, how many casualties?"

The officer, who had the name "Kim" sewn above his shirt pocket, responded: "two rebels and one soldier killed." Then strode away.

In a small group, we walked through the fence around the Provincial Hall and counted seventeen bodies. One was Yun Sang Won, the rebels' press spokesman: his body was partially burned and the magazine of a .45-caliber pistol lay near his hand.

We watched lines of students, hands tied behind them, being herded onto buses. We counted at least sixty or seventy people, including young women and one boy of about ten.

Three months later, Chun Doo Hwan was formally named president of South Korea. A month later, Kim Dae Jung, blamed for the rebellion, was put through a mockery of a trial and finally sentenced to death (to be reprieved early in 1981 in a deal with the Reagan administration under which Chun was invited to Washington, D.C.). It was the last story I covered in South Korea. I was transferred to South Africa in 1981, then to Beirut, Lebanon.

It was both ironic and satisfying, sixteen years later, to read of the trial of Chun and his successor as president, Roh Tae Woo, for corruption, under the presidency of Kim Young Sam, to be followed by Kim Dae Jung as president finally, this time in a free and democratic Korea.

As journalists we are rightly required to be neutral, to do our best to be objective. But that requirement does not mean we do not know right from wrong and cannot tell the difference between dictators and freely elected leaders, between victims and oppressors. Often that difference is unclear and muddled, and the best we can do is report what we see, what we know to be true, and hope our readers can understand. Kwangju was the first major story I covered where the difference was absolutely clear to me, and I tried to make it clear to my readers, not with opinion, but with fact. I am proud that we were able to do so.

CHAPTER FOUR

A NIGHTMARE IN BROAD DAYLIGHT

Gebhard Hielscher

Blood and Tears 1

Monday morning, May 26, 1980: I am at the Hwasung exit from the expressway, twelve kilometers south of Kwangju—at this time a beleaguered city. This is where cars, including my taxi, have to stop. Riding a rented bicycle, I mingle with pedestrians, bicyclists and motorcyclists commuting between Hwasung and Kwangju. There are young people, mothers with infants strapped to their backs, old women dressed in the traditional wide skirts and balancing huge bundles on their heads, and occasionally old men with parched brown skin, sporting black cylindrical straw hats—as if straight from a picture book of the old Korea.

At the entrance of a tunnel, this pastoral idyll ends abruptly. A burned-out truck blocks the road. On the far side of the tunnel, once through it, a rain-washed sign put up by the Kwangju Chamber of Commerce reads: "The future of the Fatherland is the responsibility of our youth!" A few meters farther on, an overturned jeep lies in a ditch. Closer to the city, the stream of people deviates from a well-paved county road, number 15, and continues along bumpy paths past villages, garbage dumps, chicken farms, and then a shallow riverbed.

I pass through a military checkpoint and find my way back to Highway 15. There, I am stopped by a group of soldiers standing near a machine gun posted in the fields. They inspect my passport, recognize that I am German, and let me pass. The passport does not indicate that I am a journalist.

Suddenly, there are no more soldiers. Instead, there are two rows of demolished city buses. They block the entire road. The shattered buses are daubed in letters of red paint: "Tear Chun Doo Hwan to pieces." The reference is to Lieutenant-General Chun, chief of the Defense Security Command and of the civilian secret service, the Korean Central Intelligence Agency (KCIA)—the strongman of South Korea. Back in December he staged a cloak-and-dagger attack, seizing the army chief of staff in Seoul and putting him on trial for alleged complicity in the assassination of President Park Chung Hee. Here in Kwangju Chun is held responsible for a bloodbath of civilians—the work of Special Forces paratroopers he despatched to the spot last week. These forces had cracked down on students and citizens when they demonstrated against an extension of martial law announced by the military.

There are four kilometers to go, to the center of Kwangju. I pass a first burned-out police station. More will follow. Most stores have their iron shutters lowered. Citizens stand about in groups on the sidewalk. The streets themselves are empty, save for an occasional bicyclist.

Police are nowhere in sight. Nevertheless, one does not get the impression that chaos rules. Market vendors hawk fruit and vegetables at tiny stalls. At the offices of *Chonnam Maeil Shinmun,* one of two local papers, the iron-bar gates are lowered. A few windows have been smashed. The local television studios—those of the Korean Broadcasting Service (KBS) and of the Munhwa Broadcasting Co. (MBC), a commercial network—are burned out.

"They didn't report what happened here," said an elderly man. "That's why people got angry."

The Provincial Hall

The seat of government in the province shines brightly in its white paint. The building is undamaged. In the wide courtyard in front, young men stand guard over captured military and police vehicles. A few steps away, a black prison van stands, its barred windows pierced through. Close by is a jeep, taken charge of by a group of carbine-toting youths complete with medieval-style riot-police gear—helmets and leather neck-protectors, a strange sight indeed.

Access to the hall is controlled by orderlies. People waiting there are admitted in groups. They are searching for missing relatives. They are led to a passageway in the courtyard. Thirteen wooden coffins stand there, the lids left half-open—they contain the bodies of young men who have been shot or beaten to death. Sobbing women and men move from coffin to coffin.

Just opposite the Provincial Hall is a small gymnasium. Here, dead people who have been identified already are being mourned, victims of the bloody massacre of Kwangju. Exactly sixty coffins are lined up in orderly fashion. Most are covered with white cloth, bound with thick rope, and decorated with the flag of South Korea. Photos of the dead, the frames wrapped in mourning crape, stand on some of the coffins. Nearby is a makeshift altar where incense is burned. A cardboard box is stuffed with donations—bank notes.

A young man beats desperately on one of the boxes. "My younger brother is in here. How could Korean soldiers shoot Koreans!"

No one looks after coffins numbered 56 to 58. Here is a whole family. A boy of only seven—barely a first-grader in school—his mother, and his father. Someone has placed a bunch of white chrysanthemums on the little boy's coffin. A group of young girls has gathered in the next row. They are students of Shuntae Economic High School in Kwangju. One of their classmates is lying dead before them. This, they cannot comprehend. Their voices choked with tears, the girls sing a farewell song. Then one of them turns round and, facing people on a platform there, makes a dramatic appeal. Seventeen-year-old Park Keum Hee shall not have died in vain. At the end everybody in the hall starts to sing South Korea's national anthem.

"Long live the Republic of Korea, long live democracy."

By making manifest their patriotism, the bereaved of Kwangju, gathered in this ceremony to mourn the dead, are rebuffing attempts by the government to defame those who died as communist agitators. They are giving voice to their rejection of the military's suffocating omnipotence—and its brutality.

A Leaflet from Chosun University

Here is part of the text of a leaflet put out by the "Committee to Fight for Democracy" of a local university, Chosun University. This is how people see events:

> On the night of May 17 Chun Doo Hwan and his gang expanded martial law and arrested and jailed all politicians and democratic personalities who do not agree with their plans. Thus the fragile hope of democracy that we had nurtured was wiped out. To meet a peaceful demonstration of democratic citizens, gathered to express their outrage, Chun mobilized more than 30,000 riot police, blocked the escape routes, closed in from front and behind, and fired tear gas.
>
> The ring was closed, nobody could flee. Thereupon 3,000 military men, rushed in from Seoul, whipped out bayonets, and like butchers gone mad, they stabbed everything and everyone in their way, like pumpkins. Streams of blood flowed. They threw the corpses onto the backs of army trucks and, as if this wasn't enough, they broke down the gates of private homes, dragged out those who tried to escape, and stabbed them with their bayonets, all this in full view of the people at large. In the face of such brutality, the citizens were infuriated and began to resist. Those who fought with bare hands were stabbed back with bayonets. An aged woman

of seventy, who saw a female student on the point of bleeding to death, grabbed a soldier by the neck and was stabbed to death with a bayonet.

The leaflet continued: "The victims killed in this massacre by special order of Chun Doo Hwan amount to more than 200. The number of wounded adds up to more than 1,000. But the mass media, whose duty it was to report this tragedy, reported no word of this nightmare. It lasted for five days from May 17 to 21."

A Hospital Visit

It is Monday evening. A doctor, who studied at Chosun University and has many friends there, comments, visibly shaken: "This is like a real civil war, just terrible."

About 300 wounded are being treated in this university hospital. Doctors and nurses on duty here take some convincing before they will show victims to a foreigner. "This is a disgrace for Korea," they say with one voice.

One of the doctors overcomes his reluctance. He takes the visiting stranger from bed to bed. He points out those who are under intensive care, who fill one large hall. The wounds: bullets in the brain or in the eyes; smashed skulls; bulletholes in the chest or abdomen; bladders in shreds. How many of these patients will possibly survive?

What will happen now in a city, whose encirclement tightens a little more every night?

The rulers in Seoul relate how a "lawless condition"—which has prevailed already for almost one week—cannot be tolerated. Patience has worn thin for the kind of "community self-rule" that has spontaneously arisen in Kwangju. The end is nigh. And how do the self-rulers of Kwangju see their own chances?

"We shall continue until Chun Doo Hwan resigns," says one of the members of a twenty-four-man citizens' committee. "That goes without saying after the many sacrifices we have made." He puts the number of identified dead at 161.

Food supplies are supposed to be sufficient for another month, some say. But the man from the self-rule committee has his doubts. He apparently considers the chances of holding out that long are rather poor. "It would be good if we could speak with the American ambassador (William H. Gleysteen) as soon as possible and explain our situation to him."

Tuesday Morning, May 27: Outside Kwangju

The state-run radio: "Last night, between 3 and 5 A.M., the armed forces and the police returned to Kwangju. More than 200 students have surrendered. Two who resisted were killed."

A group of elderly men listens to the broadcast in a location outside Kwangju. There is an uncomfortable silence. Finally one of them speaks up. "That about the two dead is certainly a lie," he says bitterly. "There must have been many more."

Fast Forward to 1999—Getting Away with Murder

Nineteen years have passed since the events in question: Will justice ever be done from the point of view of the victims of the crimes committed at Kwangju during those days of horror in May 1980? I fear not. Not in the broad sense that the word "justice" implies. Nor perhaps in the narrower framework of the laws of Korea.

Let us take stock. In terms of Korea's political and legal history, I believe it was a great achievement that two former presidents—Chun Doo Hwan and Roh Tae Woo—and some other former generals were arrested in 1995 and put on trial on charges, among others, of having suppressed the prodemocracy movement in Kwangju on May 18, 1980. That both Chun and Roh were sentenced without the armed forces interfering in the judicial process may be counted as having helped to confirm the independence of the judiciary in Korea. Here was proof that democracy was established in Korea after decades of military dictatorship.

However, the sentences passed on Chun—a death sentence, later commuted to life in prison—and on Roh, as confirmed by the Korean Supreme Court in April 1997, contained a major flaw. They were pronounced in respect of "other charges." These were: the two former presidents' perpetration of a military coup d'état in December 1979, judged by the courts to have constituted the crime of mutiny; and their demand and acceptance of huge political slush funds, while in office, deemed bribery in the eyes of the law. No one was sentenced in connection with the events in Kwangju. The judges reasoned that it could not be established beyond doubt who gave the orders for the bloody orgy committed by the Special Forces in fact commanded by General Chung Ho Yong. At the same time, charges of "suppression of the prodemocracy movement in Kwangju" were among the charges raised against the two former presidents. In the eyes of the law these charges have been "consumed" or somehow covered—in practice, done away with—by the sentences passed. Thus, legally, the charges to do with Kwangju cannot be raised once more against Chun, Roh, Chung, and the other generals sentenced at the trial. For all practical purposes, the Kwangju case has been closed without anyone having been pronounced guilty, as if the massacres never happened.

It would still be possible, in theory, to prosecute lower-ranking officers and soldiers involved in the slaughter and mutilation of Kwangju citizens, if they could be identified and their criminal acts proven. But that is almost impossible, in practice. It would seem unfair to sentence only such lower-level culprits, while those actually in command went free.

As a result, the Kwangju massacres will most likely remain completely unavenged forever. This is a gross miscarriage of justice and a terrible insult to the victims. All that one can hope for is a gradual political reconciliation and some soothing of the bitter feelings of the families and friends of the victims and of those who survived the ordeal, yet with deep wounds in their bodies and minds.

Reconciliation, I am sure, was on the mind of President-elect Kim Dae Jung when he agreed, in December 1997, to a proposal by his predecessor Kim Young Sam to grant special pardons to the jailed ex-presidents and other generals sentenced with them. Kim Dae Jung was himself a victim of Chun—arrested, sentenced to death by Chun's judges on trumped-up charges and saved only after worldwide protests—and on those grounds the people of Kwangju resigned themselves to accepting Kim's magnanimous pardon. But I am sure that, deep down in their hearts, they resent how Chun, Roo, Chung, and others literally got away with murder, torture, and mutilation, carried out to a degree beyond imagination.

President Kim continues his efforts to strengthen the democratic process and the rule of law in Korea. As he does so, the citizens of Kwangju may come to see, eventually, that the sacrifices of their relatives and friends were at least not in vain. The very excesses committed by the military against their own Korean people generated the energy that eventually drove the power-hungry generals and colonels out of Korean politics.

But even if the culprits of Kwangju cannot be brought to justice, the conclusion is still not that the issue is closed. Rather, there is work to be done. It is to record what happened for generations to come. There have been various such efforts—by the citizens of Kwangju themselves, by the National Assembly in Seoul, and by the editors of this book, to name a few. But the records and findings have to be put together. They should be cross-checked and supplemented by an investigation along the lines of South Africa's Truth and Reconciliation Commission. Anyone who comes forward and reveals what he or she knows about these terrible events and their background would be guaranteed freedom against prosecution, whatever their personal involvement in criminal acts. That way, it should be possible to get many more witnesses to open up their hearts and minds, including some from the military who, by speaking out, could also relieve themselves of some of the nightmares their memories must cause.

True reconciliation can come only after the whole truth has been revealed. Truth is a precondition for reconciliation. Only those will be included in the reconciliation who have shared to the full what they know. As for the timing of such a project, I think it would be best if the necessary legislation could be enacted by the new National Assembly elected in April 2000. The commission should start work while President Kim Dae Jung is still in office—in other words, now.

CHAPTER FIVE

I BOW MY HEAD

Jurgen Hinzpeter

Blood and Tears 6

I was in Japan on the morning of Monday, May 19, 1980, when I heard the first news of an uprising in Kwangju. My immediate thought was to inform the ARD-NDR German TV Hamburg News Center. Unfortunately our studio chief was out of the office, the decision was left up to me in this important situation. I knew that I had to cover the story. The news out of South Korea was sparse indeed. The government had declared a full-blooded extension of martial law, to cover the entire nation. The military authorities were censoring the press, line by line, claiming that there was a risk of "political instability." The information blackout heightened my curiosity. I telephoned hither and thither. I finally managed to make some direct contact in Korea. The situation was escalating. There had been student deaths, and there were ongoing clashes between groups of students and soldiers. I phoned our News Center in Hamburg once more to receive approval to commute from Japan to Korea that very day. We agreed that I should leave Japan for Korea as soon as possible.

Not that I was comfortable with the prospect. First, it would be hard to get our material out of Korea and back to Hamburg. I would be far from Seoul, far from the only exit to the outside world at Kimpo (Seoul airport). The task ahead seemed difficult. I really had no idea how it would work out. Due to martial law there was no satellite transmission in those days. On top of that a modern satellite-transmission technology like today's was not available. I should explain that I gathered everything on 16mm film that had to be developed before it was transmitted. Meanwhile, it was unlikely, in my view, that Korean officials would permit a German TV crew to go to Kwangju, in view of the complete censorship. But mulling over these problems wasn't going to get me anywhere. Never giving up I was sure that I would find a way.

The main thing was that I had obtained a go-ahead from my head office to cover the news story. In fact, the ground was thus being prepared for our eventual historical TV documentary on the citizens' uprising in Kwangju. Heartened by the approval from home, I packed up my film equipment in Tokyo. My colleague—film-cutter and sound man, Henning Rumohr—and I departed, taking minimal equipment and enough cash for an extended journey. We headed for Narita, Tokyo's international airport. We boarded the first available flight to Seoul.

Everything went smoothly that day. At Kimpo the Korean customs officers refrained from their usual time-consuming ritual of double-checking our film and sound equipment. It was as if the media were being welcomed. Very strange, I thought. Never was the paperwork handled by Kimpo customs so swiftly, without complications of any kind. I felt uneasy. As I watched the procedures going forward, I wondered: Could there possibly be any small hope of political change, given the way Korean government officials usually behaved?

Outside, our driver Kim Sa Bok was waiting for us. We greeted each other, then sped off toward the Chosun Hotel in downtown Seoul. As we drove, Kim briefed us on the situation. It was too late to set out for Kwangju—several hundred kilometers to the south. We stayed the night at the hotel in Seoul.

Avoiding the KOIS

Normally, when I checked into Seoul, I made my presence known to the Korean Overseas Information Service (KOIS), a branch of the larger Ministry of Information and Culture, which took care of the foreign press by giving us the official accreditation papers. However, the situation being downright different on this occasion—with martial law extended to cover all South Korea, and with complete censorship of the press—I thought that it would be best to give KOIS a wide berth, not to inform them of our presence in Korea. This way we could avoid being under their control in any form.

We had taken the basic decisions. Not knowing what to expect, we would head south on the expressway, traveling by day. That was preferable. Kim, our experienced driver, agreed to this.

We departed early in the morning. We left everything behind at the hotel that we absolutely didn't need. We kept our rooms at the Chosun Hotel as it was far from certain that we would reach our destination, let alone go to work.

All routes to the south were blocked, it was said. The military had cordoned off the whole area. That was the story. However, nothing would hold me back. I was determined to get through.

One extra person joined us. He was another German correspondent from the writing press, also with an office in Tokyo. I warned him. I said that there was absolutely no guarantee that we would get through to Kwangju. We saw as much as we got onto the expressway. The sign on the expressway said "CLOSED." Yet our driver Kim was not put off. We sailed down an empty highway. That deserted expressway gave me the strangest feeling. Surely, we would be stopped.

After driving for an hour, we encountered detour signs. Kim paid no attention, he kept heading straight for Kwangju. With my camera at the ready, I sat in front watching out for anything of interest. Still, we kept driving on and on. Finally, about seventy-five kilometers short of Kwangju, we ran into a roadblock manned by armed soldiers. They gave the car a thorough inspection and waved us through. We continued, barreling down the expressway. Somehow we had learned that all traffic was being halted at a tunnel about thirty kilometers ahead. Very well, we would press on.

At the tunnel entrance we encountered heavily armed soldiers. This was different. There were at least fifteen heavy tanks parked in the opposite lane. This time, we had no choice but to obey. An officer in charge had his men aim their machine guns at our car just in case we were in doubt.

Off the expressway we went, onto quiet country roads. The contrast to the expressway was total. Suddenly we were trundling toward an idyllic country village surrounded by paddies. It was a beautiful spot. Yet the last few miles into Kwangju would be the toughest. The Martial Law Command, the supreme authority in those times, was clearly trying to keep the foreign press out of Kwangju.

What should we do? Kim consulted with the local farmers. We were soon on our way again. We pressed on by small side roads, heading past more paddies. But once again, we ran into soldiers. Every possible way into Kwangju was being sealed off. That was the impression.

I decided on a new strategy. I invented a story on the spot: We were looking for our boss. We had lost him in the vicinity. We must go through to find him. That was our obligation. We couldn't abandon our chief.

The ploy worked, as was later reported on the front page of *No. I Shimbun*, the monthly journal of The Foreign Correspondents' Club of Japan (see vol. 12, no. 5). The paper reported:

> That a good story, well told, still may work miracles was proven by the German TV crew that parleyed its way past a full-fledged (Korean) army major and several other manned checkpoints by insisting with those big, blue German eyes that they were not—of course not—going to shoot any film, but that they had to enter Kwangju to extricate their boss, who was trapped in a hostile environment. Theirs was a humanitarian mission—

not a journalistic one. They kept arguing with the soldiers until they were finally waved through.

Entering the City

Back we went onto the now deserted highway. The road was partly blocked. There was a makeshift barrier or two, composed of sand, stones and other debris, dumped there by the rebel citizens of Kwangju. We made our way past these obstacles, without difficulty.

We were now only a short distance from Kwangju. We proceeded very slowly and carefully. I had fixed our German TV flag on the car. I believed that a display of the national colors of Germany would help us. It would distinguish our car from a military vehicle of any description. We drove on, and a very short time after passing the barricades we met an oncoming, motley cavalcade. It consisted of a city bus lacking side windows, decorated with the Korean national flag; a military truck, obviously captured; and a jeep, carrying five armed people. As they approached us, we could see that the bigger vehicles were crammed with young men and students wearing headbands, armed with nothing more than sticks or small axes. They sang as they came. They were welcoming us. They stopped, and we too pulled up. With my colleague Henning I climbed onto the truck. I wanted to film them as we drove into town.

Up there on the truck the students wearing headbands were singing the national anthem of Korea. They waved the national *Taekukki* flag, as they sang. The young people on the bus beat time with their sticks, setting up a rhythm. Behind the bus followed the jeep, with its helmeted crew. I felt an overwhelming sense of hope, seeing these young people.

That first impression was not to last for long.

Entering the city, while still on the outskirts somewhere, we were immediately surrounded by a large crowd. There were thousands of people, young and old. Out of that vast throng, a man approached. He spoke in broken English. He was nervous. His body trembled. He was frequently overtaken by emotion, as he described the events of the night before. Many of his friends had been shot, he said. The hospitals were crammed with wounded. There was no space for them all, no way to nurse the wounded. Calming down, he then explained that the citizens really had no way to survive. The military was using weapons with night sights, capable of seeing through the darkness. There was nowhere to go, nowhere to hide from the bullets.

We drove next to a city hospital, entering by the back. It was a painful experience. People—relatives and friends—showed me their loved ones. They opened many, many of the coffins, set out in rows. Most of the bodies were those of very young people, no doubt students. They all had head wounds. They had died as a result of brutal beatings. It was hard to hold back my tears. I filmed what I could of this sad sight. Never in my life—never in Vietnam—had I seen anything like this. I was overwhelmed by mixed feelings of anger and sympathy.

What I saw on that first day in Kwangju wore me out. Night came. None of us dared to go out. There was shooting going on, somewhere in the darkness. Machine guns, by the sound of them. The hours of darkness flew by. The night seemed very short. I got up early the next day, still in darkness, listening to the sound of gunfire.

Beating the Print Media

My colleagues had not awakened. I had time to think, as the sun rose. The shooting we had heard before had stopped. It was Wednesday, May 21, which happened to be Buddha's Birthday, usually a happy day filled with colorful celebrations. An immediate concern pressed upon me. What I had collected on sound reels and on film had to be shared with the rest of the world by being broadcast. I had to get my exposed film to the news center at NDR in Hamburg, Germany. I counted my film cans, figuring out whether my material would suffice. That afternoon, I would leave the city. I tried, once more, to telephone my head office in Hamburg. No good, the lines were dead.

Those cut-off lines put me in an unusual situation. Normally, TV could not compete with print media in those days in getting a first crack at a story. Film had to be shipped and developed. That took time. However, newspaper people needed telephones. There were none or at least they were cut off. I could beat the newspapers to it, for once. Timing is all in the news business. I was fairly certain that the phone lines would stay down for a good while. I had to get my material out of there myself to be broadcasted. What is the value of a story, what is its impact if it is not being distributed by television to the world?

Before we left Kwangju, though, I wanted to film a few more scenes. After a quick breakfast we headed for the Provincial Hall, the center of the city. Kim Sa Bok, our driver, knew the way.

The building had been taken over by the students and citizens. They were using it as a command HQ. Access was restricted. The building was in use, I saw, as a distribution point for food, drinks, and other supplies. There were big trucks. Jeeps were entering and exiting the compound. On the left side of the rambling building, people were piling up weapons and military materiel, close to an entrance way and a guard's booth. Two young people wearing fire helmets stood on sentry duty. They were armed with rifles. They had a list on hand to control incoming and outgoing vehicles. Trucks which wanted to get in just blew their horns, and were given clearance to enter. Crowds of people had gathered in front of the building, presumably to exchange news. Many were lined up along a wall. There were signboards and handwritten notices.

A blue truck came in. On the back were four bodies, stretched out. I followed it until it stopped. The truck had gone round the side of the building. At the back, I saw corpses lying in a row on white sheets. The newly arrived dead were unloaded carefully and lined up with their comrades. There did not seem to be any relatives or friends around, as far as I could see. Were these the victims of the previous night's forays? Some of the dead bodies being unloaded had been smashed beyond recognition. I was overcome by a desire to vomit.

I turned away. Back in front of the building my eyes lit on some long blue banners. They were ornamented with big white *hangul* letters (Korean written characters).

"Hopefully into the Eighties!"

A friendly young man who translated the banners for me volunteered the information that by now the whole city was under the control of the students and citizens, more or less, he said.

It was time to get on. I had to find a tall building, something higher than the three-story Provincial Hall. I wanted to shoot some general overviews of the city. We set out in search of such a place. We passed by a television station. It was in bad shape. In fact the burned-out shell of MBC-TV or Channel 9 in Korea bore signs of fire at every window. I had already filmed this building, to show what had transpired in the early days of the uprising.

At this point, still searching for the right building, we ran into two Americans. They were working for Amnesty International, they said. They had seen the first two days of the uprising, when violence had suddenly peaked. Their remarks, which we filmed on top of a nearby building, bore witness to just how violent the military had been in the opening phase of the troubles.

Theirs were important testimonies, there having been few foreigners in the city that we knew of or could reach.

Meanwhile, we had to get out of there. We had to depart Kwangju to stand a chance of reaching Seoul in daylight hours. My colleague and I decided to film just two more spots: one, an open food market; the other, a large street barricade, near an overpass, with a distant view of tanks. Unfortunately, even with my long lens, it was impossible to show that background. I concentrated on the immediate vicinity, filming a barricade built out of tree trunks.

The market, meanwhile, was nothing more nor less than a peaceful open-air market. Nothing abnormal pertained to the place. One saw no signs of grief, no uncertainty. Every sort of fruit and vegetable was on sale. That market proved that life went on in Kwangju.

It was time to go. We had a quick drink in the market. I sorted my film, putting the film I had just exposed into the original cans and boxes. I hid my exposed film in its original packaging, as if it were unexposed. I took greatest care with the film shot on the previous day. I had five crucial reels. I stuck these under my T-shirt. This film I wanted to save at all costs, even if the rest was confiscated.

Going out of Kwangju we followed the route we had used coming in. We took the highway. We passed the crude barricades. Thereupon, we had to reenter the area controlled by the military. We were stopped, and we were checked once more, very carefully. We had to get out of the car, while the soldiers examined our belongings. They looked closely at my "originally" wrapped film. Finding nothing wrong, they allowed us to carry on. Thereafter, the checkpoints were less arduous. Still, they took time. We finally arrived back in Seoul at nearly 11 P.M.

The next morning, early, I booked a return flight to Tokyo. I would travel first-class on Japan Air Lines. With luck, my status as a first-class passenger would help me. My plan was to get my film out in my carry-on luggage. I had once again repacked my film. This time in a big metal can, with the film tucked in between cookies and wrapped nicely in strong, golden metal foil, with lots of green ribbons—a wedding gift complete with decorations. The wrapping proved to be so impressive, when the moment came, that I sailed past the security officers. Once on board the plane I took stock. I had been lucky on this last stage.

Arriving in Narita, I handed over my wedding present to my staff. They in turn forwarded the film to our news center in Hamburg. The footage aired several times in Germany as well as on Eurovision and in the United States.

Taking immediately a return flight three hours later, I was back in Seoul on Thursday afternoon, May 22.

A Second Trip to Kwangju

In Seoul once more, I was preparing for a second trip to Kwangju on the early morning of Friday, May 23 and needed to get in some additional supplies. I was searching for these in one of the underground shopping arcades near the hotel when someone thrust into my hand a leaflet with an interview with Kim Young Sam, the long-established opposition leader. That surprised me. The nation was under martial law. All political activities were banned, the National Assembly was not in session, universities and schools were closed indefinitely, and the media, of course, were censored.

Yet here was some seditious literature. In an interview dated Tuesday, May 20—three days after twenty-six people, including Kim Dae Jung, had been arrested for allegedly manipulating the troubles in Kwangju and creating "social unrest"—Kim Young Sam was quoted as saying "This is really time to think of the nation's future. It is not too late for those in authority to use reason and bring martial law to an end in order to return the nation to normalcy. Before it is too late the armed forces should return to their normal duties. Kim Dae Jung and others arrested should be released immediately."

Reading this statement—I received a copy in English and another in Korean, handwritten and signed by Kim Young Sam—it occurred to me to hide a copy in my luggage, to show to people in Kwangju.

I buried the materials deep in my luggage, together with Western and Japanese newspapers I had smuggled back from Narita. I had bought the papers, eager to get hold of unfiltered reports and uncensored information on Korea. I was lucky enough to have succeeded in getting these papers through the customs at Kimpo.

The local Seoul press told one nothing. The papers carried only threats and warnings from the Martial Law Command. The headline of the *Korea Times* for May 22 read: "Six Killed—Riot Demonstrations Grip Kwangju Area for four days—Martial Law Forces to Take Necessary Steps on Riots."

The paper carried a picture of Martial Law Commander General Lee

Hui Sung. He was appearing on national TV-KBS, to deliver this statement: "The martial law forces retain the right to take measures necessary for their self-defense against violent acts undermining national security and order."

I knew what that meant. The implications of this statement were clear. The threats were to be carried out. Indeed, threats of such a nature inevitably get acted upon. It was exceedingly unlikely that the military would give way or become "rational" (in Kim Young Sam's word). The chances of any immediate move toward democracy—say the adoption of a democratic constitution—were very low.

A bloody confrontation was the only possible outcome in Kwangju, I considered, reading the press between the lines. That was unfortunate. I decided to set out for Kwangju again forthwith, determined to document the events threatened on film.

One other piece of literature came into my hands just before my departure. It came from the Korean Overseas Information Service (KOIS). Someone slid it under my door at the Chosun Hotel the morning before I wanted to leave for Kwangju again. It was no doubt intended for foreign correspondents and press people. I read it at once. The first sentence claimed that there had been no casualties resulting from clashes between the "rioters" and the military in Kwangju. The notice went on to claim that casualties had been caused by reckless firing of weapons among the "rioters." From what I had seen already, this seemed extremely unlikely to me, to put it mildly. Young people in Korea are all taught to handle weapons. They all receive military training, both at school and in the armed forces. The notice claimed that the high casualties stemmed from the general "chaos" that beset the city. These were grotesque falsifications. They made me even more eager than before to prove their inaccuracy by seeing it with my own eyes, so to speak, with my camera.

We started back down to Kwangju at 10:30 on the morning of Friday, May 23. It was another sunny day. This time, once again, I was not hopeful of reaching my destination. The military had strengthened its positions around the city. I assumed that the cordon around Kwangju must be well-nigh perfect. Yet the trip went smoothly. We joined in a convoy of Red Cross vehicles (three cars transporting medicine, blood plasma, and other supplies to the Provincial Hall) for the first 200 kilometers. Luckily, the soldiers at all checkpoints so far had just waved us through.

Some twenty-six kilometers short of Kwangju we were obliged to break away from the convoy after being stopped. But fortunately, the soldier we were dealing with spoke English. I pulled out a copy of the *Korea Herald* of May 18.

The newspaper carried on its first page the following assertion: "The freedom of travel of foreigners will be assured to the maximum." That rather shocked the soldier. With this document in hand, I was able to convince him that foreigners were permitted to travel freely, even under martial law. The man took the newspaper away with him and showed it to one of his comrades. He came back smiling. We were to pass through. The fact that Kim Sa Bok, our driver, was Korean was overlooked.

This time we drove directly to the center of town, past the barricades we had seen on our first visit. We parked on the square in front of the Provincial Hall. I was overjoyed to be back. People were, I saw, gathering for a rally. A crowd of some 15,000 to 20,000 citizens stood in front of the Provincial Hall, on the square, and in the surrounding streets. They listened attentively to student speakers, who were advocating the creation of a committee to represent all classes of Kwangju citizens.

I filmed a mother, deeply moved by the loss of her only son.

"What have we done wrong? Why did the paratroopers come? They were drunk. We should not be afraid, we too should be ready to die for the ideal of political freedom."

She carried on: "I am proud of the citizens of Kwangju, even though I am not from here. We should negotiate with the military, to seek a compromise for all of us. Everything depends on maintaining our unity."

As the rally came to an end, the crowd sang the national anthem. Everyone was deeply moved. So was I. But there was tension. What would the future bring? Would the military, having once withdrawn, now listen to proposals from the citizens?

Answers came there none.

In the meantime there was a plan to gather up weapons. Here was evidence of a wish to compromise, or at least to avoid a final clash that the military must win. Two students most probably selected from the Settlement Committee stood on a raised platform, and received weapons being handed over to them. There were piles of light machine guns and other light arms and ammunition on the ground in front of the Provincial Hall.

Yet what of the hopes for a compromise? On the next morning, Saturday, May 26, I set off early, going to the office of the Settlement Committee. It was located on the second floor of the Provincial Hall. Were they in contact with the military? In the office was a hotline, the only functioning phone in the city. Up to this time it had been little used, I understood. It was a direct line to the military.

People gathered round. There were some students, teachers, a priest and other citizens. They gathered at about 11:40 A.M. that morning. All wore sashes as badges of office. There was a spokesman, an old man. He sat near the phone and picked up the receiver. It took a while before anyone answered. The committee spokesman then explained: An effort was being made to gather looted arms. As long as shooting continued, he said, there could be no resolution of the conflict. Another committee person took the phone. He asked the military commander on the other end of the line to do nothing until he received another call.

"If you have any questions, please call again," he said. These were the last words spoken on the hotline to the military side.

As the man hung up, I noticed a clock on the wall. It was five minutes to midday—five minutes to 12. A fitting omen, so I felt.

Indeed, the line was never used again. Hopes for a political solution were dashed. They were finally destroyed a few days later—on the early morning of Tuesday, May 27—when the military stormed the city.

The hope of a political spring in Korea, a thaw, was thus destroyed. However, those days in Kwangju will live in people's memories.

An Endpiece

Since early on in my time in Korea I always kept an eye on the hard-pressed opposition and its leaders. During the presidency of Park Chung Hee and under his military successors I observed the efforts of Kim Dae Jung to strengthen his weak position. I followed his conflicts with the government of South Korea. At the same time I kept up with a range of political and nonpolitical topics, such as the intensive effort at economic development, and I followed cultural events. I excluded no subjects of interest from my coverage, especially for Germany and for people overseas.

Now looking back on those days when human rights and hopes for political freedom and justice were suppressed by the will of one leader I, as a foreign journalist, recall my own bad experience. Mostly, all the terrible things happened to Koreans. But they also befell a foreign newsman.

Six years had passed since the Kwangju uprising. On November 28, 1986, I was filming opposition New Korea Democratic Party (NKDP) members led by Shin Soon Bum on the streets in Seoul. They were being attacked by plainclothes police, while distributing leaflets near the Kwanghamun crossroads.

I was the only TV cameraman in sight gathering this news with my videocamera; besides me there was only a still photographer from Hong Kong out there. I was wearing an armband to show that I had official accreditation as a foreign newsman. My camera was clearly marked with the name of ARD NDR German TV network. That wasn't about to impress anybody, when plainclothes policemen knocked me down all of a sudden.

Some thugs and plainclothesmen hustled me across the street into the tender care of some riot police just arriving on the spot. They got me down on the ground and proceeded to kick. They broke my video camera and the battery light. Yet, that sturdy camera, I believe, saved my life. I used it to cover my face and head. They used their boots to kick at me all over. The camera served as a shield of a sort. Nevertheless, I suffered severe head, neck, and back injuries. I had bruises all over my body. I was rushed by my Korean researcher and driver Mrs. Shin Nanja to the Red Cross hospital in Pyongdong, Seoul, bleeding from my nose and my ears, struggling to breathe.

The facts of the attack on me were immediately conveyed to the German Embassy in Seoul and to the German writing press. No comment was offered, ever, by the Korean authorities either at the time or later. Despite official notifications in writing given by German TV to the German Foreign Ministry back in Bonn and subsequently to the Korean government through diplomatic channels, this was not the end of the matter for me. I suffered from increasing pains and aches. Finally, a decade later, I underwent a complex and rather dangerous operation to my cervical vertebrae. It brought only a little relief. After a year of rehabilitation, I finally had to give up my job for good.

I was being taught a lesson, paid back I should say. The Korean authorities monitored the foreign press closely in those days. Even since my coverage of the Kwangju uprising I had been a thorn in the flesh of the powers that were in Seoul. However, that same uprising was a turning point in modern Korean history. I was deeply touched by what I saw of it. Some of the images that I caught on film—a family grieving over the shooting of their eldest son; a mother who lost both her sons—etched themselves into my mind. I will never forget what I saw. I bow my head to those who lost their lives in the hope of creating a democracy in Korea and setting aside a military dictatorship serving the ambitions of one general!

CHAPTER SIX
REFLECTIONS ON KWANGJU
Sam Jameson

Blood and Tears 7

D ecades have passed since 1980, but even the word "Kwangju" still invokes an overwhelming sense of sadness and waste. The discrimination its citizens resented, the protest that only they among all South Koreans mounted against their nation's second coup in nineteen years, and the thoughtless killing that occurred there—all of it remains a senseless horror.

The tragedy towers all the more when we recall it in the context of events that unfolded after the assassination of President Park Chung Hee. His death on October 26, 1979, stirred developments that for almost five months raised hopes for an era of national reconciliation.

Opponents of Park and his eighteen-year rule spoke of putting aside the past. Supporters of the former general began consulting with political rivals, instead of jailing them. Prisoners were released, civil rights restored, purged students and professors reinstated, and criticism of the government permitted. Almost miraculously in Korea's acerbic political history, all of the established parties agreed in informal talks on a new constitution under which a democratic government would take over after a direct presidential election. Even the candidates were in place.

And then Chun Doo Hwan smashed it all.

Revelations in 1995 that both Chun—who promised to "purify" Korean society as he seized power in 1980—and his comrade in the army, Roh Tae Woo, had each amassed slush funds of more than $600 million while serving as president one after another magnified the effrontery of the coup. Not only does the task of purification remain uncompleted today, South Korea is still looking for the national reconciliation that seemed at hand before May 17, 1980.

Moreover, the "People's Power" protests of 1987—which effectively ended authoritarian rule with a toll of only two deaths—underscored what an aberration the untold killing in Kwangju represented for South Korea. No battle on the Korean peninsula since the 1950–53 Korean War took a greater toll than the three days of protest that brutality by troops transformed into seven days of insurrection in Kwangju in 1980.

The U.S. Mistake

Over the years, many South Koreans and some Americans condemned the U.S. government for the events at Kwangju.

The United States, indeed, does deserve condemnation, or at least criticism—but not for the incorrect accusations of supporting the use of troops in Kwangju that are usually hurled at it. The American government made its mistake long before Kwangju. The blunder occurred in November 1979 when Washington agreed to support a plan by the government of Choi Gyu Ha to spend twenty months—or until June 1981— writing a new constitution while in transition from authoritarian to democratic rule.

Washington backed the plan even as American diplomats in Seoul predicted that Koreans' patience with a transition government would not last longer than a year. In addition, the needlessly lengthy period offered Chun Doo Hwan, an unknown major general, exactly what he needed: time to build up a base on which to seize power.

By May 1980, South Korea was on its way toward a presidential election. Indeed, all signs pointed to Kim Jong Pil, Kim Dae Jung, and Kim Young Sam running against each other. The odds were strong that the establishment candidate, Kim Jong Pil, would win as the other two Kims split the opposition vote, just as they were to do in 1987.

If the transition had been pegged to a process of establishing the framework for a democratic government—rather than to an arbitrarily fixed period of time—Chun would not have had time to have staged his palace coup.

However, Choi, derided as a "village chief" because of his grovelling subservience to Chun, refused to alter the plan for a twenty-month transition.

When Chun, promoted to lieutenant general, had Choi appoint him as acting director of the Korean Central Intelligence Agency (KCIA) on April 14, a sense of urgency over setting a date for an election emerged. The demands of the students who launched demonstrations in May— that a date be fixed for the election, that partial martial law in effect since October 27, 1979, be ended; and that Chun resign as KCIA director—seemed only natural.

On May 15, Kim Young Sam supported those demands and called for the twenty-month transition period to be shortened by at least half a year. The next day, Kim joined with his rival, Kim Dae Jung, to demand transfer of power to a civilian government by the end of 1980.

But in Washington, two days before Chun declared full martial law and banned all political activity, State Department spokesman Tom Reston reiterated the Carter administration's support for a twenty-month transition.

Chun, directing the government behind the scenes while Choi was touring Saudi Arabia and Kuwait, seemed to encourage student demonstrations that began in force on May 13. Police uncharacteristically stood by as rows of students ten and fifteen abreast marched through the streets of Seoul, allowing the ranks of the protestors to swell to the greatest numbers seen since the 1965 demonstrations against the normalization of diplomatic relations with Japan, Korea's former colonial ruler. Only when the demonstrators turned toward the capitol did the police start firing tear-gas grenades and cannons.

Although students suspended demonstrations after three days to await the return of President Choi, Chun rammed through his "palace coup" on the night of May 17, a day after Choi came home.

Chun's Excuse

In his 1996 trial, Chun pleaded that he was forced to seize power by threats from North Korea. Indeed, the government controlled by Chun claimed at the time that two shooting incidents had occurred in the demilitarized zone in the week before the coup. But, far more threatening to Chun was the fact that the National Assembly was scheduled to open on May 20 for the first time since Choi had taken over as acting president. On the very morning of the coup, newspapers reported that the late Park Chung Hee's ruling Democratic Republican party might join the opposition to enact a resolution ordering the end of partial martial law.

Such a move would have wiped out the authority for Chun to exercise political clout.

Choi, in explaining the imposition of total martial law, cited alleged "military moves" by North Korea as well as "social unrest" caused by the student demonstrations. A U.S. military spokesman in Seoul, however, said the United States knew of no North Korean military moves.

Few foreign correspondents had any feeling that a coup was about to happen. Indeed, when Japan's ruling Liberal Democratic Party temporarily split in two and allowed the opposition to pass a no-confidence motion against the government of Prime Minister Masayoshi Ohira, both I and the *Washington Post* Tokyo bureau chief rushed back to Tokyo to cover what, momentarily, looked like a break-up of the structure that had ruled Japan for most of the post–World War II era. The two of us flew into Tokyo on the same flight Saturday morning May 17 and, after Chun imposed full martial law that night, both of us boarded the same plane in Tokyo Sunday morning May 18 to go back to Seoul.

The students who so boldly marched through the streets of Seoul just days earlier were cowed into complete silence. Except for a May 19–28 "sit-in strike" by reporters, nowhere in the capital was there a sign of any protest. Nor had word of the troubles that started May 18 in Kwangju reached Seoul.

Indeed, the protests in Kwangju and the reports of Korean Army brutality still had not attracted major international attention as late as Monday, May 19. The main news event that day was the decision by the Supreme Court of Korea to uphold a death sentence that a court martial had imposed on Kim Jae Kyu, the KCIA chief who had assassinated President Park. In the story I sent on May 19, I included only a paragraph on Kwangju. It included word that "reports reaching Seoul said at least 5,000 protestors clashed with police in Kwangju and that 400 people were arrested." I described the protesters as condemning the arrest of Kim Dae Jung.

Not until Tuesday, May 20, did the first official reports of deaths in Kwangju reach Seoul. Two protestors were reported killed, but no details were available. Only on Wednesday, May 21 did Kwangju explode into the consciousness of all of Korea and the world. Martial Law Command headquarters ended its nearly total censorship and acknowledged that what it had called a "riot" in Kwangju had gotten "out of control." The command HQ said 150,000 civilians, about one-fifth of the population of Kwangju, went "on a rampage," seizing 3,505 weapons and 46,400 rounds of ammunition from arsenals. Four armored personnel carriers, 89 jeeps, 50 trucks, 40 wreckers, 40 buses, 10 dump trucks, and 8 teargas-firing jeeps were commandeered by civilians, it added.

The military said five soldiers and policemen and one civilian had been killed—but other reports put the death toll at twenty-four, including eleven civilians who were shot to death by Korean troops perched atop the Provincial Hall building as thousands of residents tried to seize the building.

The most prominent of the other reports that day came from U.S. Ambassador William Gleysteen, who gave a not-for-attribution briefing to American reporters. It was his first meeting with reporters after Chun staged the coup. In it, he announced that the protests in Kwangju had turned into a "full-blown insurrection" and cited the attack on citizens moving on the Provincial Hall building as the immediate spur to civilians to seize weapons and launch a rebellion. He called Chun's decision to impose full martial law "oh so wrong."

In a statement that was to come back and haunt the United States in its relations with South Korea, Gleysteen also said the United States would support the use of Korean armed forces to restore order. He made the statement not in relation to Kwangju but rather in reference to a possibility that disorder might erupt throughout South Korea. But it was mistakenly interpreted as meaning that a high U.S. official, speaking for the United States, approved the initial despatch of troops to Kwangju during the night of May 17–18.

Years later, Ambassador Richard L. Walker told me that Chun, in a meeting with General John A. Wickham Jr., commander of U.S. forces in Korea, asked what Wickham thought about sending in troops a second time—to end the rebellion in Kwangju. Wickham, the ambassador said, knew that the unit that Chun mentioned was not under Wickham's United Nations command. Nonetheless, he told Chun he "saw nothing wrong" with the idea, Walker said.

Chun used Wickham's statement to claim that the United States had approved dispatching troops into Kwangju for the final cleanup, and that was why, Walker said, the United States government for years after Kwangju refused to present its side of the story. Washington ultimately did issue a long report disclaiming responsibility for the actions of Korean troops in Kwangju, but glossed over Wickham's meeting with Chun. Before the trouble began in Kwangju, however, the U.S. government clearly did not sympathize with the student protests.

One American official in Seoul condemned the imposition of full martial law as "unnecessary" but said the United States would not have objected to a clampdown focused only on students whose demands had become "very radical, very communist and inflammatory."

Responsible for covering the entire Korea story by myself with no help, I did not feel I could afford to go to Kwangju where all communications links with the outside had been cut by the Korean military. Therefore, my view of the turmoil, until the day it was quelled, came from Seoul, not from the scene itself.

Kim as a Leftist

It was not until Thursday, May 22, that the Martial Law Command got around to issuing a fourteen-page document charging Kim Dae Jung with instigating the protests in Kwangju that were sparked by his arrest.

By then the protests had spread throughout both Cholla provinces. Without offering any evidence, the document declared that Kim had leftist tendencies and had aided North Korea's cause in speeches he made overseas before 1973 (when KCIA agents kidnapped him in Tokyo and brought him back to Seoul).

I remember repeatedly asking Korean government officials to explain how Kim had managed, from his jail cell, to stage an insurrection.

My despatch of May 22 also reported that Park Chung Hoon, who took over as acting prime minister that day, traveled by helicopter to an army compound outside Kwangju and issued a statement echoing Martial Law Command claims that the insurrection had been instigated by "impure elements," a phrase that the authoritarian administration of Park Chung Hee used to mean "any opponent of the government."

Censored Korean newspapers emphasized violent actions by protestors—such as seizure of dynamite from warehouses of the Korea Explosives Co. in Kwangju—and published no reports of brutality against civilians. But they did carry enough news of such events as a protest by 100,000 civilians in Mokpo, Kim Dae Jung's birthplace, to show that Cholla residents were outraged by the arrest of their hero, a man who had been the last opposition candidate in a direct presidential election in South Korea in 1971.

The story I dispatched on Thursday, May 22, noted that protests had erupted in 16 of the 26 municipalities in South Cholla, including another demonstration in Kwangju by more than 100,000 civilians who gathered in front of the Provincial Hall after troops were withdrawn from the city. The demonstrators demanded Kim's release and the resignation of Chun, I reported.

As the first week of full martial law came to a close with no significant protests occurring anywhere else, the trouble in Kwangju assumed even greater significance as the last obstacle in the way of Chun's seizure of power. By Friday, May 23, attention shifted to efforts to work out a peaceful end to the insurrection.

On Saturday, May 24, the AP's Terry Anderson made a tour of hospitals in Kwangju and reported that the number of deaths had reached at least 107—the worst toll since the 1950–53 Korean War. Meanwhile, Chun's martial law authorities continued a business-as-usual schedule, hanging Kim Jae Kyu, Park's assassin, on that day.

On Monday, May 26, student leaders in Kwangju compiled a list of the names of 161 civilians who they said had been killed and announced that they had rounded up from ditches, vacant lots, and other sites the bodies of 100 unidentified victims.

Then, in the predawn darkness of Tuesday, May 27, it all ended. Troops moved into the city at 3:30 A.M. and killed off the diehard students in the Provincial Hall, who had stayed behind after ordering high-school students who tried to join them to go home. The doomed students reportedly told their juniors: "You are too young to die."

After filing a story on the quashing of the rebellion from Seoul, I rented a chauffeur-driven car and went to Kwangju. There was no other way to get to the city.

"Stunned residents stood before their homes and shuttered shops. Their faces told the story. Seven days of insurrection were over. Kwangju was once more under military control and its people were prisoners in their own city," I wrote. "At least four soldiers with M-16s stood at every intersection," I added.

Martial law headquarters claimed that seventeen armed insurgents and two soldiers were killed in the final attack. Although there was no way to confirm a death toll, at least 200 armed insurgents were reported to have taken a final stand in the Provincial Hall before the troops attacked.

Sixty-one wooden caskets lined the floor of a gymnasium across the street from the Provincial Hall. These were victims from the early days of the protest who had been identified by relatives. Photographs placed on the coffins showed the faces of many young men. But there were also a middle-aged woman and a child identified as seven years old.

Kwangju residents said as many as 100 unidentified bodies were being kept in the Provincial Hall. Troops, however, barred reporters from entering that building.

On May 31, the Martial Law Command issued a report on the ten-day protest in Kwangju in which it listed 170 dead, including 144 civilians, 22 soldiers, and 4 policemen. It claimed that 76 of the civilians were killed by other civilians in accidents and murders.

The most recent official count—a toll of 240—was announced in November 1995, when President Kim Young Sam ordered prosecutors to investigate Kwangju again as he prepared to put both Chun and Roh on trial for staging the carnage.

On May 27, 1980, Kwangju residents revealed how paratroopers triggered the insurrection by such acts of violence as pulling young men—anyone who looked like a college student—out of restaurants and coffee shops and beating and clubbing them in the streets. Bystanders also were accosted, they said. Brutality reached the point that even some Kwangju policemen abandoned their duties and handed over their weapons to protesters, residents said.

Adding to the rage was a belief by many in Kwangju that the paratroopers sent into the city on May 18 were from the Kyongsang provinces—the perpetrators of long-standing discrimination against Cholla.

In the city that final day, only shops selling food were open. Street after street in the downtown area was deserted except for a pedestrian here, two or three others there, a bicycle or two, and an occasional motorcycle. No buses, no cars, no taxis were running—nothing but army jeeps and military wreckers hauling away burned-out buses, cars, and military vehicles. No traffic lights were operating anywhere.

On the grounds of the Provincial Hall, army troops were busy removing destroyed vehicles on which were painted such slogans as "Free Kim Dae Jung!" and "Oust Chun Doo Hwan!" As the sun started to set, on the other side of the plaza in front of the hall, troops were dismantling a tall wooden tower. Most of the words that had been part of a slogan attached to it were already obliterated. But two words remained visible. They read "world peace."

CHAPTER SEVEN

YUN SANG WON: THE KNOWLEDGE IN THOSE EYES

Bradley Martin

Yun Sang Won, A Patriot

In a quarter-century as a journalist, I have covered such stories as the Soviet invasion of Afghanistan, the trial of China's Gang of Four, and the rioting and murder following the assassination of Indian Prime Minister Indira Gandhi. But when anyone asks which story most stands out in my memory, I answer with a single word: "Kwangju." I spent only one day in Kwangju during the rebellion there, but that single day, May 26, 1980, was enough to burn into my brain permanent images of brave people for whom the struggle against tyranny was very much a matter of life and death.

Most of the martyrs of Kwangju had already died by the time I got to the city on May 26. Relatives had identified many of the corpses. The piercing cries of grieving mothers, wailing as they embraced their children's coffins, filled the auditorium across from the Provincial Hall (*Dochung*). In the breezeway of the *Dochung* some fifteen more corpses lay bloating, turning purple as they awaited identification in open coffins. Today those Kwangju dead are buried in the May 18 Cemetery. Their graves are surmounted by portraits picturing them as their loved ones had known them in life. But I, never having known most of them in life, will picture them to the end of my days as I saw them in death. All but one of them, that is. The one Kwangju victim I can clearly see in my mind's eye is the student spokesman who held a press conference on May 26.

In the Provincial Hall

I was sitting directly across a coffee table from him in a room in the Provincial Hall in Kwangju and I was thinking that this man would be dead soon. His eyes were directly on mine and I was thinking that he himself knew that he would be dead soon. I looked at him, at his frizzy hair, unusual for a Korean, at the calm way about him that contrasted with the near hysteria of his armed, posturing, probably much younger comrades, and I had a clear sensation that he would die. His glance was friendly but, I thought, resigned. And he seldom took his eyes away from mine. I thought the spokesman was about twenty-five. He had strong cheekbones and an intelligent look. But it was his eyes that struck me with their gentleness and kindness in the face of what I thought must be knowledge of impending death.

That very morning, the soldiers surrounding the city had moved a bit closer to the center. The student militants obviously lacked the firepower to resist for long, once the army should make its move. The spokesman looked directly at me as he spoke.

"We think the United States as an ally can exercise its influence on the Korean government. Since it hasn't done so, we suspect the U.S. might be supporting General Chun Doo Hwan."

The Americans should send their ambassador (William H. Gleysteen) to arbitrate the Kwangju problem, he said, because "we can't trust the government authorities. In the case of the recent coal miners' strike [at Sabuk], the government promised no punishment if the rioters would stop—but in fact they were arrested later."

The spokesman would not give his name. He said that was the policy of the student militants, although he was sure the army knew who he was. I looked at him and could not escape the knowledge of the future that I saw in those eyes. More than 100 Kwangju people had been killed in the previous week's rioting, according to news accounts, and he was saying the real figure was about 260. Finally I asked him the question that was bothering me. It was obvious to any outsider, I said, that the army had overwhelming power to call upon whenever it might choose to strike and retake the city. Were the poorly armed student militants prepared to die in resisting or would they surrender?

He replied calmly, his eyes gently insisting that the words be believed: "We'll fight to the last man." He said the students had enough dynamite and grenades to "blow up the city."

After the press briefing, I stayed in Kwangju a while, examining the barricades, interviewing citizens. Then, at night, I returned to Seoul and sent a story to my newspaper about what I had seen. The story never ran. Before it could be printed, word came that the army had retaken Kwangju. Casualty figures released at first were low—only two dead among the students. I was relieved it was not more. They were so young, so full of idealism and determination. Later, I heard higher figures. An Associated Press correspondent, Terry Anderson, had been at the news conference. Anderson told me he counted sixteen young people dead. Among them, he said, was the spokesman, found in the same Provincial Hall office where he had held his first and last meeting with the press. The spokesman's body was partially burned in a fire that had broken out there, Anderson told me.

That young man's life and death encapsulated for me the tragedy of South Korea under military rule. After I confirmed his death, I wrote an article focusing on him for the newspaper I worked for at the time, the *Baltimore Sun*. I described what I had seen and heard, more or less as I have written above, and ended the article with the words: "If I knew the student's name I would write it here." As soon as I had sent the article to Baltimore via the Chosun Hotel's telex operator on the evening of May 27, I went out with other correspondents and got drunker than I had ever been before. I don't recall most of the places we went to that night in downtown Seoul. My drinking companions told me later they had tried to hold me up to keep me from falling, as I stumbled screaming from bar to bar, cursing Chun Doo Hwan and the other new military rulers of South Korea. My strong feelings reflected the fact that, having covered Korea for three years, I had grown to love the country and its people. I suppose I reacted to Kwangju more as a Korean than as an American.

The Top of the Front Page

My editors found the article moving and they believed readers would, too, so they placed it at the top of the front page of the paper for the morning of May 28. Certainly it is one of the most passionate pieces I have ever written. Perhaps subconsciously I had intended that passion to exorcise the disturbing ghost of the young spokesman from my mind, but he was a persistent ghost. I wondered how his life had led him to that moment. For more than a decade I was left to wonder even who he was, for I still did not know his name or anything else about him except that he had been spokesman for the rebel students.

From time to time I asked friends in Seoul, but it seemed the young man had not been famous enough for his name to become widely known. He had told us the army knew who he was, but in reality it seemed that neither the soldiers nor most other Koreans knew his name. Terry Anderson, the Associated Press correspondent, later achieved unwanted fame while covering another story, the Middle East. Working in Beirut, Terry was taken hostage by Arab kidnappers and held for seven long years. In 1992, shortly after he had been released, I wrote to Terry and asked if he knew the spokesman's name. He wrote back to say that he did not. It seemed I would have to go to Kwangju and ask around in order to fill out my knowledge of the student spokesman, so I put that on my list of things to do some day.

Then in 1993, while I was in Seoul doing research for a book, I got a call from a man I had not met. He identified himself as Eugene Soh, a Korean-born American citizen from Columbia, Maryland, a town between Baltimore and Washington, D.C. Mr. Soh asked to meet me. When we met in the Seoul Foreign Correspondents' Club, I found a smiling, casually dressed man of my own age (born in 1942). He told me that he had been looking for me, hoping to meet me, ever since 1980 when he had read my article in the *Baltimore Sun* about the Kwangju spokesman.

Soh explained that he had moved from Korea to the United States in 1970. For many years after that, he had lobbied in Washington on behalf of the United Movement for Democracy and Reunification. In 1980 Soh had distributed copies of my Kwangju article and sent it back to Korea to boost the morale of members of the prodemocracy movement. He said he had always hoped to meet me, so he could tell me that the article had had major impact in bucking up prodemocracy forces in those fearful post-Kwangju days. Naturally it pleased me to hear that. But it pleased me even more to be able to ask Soh the question that had haunted me: Who *was* that student spokesman?

"Oh, you mean Yun Sang Won," he replied. "I was born in Honam and I know his friends and family. Would you like to go to Kwangju and meet them?"

Of course I would, I replied. Within a few days Soh and I flew to Kwangju.

Yun's Family

When we arrived in Kwangju we met my host, Park Sung Hyun, former organizer of the National Democratic Students' League. Now sporting a Rotarian badge on the lapel of his business suit, Park had metamorphosed into a high-powered businessman—he had started a software company and was president of Koryo Cement, a company in which his family were the largest shareholders. A student activist in 1980, he had left Kwangju before the uprising because the authorities were looking for him in connection with his activism in Seoul.

"I admired Mr. Yun so much because he was a very intelligent, great person and very brave," Park told me. He explained that Yun had been far more than just the spokesman for the student rebels. From midway through the rebellion, Yun was actually the man in charge in Kwangju, although his central role was not widely known, Park said.

Park Sung Hyun introduced me to one of Yun's closest colleagues,

Chun Yong Ho, a Chonnam National student at the time of the uprising. After finding himself in and out of prison cells for years, Chun, like Park and many of the other aging rebels, had found a niche in business. Recently he had started an advertising and communications company in Kwangju. Chun and Soh took me to the May 18 Cemetery where I paid respects at Yun's tomb. The tombstone gave the bare outlines of his life: Yun Sang Won, born August 19, 1950. Struggle Committee spokesman in the *Dochung*. Killed at dawn on May 27, 1980, when the military advanced into the city.

Yun's photograph affixed to the tomb showed the man I remembered: older than most of the student rebels, frizzy-haired, with strong cheekbones. Someone had placed a cigarette on the tomb as an offering.

That evening, my hosts took me to a meeting of Yun's colleagues and family members. Among them, I had no difficulty at all picking out Yun's father, Yun Sok Dong: the same strong cheekbones and frizzy hair, although the hair had turned white and there remained only a fringe of it around his bald dome. I explained my connections with Korea and Kwangju and my interest in learning and writing more about Yun Sang Won. Kwangju had been the most emotional experience of my career, I told the group. The brutality had been so great I had feared it would take many years for the Korean democracy movement to regroup and stand up to the military regime again. Reassigned to open a bureau in India in the summer of 1980, right after Kwangju, I had felt relieved in a way that I would be giving up the Korea story, for I wondered if I still had the heart to cover the country now that its future looked so bleak.

When I returned to the Korea story in 1986, as antigovernment demonstrations raged once again, I was glad to see that Koreans had regained their courage. When Roh Tae Woo gave in to the demonstrators and issued his democracy proclamation, I felt as happy as any Korean. And when the Chinese in 1989 at Tiananmen Square suffered their own version of Kwangju, I felt that I knew something about indomitable fighting spirit. With some confidence—misplaced, perhaps, as so far my forecast failed to come true—I predicted that the Chinese, like the Koreans, would take only seven years or so to spring back with a systematic opposition to tyranny and force the institution of a more democratic system.

If I had anticipated before that evening began that I would encounter a certain coolness in Kwangju on account of my nationality, the reality of my meeting with the people close to Yun was just the opposite. When I finished talking, I was welcomed warmly. The elder Yun, a sunburned farmer and the chairman of the association of families bereaved by the Kwangju massacre, spoke generously and movingly: "Because of people like you, my son can live forever. Thank you."

From talking with people at the meeting and later with others—especially his close comrade, Lee Tae Bok, who had become publisher of *Weekly Labor News*—I pieced together an account of Yun's life and death. Yun Sang Won was raised in the village of Imgok, which was about an hour's drive from Kwangju before the roads were improved. There his family farmed 3,000 *pyong*—a *pyong* is 3.3 square meters—of rice paddy. The family struggled to provide their eldest son with a good education. Yun Sang Won went to a Catholic secondary school in Kwangju (where he converted to Catholicism—although his enthusiasm for religion later waned).

At Chonnam National University in Kwangju he was involved in the democratic student movement of the time. He was a political science major. Also active in the theater group, he got involved in the Korean masked-dance movement, which was becoming popular among antigovernment students. In describing his first two years of college to Lee Tae Bok, years later in 1979, Yun said he had been a simple and naïve democrat with a zeal for social justice. The student slogans of the early 1970s opposed Park Chung Hee's determination to remain indefinitely in power and opposed the corruption inevitably accompanying his near-absolute power.

After his sophomore year in college, Yun was conscripted into the army. After completing his military service, he returned to the university. There he found a new mood in the student movement. Simply opposing Park Chung Hee was not enough. Students were searching for a more all-encompassing, progressive worldview. South Koreans were not yet reading the original Marxist texts—which were still largely unavailable in the country—but it was possible to nibble around the edges of the canon. Yun and others devoured Hegelian philosophy, Third-World radical texts, and Western books on economic history and capitalist development.

Living with his younger brother in a rented room in the Kwangchon-dong slum, Yun watched the wretched daily life of the slum dwellers and agonized over what sort of career he should pursue: Would he become a well-paid, white-collar salaried man and help put his younger siblings through school, as his family hoped? Or would he perhaps go in an entirely different direction, organizing a social movement among poor people?

Not Made to Be a Banker

Yun divided his time—and his being—between the world represented by the social-science books popular among progressive students and the course work that would prepare him for his corporate employment examinations. Having done well in his studies and on the crucial employment examination, he graduated in 1977 and took a job with one of the largest banks in Seoul. But in the capital he lived in the Bongchun-dong slum, inhabited mainly by former peasants who had come to the city for factory work. Younger colleagues still active in the student movement, some of them on the run from the police, visited him there. Conversations often turned to an idea popular among student activists of the time: going into factories to become workers. Yun later told Lee Tae Bok that he had planned all along to stay in banking for only a token period and then take up movement organization work. His experiences in Seoul had only strengthened his resolve, he said.

After six months as a banker, he did resign. He wrote to explain to his father that he was committed to doing something for the nation. He had taken the bank job simply because his father had been working so hard to put him through college. He had wanted to prove by getting the job that he had made good use of the opportunity. He had been able to pass the examination for the prestigious job, and the father at least would have this to keep him from losing face in front of his friends.

"My son was a boy of strong character and will," his father told me. "Once we had quite a dialog. I thought he was too sympathetic to the oppressed and exploited people. So I told him: 'Make a lot of money and help them.' My son answered: 'How many people could I possibly help with my money? I want to change the world.' We argued repeatedly, but I never won the arguments."

The old man's voice dropped to a whisper. "After he quit his banking job my son went to work in a styrofoam factory. Around that time his mother came down with a typhus infection and had to be hospitalized. My son and a friend visited her in the hospital. She was a little feverish and told him: 'You know how hard I worked to send you to the university. And now you have become a worker.' My son answered: 'Mom, don't be too sad. Some day I will really take care of you. I'm taking care of a lot of people instead of one person. By doing so I can really take care of you some day.'"

At that stage, according to Lee Tae Bok: "Mr. Yun's ideological and theoretical background was not very sophisticated. He was moved by sympathy for poor people and a passion for democracy, and he wasn't that radical."

Still, he was ahead of his time.

"People talked a lot about being a worker, but few ever went to factories," said Lee.

In the Kwangju area only one intellectual had preceded Yun into factory work, and he had kept at it for only a short time.

Yun spent a few months studying the question of just what an intellectual could hope to accomplish as a worker, Lee Tae Bok said. According to Lee, there were three schools of thought on that question among progressive intellectuals. One group, probably the majority among Kwangju-area activists at the time, held that being a worker itself was the important thing. A second group held that it didn't matter whether you were a worker, a student, or a white-collar salaried person; the important thing was to immediately organize an underground resistance organization. This group's viewpoint tended toward starting an armed rebellion based on rural areas. Its adherents formed the South Korean National Liberation Front, whose activists were arrested in October of 1979.

The third point of view was that the general level of political consciousness among workers and students alike was still maturing, especially in the Honam region. Thus, the important thing was to be flexible and alert. Yun came around to this viewpoint. He decided that the trend toward industrialization in South Korea was critical. The times required a labor movement more than a peasant movement, and basically a labor movement would not be focused on armed struggle. For an intellectual merely to become a worker was not enough, he also decided; nothing would be solved by simply devoting his life to working in a factory.

"It is very important to note that for Mr. Yun quitting the job as a banker implied his whole future course," Lee added. "After that he was searching for a more effective, scientific way to change the world. At the moment he was not an ideologue, not a communist—rather just something more than a populist, searching for a more sincere solution than a populist solution."

I could see evidence for that assessment when my hosts in Kwangju drove me to Imgok and I had a chance to look over Yun's library. The family had rebuilt the main house in modern style in 1992, but it remained very much a farmhouse. A chicken wandered into the main room as we sat on the floor chatting with the elder Yun and his wife. Much as he resembled his father, I saw that Sang Won had looked even more like his mother. A traditional Korean farmhouse across the courtyard, in which Yun had slept and studied, remains. His room contains his photos as well as his books.

Yun's Library

The books I saw there included these titles, all in English: George Lichtheim, *The Origins of Socialism* (a pirated edition); Paul A. Baran and Paul M. Sweezy, *Monopoly Capital*; Samuel P. Huntingdon, *Political Order in Changing Societies*; Jack Gray and Patrick Cavendish, *Chinese Communism in Crisis*; John M. Hertz, *Political Realism, Political Idealism*; Maurice Dobb, *Political Economy and Capitalism*; George Lukacs, *History and Class Consciousness, Studies in Marxist Dialectics*; Sidney Verbin, *Small Group and Political Behaviour* (this book had been checked out of the local U.S. Information Service Library and never returned); Alexander Worth, *Russia: The Postwar Years*; R.N. Carew Hunt, *The Theory and Practice of Communism*.

The titles were not restricted to the topic of communism. And, far from propaganda, the books tended to be serious scholarly analyses. Yun Sang Won's reading list reminded me of my own list back in the innocent days of the early 1960s, when an interest in socialist ideas had been considered a normal phase for any American university student with compassion and a reasonably searching mentality. I had enrolled in courses like "Analyses of Capitalism" and had struggled with Hegel's dialectic, taking tentative steps along a path very much like the one Yun appeared to have trodden as he came of age in the seventies.

In 1978 Yun set up a night school with classes for workers on labor rights and other subjects. Chun Yong Ho, then a Chonnam National student, was one of his helpers. In mid-1979 Yun became an organizer in the Kwangju area for the National Democratic Workers' League, Chonminnoryon, and its affiliated organization, the National Democratic Students' League, Chonminhakryon, in 1978. When Yun joined in 1979, it was Lee who handled the interview to determine his qualifications. Yun and Lee became close comrades in the two organizations, which the police referred to collectively as "Haklim" (Student Forest).

It was Haklim that organized a strike—a celebrated labor dispute in Seoul in 1979—at YH Textile Co., owned by a Korean-American. Viewing the labor union's demands as too radical, the owner closed the company and fled overseas. When the government ignored workers' demands to save their jobs, they protested with a sit-in at the office of the opposition New Democratic Party in August of 1979. The sit-in occurred right after a court had suspended Kim Young Sam, a prominent opposition leader by then, from leadership of the party. Seeing the sit-in as collaboration between Kim's forces and the workers, the government cracked down on the sit-in participants. One worker, Miss Kim Kyong Suk, leapt to her death from the building. The "YH Incident," as it became known, helped draw public sympathy for Kim Young Sam and the democracy movement, contributing to massive turnouts for demonstrations in Pusan and Masan in mid-October of 1979. Just a few days later, on October 26, in the midst of top government disagreements about how to control the situation, President Park Chung Hee was assassinated.

The Buildup to Kwangju

Following the "12/12 military takeover"—Chun Doo Hwan's grab for power on December 12, 1979—and as a culmination to the "Seoul Spring" in the following year, at least 50,000 students demonstrated in Seoul on May 15, 1980, in what was to be a last student show of strength in the capital before Chun's crackdown two days later. They demanded that Chun resign his recently acquired post as head of the Korean Central Intelligence Agency (KCIA) and that martial law end. The demonstrators differed on what to do next. Lee Tae Bok's group wanted to occupy key points in the central area such as broadcasting offices. The majority, however, decided to call off the demonstrations on May 16 and wait to see the government's response.

"Mr. Yun, when he heard of this, vehemently criticized the defeat in Seoul," Lee Tae Bok told me.

Lee and Yun's organization thus was deeply involved in key events leading up to the Kwangju incident itself.

"Just before Kwangju, when I met Mr. Yun, we both predicted there would be a military coup," Lee said. "We expected that Pusan, Masan, and Seoul would be the hot spots for popular resistance—not Kwangju. We agreed that when the coup happened and massive resistance developed, we would fight to the end so the movement could grow up through the 1980s," he added.

I noted that phrase: "fight to the end."

Yun's Outrage

The axe fell on May 17. That was the day Chun extended martial law nationwide, banned political activity and closed the universities. When the Kwangju incident began the following day, the hardcore demonstrators were several hundred college students protesting Chun's moves. It was while they were demonstrating that the martial law troops, including "black beret" Special Forces, surrounded them, indiscriminately bayoneting and beating both demonstrators and onlookers alike. The military reign of terror continued the next day. The scores of killings ignited the rage of citizens of all ages and inspired over 100,000 to join in a demonstration on May 20.

There was no overall leader at that stage. An outraged Yun telephoned from Kwangju on the night of May 18 to Lee in Seoul, reporting what was happening.

"Yun mobilized his friends and younger colleagues to issue the *Fighter's News*, a leaflet," Lee said. "Also he prepared Molotov cocktails."

Yun was involved in that first stage as one of a number of leaders, but he had not yet emerged as *the* leader.

By May 21, when about 200,000 joined the demonstrations, citizens were seizing weapons from police stations and military depots.

"Someone would chant the slogan, 'To the police station!' and everyone would go," recalled Chun.

Yun himself led an attack on an arms depot and was involved in the offensive at the Asia Motors factory to commandeer armored personnel carriers and other vehicles, Chun said. Soon thousands of students and citizens were armed. The army retreated from the city.

The mayor thereupon called an emergency meeting of an ad hoc committee set up to negotiate with the military. Eventually, though, that committee decided to persuade citizens to return all the seized weapons so they could be turned over to the military.

"This ad hoc committee mainly consisted of bureaucrats from the city and provincial governments," Chun said. "Of course the bureaucrats tended to be very conservative."

They appealed for calm. Most of the weapons were returned. But many citizens remained in a highly emotional state after witnessing the spilling of so much blood. "They wanted some kind of compensation," Chun said. "From this point on, Mr. Yun's role expanded."

Disagreeing with the ad hoc committee's approach, Yun nevertheless made a deal with the committee, pretending to cooperate while he selected some more radical people to join its membership. The mayor soon found himself unable to lead the divided committee.

Yun said, "Let's work together."

He continued to add dissidents until, by May 22 or 23, they held the majority on the committee.

"This second phase was an organized struggle," Lee Tae Bok said. "It was fully consistent with the view of our group"—the National Democratic Workers' League.

Yun called for youngsters to arm themselves in the YWCA nearby, Chun said. "When candidates showed up, Mr. Yun held a few minutes' military drill. Then they were sent to stand guard at the Provincial Hall."

Meanwhile, a man named Park Nam Sun had already emerged as the leader of the adult fighters. Yun discussed with Park the importance of carrying out resistance to the last, without surrendering any more weapons. Because of Park's prominent role in the uprising thus far, Yun argued, the authorities already would have targeted him so that "You're going to die anyway." Park agreed to stay on as commander of the armed struggle and cooperate with Yun.

Mass rallies continued, with some 50,000 people turning out on May 24 despite rain on that day.

Yun made a speech to the crowd gathered that day, with Park Nam Sun and his armed men standing behind him in impressive—perhaps, to some, intimidating—fashion. Yun told those assembled that the ad hoc committee's stated objective of retrieving and returning all the weapons did not accord with the consensus of the people of Kwangju. The citizens wanted a "fundamental solution," Yun said. If they just returned the weapons, what next? The committee didn't have an answer, so Yun announced that his group's approach—continued armed resistance—was the alternative to submission. Anyone unwilling to go along should leave the committee. A few people left, while some among the original committee members were willing to go along with Yun for the time being. In that fashion he and his group took over the committee.

Yun did not place himself at the top of the formal organization chart of the committee. To encourage the original committee members who had stayed on, two of them were named chairman and vice-chairman. Under those titular leaders came Yun with the title of "spokesman," overseeing the departments of public relations, planning, and supply—all the operational functions except actual armed fighting, which was Park

Nam Sun's responsibility. Yun personally headed the P.R. department, which included a team broadcasting announcements from vehicles on the streets; another group printing literature (Chun was a member of this team); a third raising funds and encouraging citizens to donate blood; and a fourth group whose job was to organize public rallies.

"Mr. Yun was maybe the only one who had a strategic view," said Chun Yong Ho.

What was that strategic view? Chun and several others answered me in a rush, talking for ten minutes or so. Park Sung Hyun then summarized and interpreted what they had said: the key was Yun's long-term vision of "pockets of resistance" (an idea to which I shall return). Short term, the idea was "to make the price higher" for the regime by holding out until the last, refusing to surrender. The rebels would present the regime with a dilemma: "If you do not have the guts to kill more people, you surrender yourselves. And if you do have enough guts, then you prove yourselves barbarians."

"Isn't this," asked Park Sung Hyun at our meeting, "the only way the oppressed can prove their dignity?"

Yun and his lieutenants were willing to pay the price: their lives.

"They wanted to complete the rebellion," said Park, "to put the final touch on the rebellion. But at the same time they hoped that if they held out, other rebellions would arise." Such was the notion or strategy of "pockets of resistance."

Chun interjected to quote Jesus' words recorded in the New Testament: "If I may be spared this cup . . ."

Continuing to summarize the others' remarks, Park Sung Hyun said that the inner circle around Yun had been resigned to accepting what would come if it could not be spared the cup, but meanwhile "purposely disseminated all the hopeful news." In particular, Yun and his lieutenants put forward the hope that the Americans would intervene and avert further bloodshed, although "in their minds they did not believe in it sincerely." The purpose was to give people outside the inner circle the courage to stay the course. For Kwangju to serve as a symbol and rallying point for future revolutionaries, surrender was out of the question.

A "Poison-Needle" Scare

The people assembled for the struggle—those on the ad hoc committee—were a varied lot from disparate backgrounds. A few were well known publicly—some preachers and a lawyer—but most were unknown to one other. That made it easy for Chun's military intelligence to infiltrate the dissident and radical forces. Whenever anyone spoke out at a meeting to urge a radical response, someone in the audience would shout: "You must be a North Korean agent!"

On May 25 there was a "poison-needle" scare. Rumors were flying that agents from North Korea were carrying poison needles. The rebels blamed government agents for planting the rumors. "One person pretended to get stung by a 'poison needle,'" said Kim Yun Ki, one of the armed fighters, now working as manager of a gallery in Kwangju. Kim and others took the "victim" to a hospital. "It turned out that he hadn't been stung by anything," said Kim.

Kim told me such government provocation had been a major factor in the hysteria I encountered when I arrived in Kwangju on May 26 for what was billed as a first press conference for the foreign media. Kim had been assigned as bodyguard to Yun.

"I was one of the 'hysterical' armed people," he told me, reminding me of my 1980 description.

Looking at Mr. Kim, I did recognize his face from among the young men I had seen around Yun Sang Won that day in 1980. "I remember Mr. Yun as a very sensitive, intelligent man," said Kim Yun Ki. "His character made him so determined up to the last moment."

Relatively few others shared that determination. After most of the seized weapons had been turned in, in response to the original ad hoc committee's pleas, only around 200 remained, Chun said. Many of the volunteers who had gotten emotionally fired up enough to volunteer for the ten-minute military training session had then found their courage ebbing and had not shown up a second time. One who had lost his courage did visit the Provincial Hall the last day. The young man told his erstwhile colleagues he felt guilty for abandoning the armed struggle, but he explained that he had been badly beaten by soldiers earlier and was afraid.

On the evening of May 26, there were warnings, Chun recalled. Family members of military men stationed in the Kwangju area told the resistance fighters that the military planned to move into the city early the next morning. About 300 people were in the Provincial Hall. Yun called them together and told the women and any boys who had not yet graduated from high school to go home. That left about 150 people, who got their rifles and were assigned posts to defend. Once the fighting began, the rebel riflemen fired many rounds, Chun said, but they had M-1's and carbines—hardly a match for the soldiers' M-16s—and their negligible training showed.

Armed fighters in the Provincial Hall with Yun were despatched to the front of the building. But the military approached from the rear. The soldiers ordered the rebels to throw their weapons out into the hallway and crawl out to surrender, or they would be killed. Some complied with the order and surrendered. Yun, however, carried his gun out into the hallway, where he was shot in the kidney area, Chun told me. With Yun at the time was Kim Young Chul, who reported directly to him as head of the rebellion's planning department. Kim wrapped the bleeding but still breathing spokesman-leader in a curtain and was carrying him away when a grenade exploded and the curtain caught fire. That explains why Yun's body had been burned by the time the AP's Terry Anderson saw it.

It sounded, I said, as if planning for the armed resistance had been terrible. Or on second thought, I asked, was effective military resistance simply not that important for what Yun saw as essentially a plan for symbolic suicide? Chun nodded his head in agreement. I pressed further, asking if Chun had understood Yun's "pockets of resistance" strategy at the time.

"I'm not sure anybody understood Mr. Yun's view," he replied. He and others later came to understand and appreciate the policy, but public recognition of Yun's role has been slow to come.

Even the government apparently was not aware of the extent of Yun's role at Kwangju. Four hundred of his colleagues in Haklim were arrested in June of 1981, then subjected to what Lee described as "very serious three-month interrogations." The authorities were told during these interrogations that the Kwangju spokesman, killed at the end, had been the Kwangju organizer for the National Democratic Workers' League. But the interrogators did not pursue the matter, said Lee, who was one of those interrogated.

"The government was not that much aware of Mr. Yun's role there or his political organizing background," he added.

Lee's theory was that the government was too much preoccupied with two other versions of just who had been in charge at Kwangju to pay attention to yet a third version.

One of the government's versions, which officials did not actually believe, Lee said, was that "impure elements"—North Korean agents or sympathizers—had been calling the shots. The regime's other version, which many officials did believe, was that Kim Dae Jung and his followers had stage-managed events at Kwangju, Lee Tae Bok said. What was the relationship between Yun Sang Won and Kim Dae Jung?

"Nothing," said Lee. "They never met each other." Just before the Kwangju uprising, Yun was invited to join an organization to prepare a new political party for Kim Dae Jung, but Lee said he thought the proffered post had never materialized.

In view of the "Pyongyang fever" that developed among students in the 1980s, I pressed further on whether there might be any truth to the government's allegations of a hidden North Korean hand behind events in Kwangju. Lee Tae Bok told me flatly that the Kwangju uprising "was not influenced by the North at all." As for Yun Sang Won's views of the North, Lee said he personally interviewed Yun on the topic in 1979 as part of the vetting for Yun's membership in the National Democratic Workers' League.

"Remember the three groups we talked about. The second group, as represented by the South Korean National Liberation Front, had a tendency to be pro-North." But the third group, to which Yun belonged, had a different view. "Mr. Yun was very critical of the North. First, he felt the North Korean regime did not understand the real situation in the South."

Yun was also critical of Kim Il Sung's personality cult and of the plans for dynastic succession by Kim Jong Il—the son of the "Great Leader."

Recognition is finally, but still gradually, coming to Yun. Old comrades and others have set up a committee to grant annually the Yun Sang Won Award to people who have contributed to South Korea's democratization. Lim Nak Pyong, an old comrade now active in the environmental movement, wrote and published a biography of Yun. However, Lim told me: "The 'May issue' has not yet been resolved. That limits our activities for the Yun Sang Won Prize Committee even though there is a new government."

Kim Chang Joong, Kwangju bureau chief for *Chugan Nodongja Shinmun* (Weekly Labor News), told me of his paper's sponsorship of the first Yun Sang Won Culture Festival in Kwangju on May 16, 1993. "The background for that festival was that Mr. Yun was about the only revolutionary intellectual who fought to the death in Kwangju," he said. "He was virtually the first to lead a scientific labor movement in this area."

Ever the skeptical journalist, I asked Kim whether South Korea would have experienced the rapid economic advances of the late 1980s if labor had won its freedoms at an earlier stage, but someone else chimed in on another topic then and I never got my answer.

An Assessment of Yun?

So how do we assess Yun Sang Won's role at Kwangju? Even if he was the leader of the final phase, of course it was in the first phase that most lives were lost and it was then that the largest number of citizens rose up against the government. Which phase was more important?

"These two phases are not separate," Lee Tae Bok replied.

Park Sung Hyun elaborated: "The second phase was a matter of how to complete the first phase. You chase out the army, take up arms. Then you voluntarily put down the arms? It's just a farce."

Some believe that it was Yun's "pockets of resistance" that gave Korean protesters the courage to resume the struggle in the 1980s and ultimately overturn military rule.

"The reason why the Korean people could overcome that terrible violence so quickly in 1987 was because of Kwangju's resistance," said Lee Jai Eui, secretary-general of Chonnam Social Research Institute and one of those at the meeting.

Historians will sort all that out. Suffice it to say now that Yun devoted his brief life and consciously gave up his life to bring change to South Korea, and change has indeed come. As we left the Yun family's farm the day I visited there, I saw a police car stopping next door. Had the authorities come to check up on the onetime student radicals who were my hosts? Chun Yong Ho and Eugene Soh laughed at the notion.

"It's not like the old days," said Soh.

CHAPTER EIGHT

A SCREAM FOR FREEDOM

Henry Scott-Stokes with Shim Jae Hoon and Phillippe Pons

Fire

One of my most vivid memories of May 1980 concerns a phone call from my *New York Times* colleague Shim Jae Hoon. I received the call—from somewhere outside Kwangju—early in the evening of May 21 to my room in the Chosun Hotel in Seoul. Jae had left Seoul at 5 A.M. that day, heading for Kwangju, riding in a hired car with our friend Phillippe Pons of *Le Monde*. The two of them had just come out of Kwangju, reached a nearby town, and then found a hotel (in fact it was a brothel, they discovered) with a phone that worked. This was Jae's first call to me after leaving the city. As he read out his notes, his voice shot up into a falsetto. I scribbled frantically.

His piece ran next day as the *New York Times* page one lead of May 22, 1980:

PROTESTORS CONTROL
SOUTH KOREAN CITY;
AT LEAST 32 KILLED

NEW CABINET NAMED IN SEOUL

RIOTERS RAMPAGE IN KWANGJU
WITH ARMS SEIZED FROM MILITARY—
STRONGMAN IS ASSAILED

KWANGJU, SOUTH KOREA, MAY 21—Tens of thousands of demonstrators, many waving seized rifles, iron bars, axes, pitchforks and even light machine guns took control of this southwestern city today, the fourth day of anti-government rioting that has cost the lives of at least 32 people. . . .

Reading this piece now, I am struck by how the grey prose of the *New York Times* diluted the drama. Phillippe Pons' story, which I read only many years later, was better than ours, I regret to say. For a start he was more accurate as regards casualties. His piece began:

IN SOUTH KOREA DEMONSTRATIONS MAY HAVE LEFT 100 DEAD AT KWANGJU...

KWANGJU—Three days after the imposition of martial law a major insurrection was taking place at Kwangju in the southwest of South Korea. There, since the middle of the night, the demonstrators control the city after extremely murderous confrontations with the army.

Thousands of people—30,000 to 50,000 according to some sources; 100,000 according to others—are running round the town, some in military trucks, jeeps or armored vehicles seized from the army, with machine guns in position, flying the South Korean flag. The crowd cries out at every opportunity: "Death to Chun!" meaning General Chun Doo Hwan, the nation's "strongman.". . .

Most of the demonstrators in Kwangju carry sticks or Molotov cocktails. Many among them carry automatic rifles. Traveling out of the city for a distance of 20 kilometers one meets army trucks crammed with men, often very young, whom the demonstrators have gone to find in nearby villages.

Kwangju itself is under siege. There are barricades on the main streets, burned cars lie about, and a strong smell of tear gas hangs everywhere in the city. The army, roughly one division of troops, has pulled back from the Provincial Hall and from the university campuses. Repeatedly, one hears shots and the rattling of machine guns. The police have disappeared.

At a hospital which we visited, the emergency rooms and operating theaters are proving inadequate to deal with the wounded. Certain of these have been cruelly murdered, according to the doctors. At 1 P.M. on Tuesday the medical staff reported 30 dead in this particular hospital. Many other victims have been seen elsewhere in the city. According to demonstrators, the number of dead would have risen to 100. We saw some 70 others extremely badly injured, mostly with bullet wounds.

The city is cut off from outside. Telephone communications have been cut of. . The roads are blocked by trucks put out on the main roads by the demonstrators. Helicopters fly constantly overhead, taking in the scene, and dropping leaflets which call on the population to stop fighting. According to these tracts there would have been 10 dead on the military side.

The four radio and television stations were burned during the night. The main tax office and the Catholic Center were also put to the torch. . . .

These two newspaper articles, as it happened, focused the eyes of the world on Kwangju. Up to this time the South Korean military had pretty much kept a lid on the story.

Years later, what is there to add? There is always stuff that a reporter cannot write, notably to do with himself or herself—how the work has been done. Two points come to mind in this instance:

- Jae and Phillippe arrived in Kwangju on the key day, May 21, the day the civilian militia finally succeeded in forcing the Korean army (one of the toughest in the world) to pull back from the city. Our excellent timing was thanks to Jae. On the evening of May 20 Jae had concluded that all hell was about to break loose. We had quickly agreed that he should get a car and driver and drive to Kwangju, 385 kilometers to the south, the next day.

• The other point missing from our news stories was the fact that my friends (this was the case with all foreign correspondents) had been treated like heroes ("triumphant generals," Jae said) by the populace. Jae and Phillippe, trapped in their hired car, found themselves caught up in tumultuous crowds and swept forward, in effect as supporters of the uprising, with demonstrators chanting *"New York Times! New York Times!"*

Shim Jae Hoon recalls his experience:

The events I describe here commenced approximately fifteen minutes after we passed the toll gate and entered Kwangju. We—Phillippe and I, with the driver—were stopped and surrounded by a group of citizen-militants armed with axes and metal pipes, their faces partly hidden by cloth masks. They lifted and bounced our car up and down as if they intended to overturn it. We showed them our identification but it was useless. I thought I would die there, on the spot.

After what seemed like an eternity—we were stuck—a man appeared, introducing himself as the person in charge of information in the city. He approached us and told us to follow him in the car. He himself had a car. He also had a megaphone. He used this, as he drove, to shout at the crowds on the street.

"Citizens of Kwangju! Citizens of Kwangju! Finally, the reporters of the *New York Times* and *Le Monde* are here to report the situation in Kwangju."

The crowds standing on the sidewalks reacted immediately. The people burst into ovations, which multiplied along the way. We were received by the citizens as if we were triumphant generals. I realized, then, that we appeared as saviors to these people.

Kwangju was not in disorder, nor was there violence. Citizens, no matter who they were, provided food and water to the militants. The first conclusion I reached, then and there, was that this was no riot situation—as the military maintained, insisting on that expression "riot"—it was an "insurrection," an "uprising." My judgement was confirmed, as I looked about the downtown area for clues to explain why we were welcomed so warmly. The insurrection was taking place in complete isolation from the rest of the world, indeed the rest of Korea. The outside world, including those in Seoul, did not know the truth of the battle the populace was fighting down here. We were to be the channel of communication.

The cooperation we received was amazing. We stuck hand-scribbled notices in Korean identifying ourselves as press on the outside of our car. That was to protect us in the event of emergency. Kwangju people showed extreme mistrust toward the domestic press. By contrast, foreign news reporters had free passes everywhere.

We hurried, first, to Chonnam National University hospital. I nearly fainted the moment I entered the hospital. What I saw there reminded me of a scene in the movie *Gone With the Wind:* It was exactly like that field hospital during the American Civil War. The hospital was in a big mess, full of screaming people and reeking of blood. The corridor going down to the operating room was filled with patients, and the floor was sticky with blood. Pretty soon, our clothes were dyed red too.

We went to the mortuary. The spectacle was even more horrible than a field hospital that I had seen in Vietnam. Seeing the patients dying in great pain, I had the feeling that I might die there too. In fact, I survived several critical moments during the day. I remember passing nearby Chonnam National University and hearing a bullet hiss through the air just above our heads. I was scared to death.

Five days later—just before the end—I went down to Kwangju, traveling with Jae and Phillippe. Arriving in the city—it was by now the afternoon of May 26—was an astounding experience. I discovered that (a) it was *not* cut off from the outside world, as I had imagined from news reports, we just drove into the place, using minor roads—in other words it was completely open to attack by martial law forces at any time—and (b) those at the center of affairs in the city were immature fighters. The student leaders—Jae, Phillippe, and I went into their main offices inside the Provincial Hall and met Yun Sang Won, the spokesman for the insurgents—struck me as children. They were very tired, very young people. Being with them for only a short time, I saw that they had little idea how to handle weapons. It was alarming to discover how these exhausted students—weary after many nights without much sleep and wound up to breaking point—leaned their carbines against the wall of a room where we met the spokesman (Yun Sang Won would not disclose his name, we learned it only a decade later), as if they were popguns. Were they loaded? Were the safety catches on? I had the impression these youths had had no training. They were practically dropping asleep as they stood there. Like others before us, as I heard later, we were asked by Yun Sang Won—a mature, personable, softspoken fellow, quite relaxed compared to the students—to intervene in the situation ourselves: to telephone Bill Gleysteen, the U.S.

ambassador, who was up in Seoul, and get him to halt the bloodshed, to prevent the Korean military from coming in and killing them. I wrote a story to report this—I had no phone in the city and could not call the U.S. Embassy, nor did I ask Jae to do so—and gave the piece to Jae to file to New York.

That night I stayed alone at an inn he found for me in the middle of Kwangju, a couple of hundred yards from the Provincial Hall. Jae and Phillippe left the city with the driver, to transmit our stories for the day, stories that were never used because they were overtaken by events. Left without communications, without staff, I was unable to discuss anything with the manager in the inn. It was an unenviable situation, but one of us had to be in the city. Jae had an intuition this was the night the army would come back into Kwangju. My concern about that possibility was heightened when—at about 8 P.M.—a burly young student came clumping along the corridor to my room at the inn, to urge me, again, to get in touch with the American embassy and save the city. Or that was my immediate interpretation of the few words he uttered before he was cajoled out of the room by the manager of the inn, with many smiles and apologies.

I woke up in the small hours. What woke me, I do not know. But suddenly I was sitting bolt upright in bed. Outside—I could see nothing over the roofs—it was pitch black. Not a light showed anywhere. Certainly, the city was quiet. No one walked in the streets, that I could hear. Kwangju was not only there for the taking, it was asleep! The silence was eerie.

Suddenly, the quiet of the night was broken by a female voice. Someone up at the Provincial Hall was using the loudspeaker system. It was a young woman's voice, with a hysterical edge. As the girl shrieked on— her voice resounding over the darkened city—her words merged into a continuum, one continuous shriek, a wail that lasted for perhaps ten minutes, on and on and on. What was she saying? "This is the end." That was, no doubt, the pith of it—a token appeal to the citizens to come out and join the students, a few hundred students at most? I wish I could convey to you the passion in that voice. Imagine that famous painting by Munch, the Norwegian painter, "The Scream," with the mysterious face and hollowed mouth, and imagine that painting wired for sound at tremendous volume in an otherwise pitch-black room. Then you may have some idea of the power of that voice. There is no role in Shakespeare that calls for a scream of that power. I listened. I waited. There was no sound of doors opening, no scuffling of shoes in the street. Where were the people of Kwangju? Locked inside their homes, with their doors barred. There was no sound of doors being unbarred, no sound of steps in the street, nothing. All of a sudden the voice cut off.

Now the students were on their own. Every citizen of Kwangju must have been wide awake, listening to every slightest sound outside. (The contrast with the city then, and the Kwangju of a couple of days before, when 100,000 people surged onto the streets, was total; but then everybody had had a chance to weigh up what coming out into the open could mean.) Shortly thereafter, the sound of gunfire approached from the outskirts of the city. I heard the dom-dom-dom of heavy machine guns in the professionals' hands, a whoof or two from some heavier weapon, and then in reply an occasional pop from a carbine on the students' side. It was a one-sided fight.

A few hours later, Shim Jae Hoon and Phillippe Pons came back into the city and we were reunited. Jae has remembered that I looked "scared," when he rejoined me—I was distraught. The wrong side had won. The students who had asked for our help were now, however many of them, dead. We had not lifted a finger to protect them. Worse, I had written no story on the fall of the city. Without that indispensable phone, I had been sunk. That morning, not far from my inn, I had found a burly student lying flat on his face in the street. A trickle of bright red blood ran away from his body into the gutter. The boy who had come and rapped on my door the night before? I would never know.

Let Phillippe describe what Kwangju looked like:

> Kwangju seemed dead as a city. The streets, all the main traffic arteries, were blocked by tanks. Soldiers checked the papers of occasional passers-by. They were searching the houses, using their fists. This city had just been conquered by an alien army, that was my impression. In every main square, machine guns were set up, ready to fire. Armour and trucks dominated the city center. Soldiers, with fixed bayonets, were prowling into the side-streets. Outside the Provincial Hall, the men stared at the corpses. There was sporadic gunfire carrying on into the afternoon. The radio made an announcement: to leave the city was forbidden. . . . Hours later, we left in the *New York Times* car. We gave a helping hand to one man, who was desperately seeking to flee the city. We put a press armband on him.

Yes, I remember. That gambit with the armband must have been Jae's idea, enterprising fellow that he was. We jammed that mysterious man—a tall, good-looking fellow with a smile on his lips, very different from our tense selves—between us in the back of the car. We did not know that person, but we wanted to help. He was in trouble for all that his demeanor was that of a cheerful chap returning to the city after a weekend in the country. We got that unknown man out of the city and all the way to safety through the army roadblocks on the expressway outside Kwangju.

I was glad that we could do something for someone on the losing side. Yet I should have known, listening to that girl's voice shouting out into the night over the dark roofs of Kwangju, that all was not lost.

Hers was no ordinary cry. It was a scream for freedom.

CHAPTER NINE
"LET'S LIVE AND MEET AGAIN"
Norman Thorpe

The Rally at the Square in Front of the Provincial Hall

Probably for almost everyone who was in the city then, the Kwangju uprising was a powerful event.

When I arrived in Kwangju on Wednesday, May 21, 1980, the city was in turmoil. As I walked down the streets, identified as a reporter by my armband and cameras, person after person came up to tell me urgently what was happening.

"They're killing the students! They're shooting the students!" they told me time after time.

In 1996, sixteen years after the events, I visited Kwangju again. As soon as a resident heard that I had been there in May 1980, the person would tell a story about what he or she had experienced then, when South Korea's army sicced its paratroops on their own countrymen and countrywomen.

Several times I have been asked to give speeches about what I saw in Kwangju. When I do, emotional memories well up. As I tell about the soldiers' casual brutality and killing, about how the citizens rose in outrage, about the first schoolboy I met with a bullet wound, and about going from hospital to hospital to count the dead, I get a knot in my throat and it's difficult to keep speaking.

For a reporter, personally seeing the bodies and verifying the deaths was of paramount importance. In Seoul, the government was saying no civilians had been killed—one of the many lies it told about Kwangju over and over. I think seeing those bodies and hearing those lies are the reasons why memories of Kwangju are still so emotional for me. A government's foremost duty is to protect its citizens. To kill them is an atrocity, and to deny the deaths is an even greater injustice.

During my first hours in Kwangju I took many pictures, including photographs of many of the bodies I saw. On my second day there, when I found a Westerner who was leaving, I sent most of the film out with him. I wanted to be sure proof of the killings would get beyond Kwangju. I've never been able to find out what became of the film. Today I wish I still had my pictures of those turbulent hours. At the time, however, the most important thing to me was to tell the world the truth in the face of falsehood as quickly as possible: one of a reporter's most important objectives.

Today, when I hear or read of some other great injustice where innocent people are helpless against some overwhelming force, it can suddenly bring Kwangju to mind. Stories of the Tiananmen massacre, for instance, did that.

A Bicyclist's Solitary Journey

Some of my memories of Kwangju are like photographs. One is a moving photograph—a slow-motion picture of a scene I saw. In it, a man, perhaps middle-aged, steadily pedals a bicycle down a Kwangju side street. Like most Korean bikes in those days, his bike had a strong cargo rack built over the rear tire. Strapped onto this rack and extending out behind his bike was a pine coffin.

Someone in this man's family was dead—most likely the victim was one of the many people who had been killed by the soldiers—and the man had gone by bicycle to fetch a coffin.

I had already been to the various hospitals in Kwangju and seen the stacks of unpainted pine coffins into which the victims' remains were being placed. I saw mothers publicly wailing with grief over their children's coffins, draped with Korea's national flag.

It is this bicyclist's solitary journey, however, that has stayed in my mind as one of the most poignant images. As the rider leaned forward to get leverage on his pedals, I was reminded how each family had had great hopes for whomever had died, especially for those who had been students. I had just met some of those students in hospitals—lucky ones whom the bullets had only wounded. But here was something I hadn't thought about. Some of the families were so poor that they could bring a coffin only by bicycle. Now in a wrenching upheaval, the focus of their hope was gone.

I glimpsed the bicycle for only a few seconds while riding through Kwangju with several other people in a trailer behind a farm tractor. I wanted to photograph the scene. I wanted to chase after the man and ask him to tell me his story. There was not time, however, to get the tractor to stop before the bicycle with the coffin was gone. The image has been riveted to my memory ever since, more powerfully than the most moving photograph.

Kwangju wasn't just an event in history. As I contemplate the bicycle rider's personal tragedy, I think of what a frightening time Kwangju was for parents. Young people feel invincible; they don't recognize danger or their own mortality. What's more, much of the soldiers' violence was indiscriminate. Many of the more than 2,000 people who were wounded or killed were simply spectators. Others weren't even that. They simply happened to pass the wrong place at the wrong time. Often, parents had no way of knowing whether or not their children might be involved.

On the Mokpo Road

In Kwangju, after a couple of days, the situation had become a standoff, with the rebels within the city and the army without. Negotiations were going slowly, so one day I set out from Kwangju for the port city of Mokpo. I had heard that the rebellion had spread, and I wanted to see what was happening elsewhere.

Initially, I walked, hoping I could find some kind of ride. Along the road I met a farmer from Muan. He had ridden his bicycle thirty-three miles to Kwangju that morning to find his two sons, who both worked there. He was afraid they might have been caught up in the violence. Fortunately, his sons were all right. So he had sent them on home ahead of him, giving them his bike. Now he was walking back home himself, unconcerned about the distance, simply relieved to have found his sons safe.

That evening, although I had gotten several rides, I still hadn't reached Mokpo. I was walking on the road out in the countryside when darkness fell. I met some high school students talking by the road in the dark. One of them took me to his parents' farmhouse. His parents kindly fed me and gave me a place to sleep. But, when I said I was planning to go to Mokpo the next morning, the boy's mother became quite nervous. She feared her son would go with me and get caught up in the violence there. In the morning, the son showed me a way to Mokpo along the coastline by which I could avoid passing an army unit. After being shown the way, I sent him back home to alleviate his mother's fears.

Kwangju even generated worries for the parents of my assistant, John Marcom, a recent university graduate who was working for me as an intern. When the disturbances in Kwangju first began to break out I was fully occupied covering news of the military's takeover in Seoul, so I sent Marcom to Kwangju to monitor events there. After I reached Kwangju, we sent out a story with both our bylines. When it was published in the U.S. edition of *The Wall Street Journal*, Marcom's parents saw it, learned he was in Kwangju, and began to worry that he was in danger. Fortunately, I had already sent him back to Seoul by then.

Throughout the time I was in Kwangju, including my last day there, I saw parents and family members searching for relatives and worrying about people who were missing. Even a few years ago when I visited the Kwangju cemetery, where the victims of the massacre are buried, a display listed more than forty people who still were missing. Their families believe they may have been killed in the violence and their bodies hidden by soldiers.

Kwangju left many mysteries. For me, one of the most vivid was something else I encountered on my trip to Mokpo. Along the shoulder of the road south of Kwangju, I found a group of people staring at a heavy-duty wrecker truck painted army green. Several bullet holes perforated the gas tank and the fender near the driver's seat. The front of the truck was smashed in from a collision.

The mystery, however, involves the left rear wheel. Hanging from it was someone's complete scalp, apparently ripped off when hair was caught between the rim and the tire. The people standing there gawking decided the scalp must have belonged to a male civilian, because they thought the hair was too long for a soldier and too short for a woman.

Was the truck an instrument of some horrendous torture or punishment? Or did some unfathomable accident occur? I don't know, but whatever happened was horrible.

Not all of my memories of Kwangju are painful, however. One thing that touched me was how much people helped each other, such as the farmer's family that sheltered me for the night. People helped me, especially, because I was a reporter, and they wanted me to get my story out. But they also reached out to each other. Townspeople gave the demonstrating students food and shared transportation and information. While I was on the road to Mokpo, people said to follow the railroad track for part of the route. At one place along the track, I was surprised to find a large earthen jar filled with water.

Someone had put it there so that weary passers-by could get a drink on their dry journey.

A Haunting Memory

One of my most haunting memories, however, is of a body I found in an upstairs room of the Provincial Hall immediately after the battle there ended on Tuesday, May 27. The room was some sort of auditorium, and the body, that of one of the rebels, lay in the middle of it. The body had been scorched by some kind of fire, and some of the hair seemed burned away. A pile of some unknown substance, melted but also like ashes, was heaped around the body.

As I recall, the rebel's eyes were still partly open, which was one of the things that made the scene so haunting. I wanted to reach down and close the eyes, as characters do in a movie, but I felt as a reporter I shouldn't alter anything. In particular, the face had been burned. At the time, I imagined he had been burned by one of the rocket-propelled grenades being used by the army in their attack, or perhaps by some kind of stun grenade. In this case, the mystery has been solved.

I didn't know the young man's identity, but the image of his face stayed with me so strongly that over the years I wanted to know who he was. My family and I visited Korea a few summers ago, and I took them to Kwangju. When we went to the cemetery, I stopped at every grave to look at the deceased's photograph beside each tombstone and read the information there. I didn't tell my family what I was doing, but I was searching for a photo that matched the burned face etched on my memory. I wanted to learn the young man's name, his occupation, and why he had chosen almost certain death facing the government troops as they retook the Provincial Hall.

Many of the gravestone photos had been damaged by the weather, though, and as much as I looked, I never found a face that matched my memory.

Ironically, Bradley Martin of the *Baltimore Sun* remembered the same man—not in death, but when he had functioned as the rebels' spokesman. Martin also had wanted to know the man's identity and what had happened to him. From Kwangju survivors, Martin, not long ago, confirmed that the man was Yun Sang Won.

Martin learned that one of Yun's friends, Kim Young Chul, was with Yun during the Provincial Hall battle. During the battle, Kim said afterward, Yun was shot in the abdomen. Kim wrapped the bleeding Yun in a curtain, which then suddenly caught fire when a grenade exploded. That's how Yun came to be burned.

For me, the story reveals the panic and helplessness the rebels must have felt in their final lonely hours and minutes facing death as the army closed in on their undermanned and poorly armed positions: When Yun is gravely wounded in a burst of gunfire, his companion desperately wraps him in a curtain. The curtain probably came from the auditorium's stage. Then there's another blast. The curtain bursts into flames, and there's nothing more Yun's companion can do.

The rebels' last stand had begun only a few hours earlier. For five days, they had occupied the Provincial Hall in Kwangju, using it as their center of operations while negotiations were conducted with the government. They had manned blockades and defense lines where highways came into the city.

Most of the foreign reporters in Kwangju were staying at an inn behind the Provincial Hall so they could keep close tabs on developments. At about 2 A.M. that morning, I was awakened by someone's voice outside the inn.

Hey Mister!

"*Ajossi, ajossi* (Mister, mister)," a young man called, "the troops are going to attack!"

I hurried out to talk with him, and he said the rebels had been told to surrender by 4 A.M., because the soldiers would enter the city then.

I wakened some of the other reporters and then went up to the roof of the inn to see if I could see or hear anything. The city was mostly dark, and stars shone brightly in the clear night sky. I even saw a falling star. Small planes flew over the city, and loudspeakers warned citizens to stay indoors. After a while, the rebels turned out a group of forty to fifty high school students from the Provincial Hall, saying they were too young to give their lives.

"Let's live and meet again," I heard someone say.

Rebel leaders told us that they had no alternative but to fight. If they surrendered or were captured, they probably would be executed, they said. One of them said their forces numbered about 100 in the Provincial Hall, with about 200 others elsewhere around the city. Using a loudspeaker, they began to appeal for any brave citizens to come and help them, but there was no response. As four o'clock neared, they broke windows out of the provincial headquarters to facilitate shooting and took up positions. A few rebel trucks darted through the streets; then there were the sounds of distant sirens and dogs barking.

At 4 A.M., as Korea's traditional curfew ended, church bells began to peal. Then, mixed with the pealing bells, gunfire erupted, including the sound of automatic weapons, as the army invaded the city.

Soon, I realized I better leave the inn's roof, where in the dark I could be mistaken by either side as one of the enemy. I went inside, joining the reporters clustered there. We listened as the gunfire got nearer, intensified, and seemed to focus on the Provincial Hall next door. Soon there were the sounds of a heavy battle, and the shooting was punctuated by large booms that someone identified as the sounds made by rocket-propelled grenades. We heard armored vehicles moving in.

Getting Shot at a Bit

Dawn was providing some light now. From one of the upstairs windows of the inn, we had a poor view of part of the Provincial Hall. A small group of us gathered there, trying to catch a glimpse of the battle through the open window. Suddenly we saw a government soldier only fifteen or twenty yards away from us, on the Provincial Hall roof—our first view of what was happening.

When the soldier saw us, he quickly motioned for us to get away from the window, which we did. However, Terry Anderson, of the Associated Press, wanted to get photos of the soldier; we hadn't been able to photograph any part of the battle thus far. Anderson adjusted the settings on his camera, then rose to the window again, and focused on the soldier. As soon as the soldier saw him, the soldier swung his M-16 around and fired off several shots toward us, which crashed into the window casing and the wall behind us.

Fortunately, none of us was hit, although we could very easily have been. We were all shaken to have shots aimed in our direction, and I found the close call very scary. I realized that being next to the window was foolhardy, that with grenades and possibly heavier armament being used, any of the outer rooms might be unsafe. I moved to an interior hallway, which I felt was more protected, and waited there for a while for the battle to ebb.

By 7 A.M. the battle and the Kwangju insurrection were over. Thousands of troops were deployed throughout the city, and fifteen tanks occupied the central plaza in front of the Provincial Hall. There, soldiers guarded groups of rebels who had surrendered and who were lying on the ground at gunpoint. Other young men were marched up after being captured elsewhere, and eventually I saw forty to sixty of them loaded onto buses. Later, the army said it arrested 295 people as instigators and participants in the revolt.

Soon, reporters were allowed to walk through the Provincial Hall. In it, I saw the bodies of rebels scattered where they had died: Yun's body in the auditorium, another body in a tangle of folding chairs, others within a few feet of coffins where the embalming of Kwangju's earlier victims hadn't been completed, and two sprawled upstairs in a pool of blood. Soon, soldiers took the top from a Ping-Pong table, dragged those two bodies onto it, and used it as a stretcher to carry the bodies downstairs.

I walked several blocks around the area and found more bodies along the street and one in the foyer of the YWCA, which showed heavy damage from gunfire. A settee inside held a large pool of blood. I was told that about twenty men and women had been taken prisoner there. Women students had earlier planned an all-night vigil there, which apparently was in progress when the army attacked the city. In all, I counted eighteen dead in and around the Provincial Hall area.

For a while, citizens stayed indoors, having been warned that anyone on the streets was subject to arrest. Eventually, however, they began to drift out to see what had happened. Many were sympathetic with the rebels. Time after time, they spoke with me, urging me to tell the truth about the events. The reason the students had taken up guns, they said, over and over, was because of the army's initial brutal and indiscriminate attacks on civilians.

"The students got guns because they saw so many people killed," a middle-aged white-collar worker told me bitterly.

After seeing all this, I was appalled by the needless bloodshed and use of naked military force I had witnessed. It was time to write my story, but my mind was numb. I was emotionally overwhelmed. I felt dirty. In order to fulfill my duty—telling what I had seen—I had to go somewhere peaceful. I didn't want to be around the bodies, or the prisoners, or the soldiers that were on every street corner.

Somehow I walked or hitched a ride, I can't remember which, to somewhere on the outskirts of Kwangju, where the urban landscape ended and placid rice paddies took over. I found a seat on a low hill, away from any people, facing where I couldn't see anything but nature. There in the May sunshine, I cleared my mind and composed a description of events for my editors.

I didn't go back to Kwangju again for sixteen years. When I did, I was amazed by the heavy traffic and bustling streets, the new buildings, and the huge underground shopping mall that's been built in front of the Provincial Hall. Downtown is attractive and inviting, and, except for some of the space around the Provincial Hall, the streets don't seem the same. During the uprising, I had walked everywhere because there was no public transportation and there were almost no cars. It was hard to make any of my memories fit and harder still to expect my wife and children to envision what I had told them.

When we talked with the people, though, we discovered they hadn't forgotten what happened. When we went to the Kwangju cemetery, I became sure they will never forget. Those who died have been memorialized well. The cemetery tells their many different stories straightforwardly, and visiting it leaves a strong impression. It's a site that Koreans and foreigners alike should try to visit to understand more about how Korea threw off the yoke of dictatorship and achieved a more democratic government.

Memorializing missing classmate.

A youth being beaten to death.

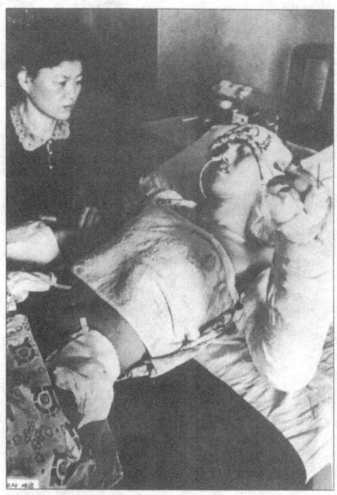

Wounded protestor in hospital.

Troops on the move.

Soldiers advancing with batons.

Fighting in the streets.

World media expresses outrage.

Citizen Settlement Committee in session.

Captors and demonstrators.

A peaceful rally in front of Provincial Hall, May 22-26.

Former presidents Chun Doo Hwan (right) and Roh Tae Woo (center) on trial in Seoul, 1996.

Soldier beating youth.

Arrested militants.

PART THREE
THE KOREAN PRESS

Introduction

The Korean press had a terrible time in Kwangju. For the foreign correspondents it was a major story—few foreign correspondents were in physical danger for more than very short periods of time; their stories were published as they wrote them. The domestic press operated—or not—under martial-law censorship. They were, of course, not permitted to acquaint their readers or viewers with the fact that they were being heavily censored and, moreover, forced to slant their stories, once the fact of the clashes at Kwangju could no longer be kept quiet.

The first piece among the contributions that follow is by Kim Dae Jung, a senior editor at *Chosun Ilbo*—a national daily with head office in Seoul—at the time of the Kwangju troubles. Kim Dae Jung (a namesake, no relative of President Kim) self-criticizes, yet he, like editors at all the newspapers, couldn't publish a line from Kwangju; any Seoul-written pieces he ran were slanted to satisfy the censors. The latter were army officers; they were posted in newspaper head offices and broadcasting stations and were on duty at all times, working in relays. Slanting of the news was achieved by crude but effective means. The demonstrators—citizens and students—must be identified as "rioters" and as "hooligans." Nothing could be said of the brutality that provoked Kwangju into an uprising. Casualty figures were reduced to a minimum, and ascribed to fights among the citizens or to accidents, never to the military. News control was kept tight.

The lid was kept screwed down, especially when it came to news photos out of Kwangju. Hwang Jong Gon, a staff photographer for *Dong-A Ilbo*, another national daily, mentions in his piece, with pride, that his newspaper was permitted to carry a single photo from Kwangju on May 23. One photo! The censors were not content with cropping pictures, to cut out bits they didn't like; or with choosing benign photos of smiling schoolchildren or of citizens seated in the big square in front of Provincial Hall, listening to speakers. They cut out the lot. No pictures could be published. The newly installed army junta was strict, because a lot was at stake. If all went well—the lid was kept on the news, and the press was held in check—it looked as if they had the presidency in the bag (General Chun Doo Hwan would seize the presidency for himself without further ado in August 1980). The last pocket of resistance in the nation was Kwangju. Just fix the "rioters" there and South Korea was the junta's for the taking.

In journalism, once you've missed the news, that's it. Journalism is about news. Nothing is older than yesterday's newspaper. Members of the Korean press who missed the boat at Kwangju had to wait years, if not decades, to see their stuff in print. Hwang Jong Gon, the *Dong-A Ilbo* photographer, eventually saw his pictures published in book form, along with those taken by a colleague, fourteen years after the events. Kim Yang Woo, the author of the last contribution to this chapter, waited sixteen years to get a book out, finally using the material he had kept untouched all that time. Several contributors to this chapter—Ryu Jong Hwan of the *Pusan Ilbo* is one—mention their chagrin; on returning from Kwangju, Ryu discovered that his paper had not used one line of his as he wrote it. A news blackout was in operation nationwide. The biggest news story out of South Korea in the 1980s was never accurately reported as news by the Korean media, because by the time reporters were free to write, Kwangju was no longer news. Officers loyal to Chun ensured that there was not a peep in the press to discredit their man.

This was possible under martial law. Was there no recourse? None. Meanwhile, part of the explanation of the great delays in getting out the facts—or publishing photos—lay on the shoulders of the newsmen and photographers themselves. It is unpleasant to admit that you have fallen down on the job. Yet our contributors admit they did. They failed in their duties. One after another, the writers in this section wring their hands over what they did not write. An explanation is not hard to find: When censorship is prevalent, a reporter learns to sense what he can write and what he cannot. Self-censorship enters the picture. See the piece by Kim Dae Jung of the *Chosun Ilbo*. Reading between the lines, he is doing the censors' work for them. He writes that he went down to Kwangju, met his chief reporter on the spot, Suh Chung Won, and spent twenty minutes with him on a lawn. Kim then returned to Seoul. Both he and Suh describe this encounter as an emotional one. What did they say to each other on this occasion? Kim gives a record of things said to him that he was going to ignore.

Covering the Kwangju troubles was a traumatic experience. Every contributor states as much. For a reporter to blurt out what he had seen to his colleagues—to be fair to the *Chosun Ilbo* staffers—was to jeopardize his livelihood. See the piece by Oh Hyo Jin, a broadcaster with MBC, whose career at the company ended to all intents and purposes with his coverage of Kwangju. Oh states that within a short time of arriving in the city—within minutes—he supported the citizens' side. He forgot that he was a reporter. He arrived on the plaza outside the Provincial Hall and at once he joined in the shouting of slogans, raising his arms to the skies.

"Tear to Pieces the Murderer Chun Doo Hwan!" was the big slogan, according to Kim Yang Woo of the *Kukje Shinmun*, a Pusan paper. (Kim and Gebhard Hielscher were the two reporters who picked up on this slogan in their contributions.)

Now, wait a moment. That square was full of informers, scattered among the crowd. Oh Hyo Jin blotted his copybook in public. This was before he made the calls he describes to his colleagues in Seoul, in which he blurted out everything he had seen. Yet to say nothing, to bottle up the truth inside, could be damaging too, as the case of Ryu Jong Hwan of *Pusan Ilbo* suggests. Oh got the poison out of his system, he 'fessed up in Seoul, he hid nothing. Ryu, compelled to keep stuff to himself in the relatively claustrophobic atmosphere of Pusan, could no longer function as a journalist when he got back to his newspaper, he writes. He had seen too much, he was burdened with a knowledge he could not share.

Easily the most disturbing piece among those that follow is Kim Yang Woo's. The Kwangju uprising, we now know, from the testimony of Kim Yang Woo of *Kukje Shinmun*, ended with cold-blooded killings of bound captives—students taken prisoner at the Provincial Hall, bound, and beaten to death on the morning of May 27, 1980. It took Kim sixteen years to write the story. Had Kim shared his information with the foreign press at the time (he was with other reporters from his newspaper), it would have gone round the world in two seconds.

A word is in order on two expressions peculiar to the Kwangju uprising, which are often used in what follows. One is "Settlement Committee." Another is "Citizens' Committee." We have edited the reports that follow so as to distinguish between the two and to correct writers' use of the nomenclature where they were being confusing. The Settlement Committee was composed of people who wanted to settle, i.e., strike a deal with the military, as the name suggests; there were older government officials on the committee, formed immediately after the armed forces left Kwangju on May 21, and there were pastors and lawyers. They wanted an accommodation with the military under which arms would be handed over and the citizens would then surrender themselves to the mercies of the military, i.e., Chun. That was what it boiled down to. There was a student softliner, Kim Chang Gil, who served as a student representative on this "ad hoc committee" to use the expression favored by Brad Martin (see chapter 7). The Citizens' Committee was, or emerged as, the hard-line ad hoc body, with Yun Sang Won taking over control behind the scenes on the morning of May 26. The group renamed their committee, calling it the "Struggle Committee for Democracy." By this time the original "Settlement Committee" had collapsed or was powerless. The softline student leader Kim Chang Gil, sometimes described, confusingly, as head of a "Student Settlement Committee," was ousted from control. By that time, however, many of the original student militia and the citizens had handed back their arms, and many of the student and other militia members had disbanded or disappeared, leaving just the hardline student elements headed by Yun Sang Won in place at the end. See *Kwangju Diary* (p. 130) for further notes on this situation. The crucial issue was the handing in of arms, which became tantamount to surrender.

One other expression may be mentioned, "Citizens' Army." These were people, students and ordinary citizens, including workers, who took up arms. They were never very coherently organized as such. They did not have a distinct headquarters and uniforms of their own. In the end Yun Sang Won emerged as the leader of this group also. There is, however, very little written about him in the contributions that follow. Few Korean journalists were aware of his role until many years later. The military also was in the dark.

A final note is in order here on cutting. On the whole the foreign correspondents' contributions were not cut. The pieces by Korean writers that follow were in several cases heavily cut. There is still much repetition. However, different reporters had differing perspectives—and sometimes different facts. An effort has been made to align what remains, and to remove mistakes of fact.

CHAPTER TEN
AN EDITOR'S WOES

Kim Dae Jung

Flag

I was provincial news editor of the newspaper *Chosun Ilbo* and responsible for coverage in the provinces, outside Seoul, at the time of the "cruelest month"—the expression Koreans use for this hot and sticky season—namely May 1980. As such I was responsible for our coverage of the Kwangju Democratization Movement, as it became known—the Kwangju uprising. Prior to taking on a news editor's desk job I had served as the newspaper's Washington correspondent for six years from 1972 to early 1979. Thereafter I was briefly foreign news editor, before being made a provincial news editor in early 1980.

A knowledge of my desk functions at the time of the uprising is integral to my piece, so that's where I start. Mine was the desk where the buck stopped as regards provincial news at one of South Korea's leading daily papers. What then was the view from that desk?

During May that year our regional news coverage focused on student demonstrations from the start. Even when there wasn't that much student activity, martial law was pretty much asserted and in place. Then in mid-month the demonstrations intensified. All of a sudden there were casualties. The military quickly tightened censorship. Our front page looked like a gap-toothed horror some days, with entire stories blacked out by the censors in our office.

Naturally, we covered the big demonstrations in Seoul on May 16. On that day 20,000 students from nine universities demonstrated from 3 P.M. all the way through the evening to 11 P.M. On the following day, the military struck. Full martial law was proclaimed. Decree Number 10 under this intensified rule said that all political activities must cease forthwith. The universities were closed until further notice. What happened thereafter needs no stressing, but let me recall the basic facts. That day twenty-six people were arrested, including my namesake (but no relative) Kim Dae Jung, today the President of the Republic of Korea. Thereupon demonstrations stepped up in Kwangju. Park Rae Myong, our correspondent down there, reported that there was violence. Immediately, I sent Lee Young Bae, a young photographer, and Suh Chung Won, a seasoned reporter, down to Kwangju to beef up our coverage.

The first stories they sent on May 19 were grim. Everyone was upset. We had photos of soldiers pressing their boots down on the heads of half-naked youngsters kneeling down with their hands on their heads in the street. They looked like prisoners of war rather than demonstrators taken in for misdemeanors. These pictures enraged the younger reporters on our staff. However, we were forbidden to publish the photos or the article that went with them. The military insisted that anything on Kwangju had to be written by them or under their control anyway. The result was that we couldn't cover Kwangju, basically, from May 17 through May 21. We missed the crucial period when tension was escalating to fever pitch in Kwangju. We followed what the Martial Law Command told us to do. We stated merely that "riots" were going on in Kwangju. We cut back the number of deaths to five soldiers and one civilian. We mentioned that "rumors" had been spread along different lines, but that was all.

The censors kept Kwangju off our front page until May 22. That was the day the enraged citizenry drove the paratroopers out of the city. We were obliged to call them "hooligans" and "rioters," terms that were imposed on us from the very beginning of the uprising on May 18. Frustrated by this turn of events I asked the team down in Kwangju to write down everything they had in a notebook. When the right moment came in the future, we would publish the material. For the time being, I kept the project secret. (Later, even just the existence of the notebook caused me a lot of trouble when I tried to get its contents into the paper.)

On May 24, finally, the Martial Law Command took the editors-in-chief of all the main newspapers down to Kwangju on a tour. So that we could see with our own eyes. We were given a briefing in the local military headquarters. We were then invited to go up to a look-out point, a hill in Hwajung-dong, to observe the barricades erected by the citizens, blocking the streets below. Next, we went to a hospital. The sight of the coffins lined up there choked me up.

"How much more blood must be shed for democracy to take root in Korea? Why did these young people have to die?"

I trembled as I asked these questions of myself.

I then received our four staff covering the story. They were Suh Chung Won, Lee Young Bae, Park Rae Myong, and Cho Kwang Hum.They brought a list of demands from the Kwangju citizens' committee. The first thing I noticed was how soiled their press armbands were. Obviously, I was happy to see them, but I was disturbed by their appearance. Suh and Lee looked thoroughly worn out from lack of sleep. They begged me to ensure that the newspaper reported that there was never, from the start, a "riot" (the favored phrase of the military censors). They pleaded for the truth to be told. What a precarious situation we press people were in! I told them that the authorities in Seoul sought to portray events in Kwangju as a riotous uprising. They gave out false information to justify their stand. I promised to do my best and asked them to support one another and hang in there, however bad the situation became. I gave them all the money I had on me. They climbed back down the hill after our meeting, leaving me weeping as I gazed after their forlorn figures.

A Useless Piece

When I got back to Seoul I wrote an article. My aim was to describe the general atmosphere of the place. It was a useless piece. No one reading it could understand what was going on in Kwangju. It was filled with vague and ambiguous expressions. Even this piece was passed by the censors on condition that I used the word "rioters." After much argument over this, I finally gave up and put it in. I thought it was better to have something in the paper rather than nothing at all. I rephrased one particular sentence to change "citizens were seen carrying guns" to "rioters were seen carrying guns." Looking back, I regret having done that. But I console myself with the thought that, even so, the piece became the subject of hot debate at the time.

Five years later, by then chief editor of *Chosun Ilbo*, I had a first chance to face the citizens of Kwangju in person. My job required me to supervise publication of *Chosun Monthly*, a publication of the group. We were working on the June 1985 issue. I decided this was the moment to repay the people of Kwangju by writing about what really had happened five years earlier in 1980. I was asked to do this by two of the reporters who had covered the events.

I sent these two, together with a third young reporter, back to Kwangju to collect material having to do with the events of 1980. I asked them to write up a revised account of what had happened there under the title *Ten Days on Gumnam-ro*. That choice of headline had been on my mind since 1980. I felt that the time had come to tell the truth. It was a judgment call: Even the horrible Chun Doo Hwan lot could not suppress the truth forever, I thought. However, before we went ahead with the piece I thought it best to sound out some of those in authority first. I reasoned with them as follows: "Many people know already that there were allegedly over 2,000 deaths in Kwangju, counting both dead and injured.

Five years have passed, the wounds have almost healed, but still many know that there were supposedly over 2,000 victims of government wrongdoing. In fact, our reports show the number went as high as 3,000. Surely, such high numbers cannot be held back anymore? People are going to go on talking about this. Sooner or later you will be held to account. Why don't you let me write about those fateful days?"

I believed that I had obtained a tacit go-ahead. I went ahead and wrote the piece. My aim was to write as objective and factual an article as possible, because I knew that the general public was not going to believe in such large numbers (even at that time). However, this attempt of mine to redress a wrong went horribly awry. At the very last moment, when we were about to go to press, we were ordered to reexamine the articles. I saw then that what I had believed (that we were being allowed to go ahead) had been too good to be true. I had been a fool to believe that the government would permit us to write about such a taboo topic. From the very start the authorities knew what they were going to do; they intervened at the last moment, an excellent piece of timing from their viewpoint.

Still worse from my viewpoint was the deletion by the authorities of the most crucial parts of our reportage: They struck out statements to the effect that the paratroopers used excessive force from the outset, and they eliminated the original headline. With that second decision I lost the will to resist. The piece had been so manhandled as to eliminate the point that cruelty and brutality by government forces had led to an explosion of rage on the part of the people of Kwangju. I tried to fight back against the threat of censorship, hinting that I would discard the whole effort. But in fact, as time passed, I was losing ground. Without the censored piece, the magazine itself could not be published (not with a huge hole in it). To find something else to go in there—were we so lucky—would have needed time too. We had no more time. To delay further meant loss of revenues and loss of sales. In a cutthroat industry such as newspapers you cannot afford that. Timing is all. I could not afford to miss the deadline. My good intentions failed. I ended up with a big net negative. The article originally headed *Ten Days on Gumnam-ro* was heavily censored and the number of victims reduced to 200. My intention had been to state the facts. But I failed due to my naïveté.

I set about trying to find excuses. There weren't any. I had lost the game of wits with the government. I had to live with this failure. Just to make my defeat all the more excruciating, our rival *Shin Dong-A* came out with an article titled *A Reconsideration of Kwangju* on the very same day our censored piece appeared. Their monthly published just the sort of exposé I had had in mind originally. This was bitter medicine. Later I found out that *Shin Dong-A* had learned of my plans in advance and had asked Yoon Jae Gul to write their own exposé. They kept their plans secret and then at the last moment, without fearing reprisal from the authorities, they slipped the piece into print. The reaction in Kwangju was immediate: *Shin Dong-A* was feted for its heroism, and *Chosun Monthly* was castigated as evil. It got worse. People in Kwangju launched a protest against our piece.

If only *Shin Dong-A* had not published their article, the backlash against ours would not have been that strong. The matter could have blown over. This was not what happened. I had to face a storm of criticism. If I could have found a scapegoat or a loophole in the charges made against me, I could have avoided a disaster. Unfortunately, it was not to be so. Conscience required that I go no further. My integrity was at stake. I faced up to the situation: A backlash was to be expected and was only too well deserved in view of my cowardice. The honesty of the *Shin Dong-A* article made a glaring contrast as compared with our piece. It was only too clear that no mere face-saving measures could make up for what we had done. In comparison with the *Shin Dong-A* piece our doctored effort was an insult to the survivors of the Kwangju uprising. It was only natural that a protest down there escalated into a boycott of our daily, not the monthly. I considered that the monthly, not the daily, was responsible for the mess. But that was not the view taken in Kwangju. Until the boycott began *Chosun Ilbo* had a good number of readers in the Honam region (the Cholla provinces). The boycott quickly cut into our readership. The head of the Kwangju branch of *Chosun Ilbo* screamed bloody murder. That deepened our sense of crisis. Park Rae Myong, the head of the Kwangju office, sent an urgent cable to the head office in Seoul, calling for something to be done. I went down to Kwangju to try to resolve matters.

I do not remember the exact date of my visit to Kwangju. It must have been late August or early September 1985. What I do remember is a visit Park and I paid to the citizens' group that had initiated the boycott. There were seven or eight people in the office when I got there. One of them asked me to bow down on the floor, to show my apology was sincere. I rejected this demand as calmly as I could, and proceeded to explain why I declined to go that far. There was no need to inflict a physical humiliation on me, I said. An oral apology, I maintained, was enough to show that I was sincere in my regrets.

Fortunately for me, my point was accepted. We then launched into a discussion of the matter at hand. I explained what had happened. I told them that I was responsible for the unfortunate outcome. Then, I requested an end to the boycott. In response, the representatives of that organization made general remarks, saying that there was prejudice against Kwangju in Korea and that the press gave a distorted view. They pointed to the media in general and to me in particular as partially responsible for this situation. I could not refute this. I ended up repeating my apologies over and over again.

I did my best to assuage their feelings by writing an apology in the name of *Chosun Ilbo*. However, the people I met with said that I was only the chief editor of the monthly. They wanted an apology over the signature of the owner of the publication. I was at a loss as to how to respond to this petulant demand. I did not know whether to laugh or cry. After some further deliberation I once again begged them to accept my apology and pleaded for permission to start the apology with these words: "As the representative of *Chosun Ilbo* I, Kim Dae Jung, the editor-in-chief, most sincerely regret. . . ." When the ordeal was over, I stepped out of the room feeling completely spent, with sweat pouring down my back and my legs shaking.

How Can I Make Up to Kwangju for What I Did?

I have loved Kwangju. I still do. When I am there, I feel at ease. That might be because my family name comes from Kwangsan, a place near Kwangju. I love the natural beauty around there, the people, and the cuisine. I first came to Kwangju in 1971, when I was covering my namesake Kim Dae Jung's bid for the presidency in the elections of that year. After that, for some strange reason, I was often assigned to that Honam region. I didn't have to do so as editor-in-chief, but when there were elections, I visited Kwangju and Chunju to oversee the election coverage.

During one election I went to Kwangju and met Ms. Cho A Ra, the celebrated "mother of Kwangju." I appealed to her common sense as regards Kwangju and its sense of being victimized. I said that the city had made a noble sacrifice and yet the people of Kwangju were still regarded as troublemakers in the rest of the country. That must be very painful for Kwangju people, I observed.

I believe I understand the Kwangju movement for democracy more deeply than many others. Yet despite this, every time I covered Kwangju I seemed to cause harm: whether as the chief person covering the democratic movement there; whether as the editor-in-chief responsible for that article I mentioned; or whether as the chief writer covering the feud between *Chosun Ilbo* and the Pyongmin Party established by the politician Kim Dae Jung in autumn 1987. My discomfort with Kwangju always seems to produce a negative result.

In sum, my deepest regret is over my failure to keep my promise to write a factual, objective account based on reporting of what happened in Kwangju in 1980. After I left the company, *Chosun Ilbo* published an in-depth account in 1988. More truth came to light during the trial of the two former presidents Chun Doo Hwan and Roh Tae Woo as reported by my old newspaper in 1996. However, my guilt over my failure to write an honest report of my own on the events in Kwangju in 1980 remains with me to this day.

CHAPTER ELEVEN

HOW THE PROVINCIAL HALL WAS TAKEN

Cho Sung Ho

Citizens' Army-The Holy General

Every year, when May comes along, I hear again the heart-wrenching cries. I see, once again, the bloody struggles, the bodies along Gumnam-ro.

When I think of Kwangju, I get a suffocating feeling. I remember those young men who stood for democracy, who resisted violence, and who fell before the clubs of the soldiers. Then there were plain folk, citizens, who had lived peacefully up to that time and suddenly fell victim to the bayonets and guns and sacrificed their lives. I hear again the cries of parents, maddened by the loss of their loved ones. It's hard for me to breathe when I remember what I saw.

I think again of Gumnam-ro. There is the whistle of bullets, the ear-splitting crack of the rifles, the metallic buzz of the helicopters above our heads, and the cries and screams down below. The loudest sounds—the ones I remember most vividly—were the enraged cries of the citizens. In a compressed vision I see before me the images of the dead and the cries of the living, the latter making the former come to life once more.

There are many records of what happened in Kwangju. I feel a bit ashamed of my own belated contribution. Through many witnesses we know what happened. Compared with what reporters from Kwangju know, we from Seoul—I from *Hankook Ilbo*—have relatively little material. However, as a means of self-discovery, I would like to put together a few fragments of memories, to see what happened.

I myself witnessed the historic uprising from the front lines, as it were. I arrived in Kwangju on the afternoon of the May 19, after the first clashes had taken place, and I stayed on in the city for ten days. At that time the students and demonstrators referred to May 18, the first day of violence, as "Bloody Sunday." They called May 21 Bloody Buddha's Birthday, and May 27 Bloody Tuesday.

The day when the most casualties occurred was May 21. Through my diary I look back on it as one of the longest days of my life.

The Cries of the People, Raging through Gumnam-ro

The fourth day of the Kwangju uprising dawned. From early on that morning the army choppers were exceptionally noisy. The citizens started heading toward the Provincial Hall. All through the night they had fought against paratroopers in the streets of Gumnam-ro, Chungjang-ro, and Jebong-ro, and around Kwangju Station and Gyerim-dong. There was a rumor that a total of ten people had been shot at that time, including one who died in front of Kwangju Station.

The cries of anger grew stronger in the streets. Finally, the paratroopers, sensing danger, backed toward the Provincial Hall. Tension mounted.

Around 6:20 A.M. a cart carrying two bodies appeared on Gumnam-ro, pulled by a truck. The two dead were covered with a Korean flag. Their bloodied feet poked from beneath the flag. Demonstrators had discovered these two bodies near the station early that morning. These were casualties that had occurred during the night. Marching with the two bodies in front, the citizens headed from the square in front of Kwangju Station over to Gumnam-ro via Yangrim Bridge and Kwangju Park. People who watched this parade let out angry cries.

"Down with Chun Doo Hwan, the murderer!"

"We need compensation for the blood of the citizens of Kwangju!"

"We'll protect Kwangju with our lives!"

The crowd swelled in size. From early that morning all the vehicles that could be seized—coaches, buses, trucks, and cars—were driven toward downtown Kwangju. Inside the cars there were young men armed with axes, clubs, and short scythes. Cars were driven from the suburbs into the downtown area.

Around 8 A.M., the young men who were in front of the Catholic Center suddenly began to shout. "Let's get the cars from the Asia Motors factory!" "Let's get the cars and arm ourselves!" These young men disappeared. They reappeared on Gumnam-ro with seven or eight buses. The people watching were pleased.

"Come on! Come on!" someone shouted.

Many young men climbed aboard a bus. They returned pulling more buses. They brought army trucks and some armored vehicles as well.

Standing in front of the Provincial Hall, the paratroopers were by this time in a very tense state. The demonstrators were squeezing into the paratroopers' defense lines with their armored vehicles. A sense of terror stalked those streets. There was terrible bloodshed to come.

About 9 A.M.—again close by the Catholic Center on Gumnam-ro— a crowd of about 10,000 people confronted the paratroopers, protesting the atrocities committed by them between May 18 and May 20. By 10 A.M. the crowd had swelled to 20,000 people or thereabouts.

On the roads leading to Gumnam-ro there were many people struggling desperately with the paratroopers. The latter fired tear gas indiscriminately.

Around 12:30 P.M. the head of the demonstration came up head-to-head with paratroopers who were by then only thirty or forty meters away from the Provincial Hall. The paratroopers started to retreat.

Police helicopters overhead announced the words of the governor of South Cholla province and the mayor of Kwangju—the region's two top dignitaries. Both called for order, using such slogans as "Citizens, let us save Kwangju!" Their announcements simply were not heard.

Already at about 10 A.M. officials had started to smuggle key documents out of the Provincial Hall, obviously preparing for an occupation by the demonstrators. Already then, some secret plans (for retreat) were being carried out.

Bloody Buddha's Birthday

It was just after 12:50 P.M.

Suddenly an armored personnel carrier, one of those that had been commandeered by the citizens, started to move toward the perimeter set up by the paratroopers. A shirtless young man in a white headband stood on the vehicle waving a Korean flag.

"Long live Kwangju!" he cried out.

A shot rang out from Provincial Hall. The young man fell, spewing blood everywhere. (Not long after this, I heard that two paratroopers had been killed.) Trucks and buses followed behind the armored personnel carrier. The resistance of the army finally crumbled.

Rumors of clashes and of bloodshed near the Labor Office—a branch of the Labor Ministry in Seoul—and the YMCA building nearby started up. The word-of-mouth stories changed every minute. Ten minutes after the incident with the armored vehicle, there was a crash of guns. The paratroopers in front of the Provincial Hall had fired. There were rumors of paratroopers hidden around the office.

Next there came reports of casualties at *Chonnam Ilbo*, the local daily newspaper office, at the Labor Office, and at the YMCA building. The injured were all taken to hospital, it was said. Then there was word of clashes at Chonnam National University and of major casualties there. That afternoon, all hospitals in Kwangju were on emergency status, as mangled bodies were brought in.

I was caught up with demonstrators close to the Commercial Bank in

Gumnam-ro. Around 2:10 P.M. I thought I heard a shot fired. A citizen close to me suddenly spewed blood and fell. My heart stopped, I thought. (The man was Kim Hoo Sik, thirty-nine, a resident of Sansu 2-dong.) I realized that I could die here.

In this desperate situation, I looked frantically for an intern reporter who had come with me to Kwangju. I wanted to get a report out of the city before it was cut off. I handed my diary carefully to him, as if handling precious treasure, and instructed him to get out of Kwangju and go straight to head office in Seoul.

From early on the morning of May 21 it had been impossible to send out or receive any articles. Kwangju was isolated from the outside world. As of 2:40 A.M. long distance lines had been disconnected. The night before Kwangju Station had been paralyzed. That afternoon the main highway into Kwangju was blocked, enforcing a complete isolation. Every institution and every shop closed. Without students showing up, the schools were also closed. Police stations were empty. The policemen hid. Reporters were advised by their papers to get out by 2 P.M.

Between 2 and 2:30 P.M. some demonstrators handed weapons to the people gathered in Gumnam-ro. Those who came later had AK-47 rifles with them. Armored trucks with weapons started to enter the city, also in demonstrators' hands. (Later it was learned that they smuggled the weapons from police stations, mines, and armories in the Hwasun and Naju areas.) On one side of the street they were handing out bottles filled with gasoline. Armed young men climbed up on the buildings in the area. An astounding situation was developing.

Around 2:40 P.M. the demonstrators on Gumnam-ro rolled what looked like big cylindrical containers, already lit on fire, toward the paratroopers. They pushed their trucks from behind the containers. The paratroopers fired and a battle ensued. The sounds of guns and of screams echoed around. The raucous sirens of ambulances mixed into the chaos in Gumnam-ro.

The demonstrators went up against paratroopers who painted Kwangju with blood. The citizens called themselves a Citizens' Army (*shimingun*). Those who had been scattered by bullets and tear gas massed together once more, pressing toward Provincial Hall.

At 4:40 P.M. demonstrators finally set fire to their trucks and pushed them forward. Paratroopers who had held out now retreated hurriedly. Officials in the Provincial Hall had already retrieved personnel files and other documents. (The paratroopers looked as if they were retreating under attack, in fact they had already been ordered to retreat by 4 P.M.)

Demonstrators finally entered the Provincial Hall. It was 5:30 P.M. The citizens were triumphant and drove their trucks around the streets, firing their guns into the skies. The streets were flooded—one could not recognize where one was—with people shouting out hurrahs.

"*Manse!*" ("Live for One Thousand Years!")

"Victory!"

The citizens had indeed driven the paratroopers out. That day, May 21, happened to be Buddha's Birthday. That sacred day in Kwangju turned into a bloodied hell of screams and corpses. There were rumors that at least sixty or seventy people had been shot and killed, while the injured were too numerous to count. (Including those who died later, the number of casualties was at least seventy.)

The Cries from the Mortuaries

From May 19 onward, the hospitals in downtown Kwangju were in chaos with incoming casualties. The casualties started to increase as the conflict between the demonstrators and the military stepped up.

On May 22, the day after Buddha's Birthday and the fall of the Provincial Hall, a temporary mortuary was created and forty-six bodies were laid to rest inside the Provincial Hall itself. Students bought cheap coffins with their own money and wrote down whatever details they could about unidentified bodies, to try to establish who they were. To prevent decomposition, they bought disinfectant and used it in each coffin. Meanwhile, the hospitals were short of blood supplies and of places to lay out the dead. They were also filled with families trying to identify bodies. Many people went from hospital to hospital to find their loved ones. At Chonnam National University Hospital on May 22 there was similar chaos, as families pulled aside cloths covering the corpses, trying to see whether these were their relatives. The mortuary and the hospital back yard rang with the cries of people who found their family members dead. Inside the hospital there were sounds of people crying out and of nails being driven into coffins.

That day, a young man in his twenties rushed in from a group of armed demonstrators, scaring the people in the hospital and shouting. "I don't want to live alone. Fellow Citizens! Let us all die together!" Thereupon, he fired his gun into the air wildly.

On that same day blood from thirteen bodies that were placed in the Kwangju Christian Hospital mortuary mingled together with blood from the injured, making a small pool in the middle of the floor.

One student, apparently in his late teens, had lost half of his face. Choi Pyong Ung, the deputy director of the hospital, shouted out, with his body trembling: "How can this happen on the face of the earth?" Atrocities went on without limit in Kwangju.

The Media: Enemies of the People

That evening, when the demonstrators entered the Provincial Hall, a student stopped me and told me with a glare: "The reporters are also the enemies (of the people)." Such was the anger of people who were disappointed by the failure of the press to report other than distorted information from the military side. That student spat out a summary of what had happened in the previous few days.

First, there had come a cry for an end to the military dictatorship and martial law and a continuation of the democratization process. Next, there had come the expansion of martial law, the occupation of the universities by the martial-law authorities, merciless physical attacks on students, many of whom were clubbed close to death on May 18; and finally this had been followed by the students fighting back, joined by citizens on May 19; this was followed by a massive uprising and mounting casualties on May 20. Such had been the course of events, the student remarked, summing everything up.

The day following this encounter with a student in Kwangju, this was how the media reported developments in the city, as of May 22:

> At the start of this chaos, some 600 Chonnam National University students came out onto the streets, calling for an end to martial law. On May 20 many rumours circulated in the city as to regional hostilities. Angry citizens joined in the demonstrations, making the situation worse. As of 7 A.M. on May 21 fatalities numbered five military personnel and one citizen.

Such incredible distortion of the facts left many in Kwangju speechless. "One citizen dead"? Thereafter critical expressions frequently appeared in the press to describe what was going on in Kwangju. The key words were "rioters," "riots," "theft," "rumors aplenty."

Fortunately, the newspapers were not delivered to Kwangju. Reporters were spared a tragic outcome. Newspaper reporters who had been sent to Seoul were obliged to beg their head offices on no account to send the newspaper down to Kwangju. This was a shameful page in the history of Korea's press.

Suspicion of the media ran very deep. It was more like hatred. The Kwangju KBS TV station was attacked and the window panes broken on the night of May 19. On the night of May 20 and the morning of May 21, the MBC and KBS buildings were set on fire. Citizens went to the broadcasting stations and demanded that correct reports and casualty figures be reported on the news. However, these organizations did not broadcast along these lines and simply played music on TV. People threw stones at CBS located on Gumnam-ro.

A nearby big newspaper office and other newspaper buildings were attacked by angry demonstrators. Windows were broken and company cars stolen. Perhaps for these reasons many reporters sent from Seoul refused to cover the demonstrations and spent most of their time in the Provincial Hall. Suspicion of the media left an indelible mark on their reputation.

The Final Page of a Reporter's Notebook

The Kwangju uprising came to an end with the attack launched by paratroopers on the morning of May 27. On that day, all reporters put on a lapel button given to them by the martial-law authorities. They had started the day with an ID armband approved by the Citizen's Army.

Inside the Provincial Hall, the bodies of demonstrators were scattered around, bleeding. The last page of my reporter's notebook features the death of one student in particular. I kept thinking of his face on the occasion of the fifteenth commemoration of the uprising in 1995. That day I wrote a column about the student in the *Korea Times* under the title "Echo":

> When May comes round, many images of Kwangju come to mind. What I experienced over ten days fifteen years ago in Kwangju has been buried within a silent me. But whenever that day comes around, it screams back to life: the fierce battle between the military and the demonstrators, the blood on the bullet-ridden main square, the chaotic mortuary full of screams and angry people, the desperate scenes that unfolded in the Provincial Hall on the last day, the time when bullets whistled past my head in Gumnam-ro and Nongsong-dong.
>
> Suddenly, I think of that time, and I take out my reporter's notebook, with its record of the death of one student:

It is the afternoon of May 27 at the operations control room of the Provincial Hall. A young man has bled to death, his face looking up at the sky and his body set down among flowers that lack leaves. He is wearing an army jacket and a pair of brown pants with a little notebook stuck in the back pocket. Beneath his legs fresh white sneakers and bloodstains are scattered. Close to his head I find an iron plate, with a bullet hole in it. The student was later identified as Park Byong Gyu, a freshman of Dongguk University in Seoul. Possibly, the student tried to stop the bullets with that plate. What led this young man to die here?

His tragic death engraved itself on my mind. The irony of the time is that this dead young man would have been labeled a "rioter" and is now called a "martyr." Fifteen years have passed, and the Kwangju rebellion is now called the Kwangju Democratization Movement or the Kwangju people's uprising. The official vocabulary has changed from "rebellion" and "rioters" to "popular uprising" and "Citizens' Army." Those who have been buried have turned into martyrs resting in the (state-founded) Mangwol-dong Cemetery.

When I think of Kwangju as it was, an old residue of bitterness and the pride today in seeing the fruits of the sacrifice intersect within me. The Kwangju uprising did not end as a tragedy alone. The spring uprising laid a foundation for bigger uprisings in the 1980s and acted as the mother of all prodemocracy movements to come in Korea.

The sacrifices of those buried in Mangwol-dong have borne fruit indeed. I now sing the song that was sung by a poet on the seventeenth anniversary of May 18:

> *Here it comes, the month of May,*
> *The person with blood on his chest rises afresh*
> *His face shines brightly.*
> *See those who return*
> *Sighs overflow Kwangju River*
> *The grass reaches up to the shoulder of the hill*
> *The asphalt of Gumnam and Chungjang awakes and rises*
> *Your proud face sears into my heart.*

CHAPTER TWELVE

BANG! BANG! BANG!

Suh Chung Won

The Battle at Dawn

Twelve fifty-five P.M., May 21, 1980. Bang! Bang! Bang! The shots cracked out in the street at Gumnam-ro. Thousands of demonstrators ran for cover in buildings and alleys.

I witnessed—I had a clear view—of the soldiers who fired from the Provincial Hall. The Kwangju bureau of *Chosun Ilbo* was only 200 meters away.

Except for the gunshots, the streets were deadly calm.

We were trapped in the newspaper office, unable to leave. Time passed. Leaning against a filing cabinet, I observed the area around the Provincial Hall. A group of soldiers was seated in front of the fountain on the square, pointing their weapons down Gumnam-ro.

At that moment a young man standing on an armored personnel carrier took a bullet in the body and tumbled over. The gunfire was repeated, from time to time. We were frozen on the spot, we were paralyzed by fear. Spellbound. The soldiers—ordered to do so by their officers—had started shooting demonstrators in broad daylight.

Ten Days and Nine Nights of Coverage

It is nineteen years now since the uprising. That old piece of writing, with which I begin this piece, is something I dug out from my files. I was in my thirties in May 1980, when I witnessed the events at Kwangju. Now I am a middle-aged man in my fifties.

Ever since the uprising, efforts have been made to bring the truth to light, though it was concealed earlier on. After many twists and turns, the uprising has finally been given an official name: the Kwangju Democratization Movement (as of 1988).

I myself witnessed the events as a senior reporter of *Chosun Ilbo*. I wrote a piece on the uprising at the time, in terms intended to get it published even under martial law censorship. My article wasn't outstanding. Later it appeared in the July 1985 issue of *Wolgan Chosun* (Chosun Monthly).

Just as when I first wrote a piece on this subject I find it hard to conjure up memories of what I saw during the ten days and nine nights of the uprising—it is easier for me to say what I felt than what I saw.

The First Day of Coverage

I departed Seoul for Kwangju at 4 P.M. on Monday, May 19 in the company of Lee Young Bae, our photographer (he passed away in 1996). When we got to the Banpo Express Bus Terminal in Seoul we found that the service had already been stopped because of the curfew in Kwangju. All we could do was to take a 5 P.M. bus to Chonju. We spent a night there at Chonju—we were impatient over this delay—and left for Kwangju at 8 A.M. the following day.

When we got into Kwangju it was about 9:20 A.M. We could not go as far as the terminal. We got off at a downtown stopping place. That made me feel the situation had deteriorated. It had been raining slightly since the previous afternoon. We took a taxi. The driver, a man in his twenties, told us that tens of people had been killed during the student demonstrations the day before, May 19.

"Four taxi drivers have been killed," he added. "Numbers of students have been arrested."

We entered Gumnam-ro at that point. Two-thirds of the shops were closed. We saw broken windows here and there. Almost all the windows of the Catholic Center on Gumnam-ro were smashed. We got out at the Kwangju bureau of *Chosun Ilbo*, our newspaper, in Gumnam-ro. It was hard to keep our eyes open, the pain from the tear gas was so great. It was worse inside the building, going up to our third-floor office. Tear gas remained in the buildings after the demonstrations thereabouts on May 18 and 19.

My first move was to discuss plans for coverage with our reporters there in the Kwangju bureau. I made a decision. I would personally confirm the number of casualties that people were talking about. Leaving the bureau I headed for Chonnam National University Hospital, going past the Dongsan police station, which was damaged, and the Gyerim police station, also burned, and Kwangju Park.

It was extremely difficult to collect information. The hospital would not say a word about the numbers of dead and injured. The man in charge let someone else handle my inquiry. All the latter would say was that "there are not many casualties." Or again: "I haven't received any report yet."

I managed to find one injured person. He was Kim Young Chan, nineteen, a third-year student at Jodae High School. I found him up on the eighth floor of the hospital. He had been shot through the right wrist and on the right side of his body. He had been injured at about 4 P.M. on the afternoon of May 19—the day before—in front of Gyerim police station and was brought to the hospital. The boy was in a coma and was being given oxygen through a mask. According to his father Kim Hyong Gwan, fifty-one, Young Chan had been caught in a confrontation between demonstrators and martial army soldiers on his way home from school with friends. Approximately 100 demonstrators had surrounded an armored car in Gyerim-dong. After a while the demonstrators tried to pull one of the army crew from the vehicle. Shots were fired. Unfortunately, one of them hit Young Chan.

We moved on to another hospital. It was just as hard to report as before. The most we could confirm was that there had been a few casualties. Looking around the hospitals and seeing the burned police stations, though, I could easily imagine how fierce the two days of demonstrations had been.

Having arrived in Kwangju on the morning of May 20, I realized that the quickest way for me to find out how everything had begun was to ask our reporters who lived in Kwangju to help me out.

May 20: Outraged Citizens Stream onto the Streets

On the day I arrived, as mentioned, my first move was to visit the hospitals. I got back to the office in Gumnam-ro at about 1 P.M. Citizens were spreading out along Gumnam-ro. They were extremely indignant over what happened the day before. As time passed, more and more people gathered on the sidewalks in the downtown section there.

Citizens and students started a fresh demonstration on Gumnam-ro at about 3:40 P.M. They shouted slogans: "End martial law!" "Release the students under arrest!"

The soldiers countered with tear gas. At about 5 P.M. the demonstrators retreated about 300 meters. At that point there was a stand-off. Some 2,000 troops stood face-to-face with the demonstrators in front of the Kwangju branch of the Bank of Korea on Gumnam-ro. From that point on the streets of Gumnam-ro were filled with tear gas. People barricaded the streets, using oil drums and wire.

At 6:40 P.M. about 200 taxi drivers gathered at Moodeung Stadium, to protest the killing and wounding of their colleagues. They marched toward the Gumnan-ro section, with one truck and five buses, including one taken from the Gwangjin Transportation Co. with the license plate Chonnam 5 Na 3706. All the vehicles had their headlights on. The combined forces of the military and the police had by now been pushed back to a spot near the Kwangju Tourist Hotel. They sought to establish a last line of resistance there, using pepper fog and tear gas. Tear gas filled the Provincial Hall and the square in front of it. The demonstration began to heat up.

About that time four police officers from Hampyung County Police Department were killed and two others seriously injured in the course of a headlong clash—and finally a traffic accident—in front of the Office of Labor. Even the county police had been called in to help calm down the demonstrators. It was nothing less than a tragedy.

The outraged demonstrators were beyond police control. In the clash in front of the Office of Labor alone, twelve vehicles, including two buses and some taxis, were set on fire. The anger was intense. About 10 P.M. some high-ranking officials and others in the building prepared to evacuate. The rumor was that the demonstrators had already broken in through a wall at the back of the building. It was not hard for demonstrators to sneak in through the weak police protection on one side of the building, but getting out on the other side was hard. We needed to escape from that building; otherwise the enraged crowd could mistake us for office workers there. We managed to escape, going toward the governor's official residence on the right-hand side of the Provincial Hall. Demonstrators passed by on all sides. While we hesitated—we were stuck for about ten minutes—more demonstrators passed by. Out of options, we ran toward the Provincial Hall. We took refuge in the Provincial Board of Education to send our reports from there to the head office. It was already 10:30 P.M. I was petrified. I realized only then that I had not eaten all day.

While I was sending in our reports to the head office in Seoul, I heard gunfire coming from the direction of Kwangju Station. It was about 10:55 P.M. There were hundreds of shots, in a stream. When I stepped outside, I saw fireballs flying toward the west. It was a bad omen.

May 21: The Early Hours and a Woman's Voice

The demonstrations continued until well after midnight. They reached a greater pitch than on the previous day. I decided to chase over to the spot where the MBC building was burning, drawn by the powerful voice of the woman still using the loudspeaker system I mentioned. The streets were in a terrible mess. Shattered window-frames, rocks, and broken office fixtures snatched away from the police stations and government buildings were scattered everywhere. It looked as if there had been a war.

The demonstrators constantly moved back and forth between the Office of Labor, Kwangju Station, and the MBC building, following the woman's instructions. They were mostly young people in their teens and twenties. They carried an assortment of weapons: sickles, iron pipes, sticks, pickaxes, gasoline bombs, and so on. Girls in school uniforms were even there, nursing injured young men.

A number of buildings were put to the torch in the streets ranging between the Office of Labor and the MBC station. At about 1 A.M. the main building and the annex of the Kwangju Tax Office in Susok-dong, just behind the Provincial Hall, began to burn. Next, the parking facility of the Provincial Hall was set on fire. Three vehicles there were burned.

Meanwhile, some of the demonstrators got guns for the first time— they obtained seventeen carbines from an army reserve armory in the Kwangju Tax Office. The citizens armed themselves with firearms at last. Until that time they had had nothing with which to shoot back at the army and the police.

I went back to the night-duty room at the Provincial Board of Education to finish sending my reports. But the phone was suddenly disconnected. Long distance calls were stopped altogether at about 2:20 A.M.

Demonstrations continued through the night. As the sun came up, I heard the woman's voice once more: "Citizens of Kwangju! Let us all gather in front of the Provincial Hall this morning!"

Yet another fire had been started over toward Kwangju Station. People said that it must be the Kwangju branch of the Korean Broadcasting System (KBS). That was at about 5:30 A.M. We headed in that direction. By the time we got there the building had been entirely destroyed by fire. I heard that three bodies had been found when the military evacuated Kwangju Station. The discovery of these dead had outraged the demonstrators, and they had set the KBS building on fire about thirty minutes after the soldiers pulled out of the station.

At 6 A.M. approximately 1,000 protesters were gathered in the MBC building area, demonstrating at the intersections on Gumnam-ro. Others raced around town with the vehicles they had purloined. The atmosphere was terrifying.

Demonstrators appeared pushing a bicycle cart with two bodies on it. The citizens began to gather once more, as early as 7 A.M. The mood seemed a bit calmer. A group of demonstrators then appeared with trucks, bringing bread. They distributed the food among the people. Then at about 8 A.M., Chun Ok Ju, thirty-two, a woman leader well known at that time, made a speech. She urged the citizens to mourn for the dead and maintained that the demonstration was righteous. She proposed a meeting with the mayor of Kwangju.

From that day on, offices and shops were closed. All the schools were closed, naturally. *Chonnam Ilbo* and *Chonnam Maeil*, the two local newspapers, stopped publishing daily. Local broadcasting was discontinued. In addition, foreign tourists staying at the Kwangju Tourist Hotel left the city.

From 9 A.M. people gathered in larger numbers at Gumnam-ro. They shouted out demands for an apology from the martial-law authorities for excessive repression. They also voiced criticisms of government leaders. Meanwhile, some demonstrators had obtained armored cars and jeeps from the Asia Motors factory in the Kwangju industrial complex. They drove the vehicles into the downtown areas around 10 A.M. Using the armored vehicles they began to press back the army lines. They pressed toward the Catholic Center. Pepper fog and tear gas were useless to hold them back. From 10:30 A.M., as on the previous day, the demonstrators squeezed in toward the Provincial Hall from three sides.

At 10:50 A.M. the governor, Chang Hyung Tae, and the mayor, Ku Yong Sang, made an appeal: "We will withdraw all troops. Kwangju citizens, please keep order and save the city."

But the people did not respond to this request. The whole area began to seethe, as on the day before.

At noon, a rumor spread that demonstrators had occupied the Provincial Hall. Accordingly, demonstrators at the Catholic Center moved forward about 200 meters, with the armored cars and trucks leading the way. They came to within ten meters of the army defense lines in front of the Kwangju Tourist Hotel. Government and local officials immediately escaped from the Provincial Hall, going over a wall at the back. Our team also evacuated. We moved our branch office to a new location near the Kwangju Tourist Hotel.

Some people were now distributing leaflets that said that the Provincial Hall had been taken over. The leaflets said: "Let us rise for action and gather in front of the Provincial Hall at 2 P.M., as the organization 'The Students' League of South Cholla Province.'" From this point on, anything could happen.

We were just arriving in our new office on the third floor of a building that housed the East District staff of City Hall. It was 12:30 P.M. The confrontation between the soldiers and the civilians was peaking just in front of the Kwangju Tourist Hotel, close to where we were. At that moment a commandeered armored personnel carrier with a young man standing on it headed it straight toward a line of soldiers in front of the Provincial Hall. He was shot and fell, as did several soldiers. That triggered an outburst of tear gas fire. For a moment the demonstrators hesitated. The troops retreated back toward the fountain in the middle of the square in front of Provincial Hall. The building, it seemed, was going to be seized at any moment. The situation was extremely tense and horrifying. The troops lined up in front of the fountain, facing the crowd.

Bang! Bang! Bang! The martial-army forces opened fire at about 12:55 P.M. on May 21.

The demonstrators in front of them, mostly unarmed as yet, hastily took refuge in side alleys and in nearby buildings. Seeing the young man on top of the armored car shot down, our team of five decided to beat a retreat. Using an alley at the back of our office building we ran to Kwangju Police Station, which was about 150 meters from our branch office. We could not, at that time, confirm how many casualties there were. All we could do was to report the situation to Seoul, using a phone in the entranceway of the police station.

Thereafter, from 3:40 P.M. onward, the situation was indistinguishable from wartime. Some demonstrators, who had obtained weapons, started shooting back at the soldiers. This was streetfighting. At 4 P.M. I received a message saying that demonstrators had acquired weapons from an armory at Hwasun and were heading for downtown Kwangju in trucks. At 4:05 P.M. calls came into the police saying that 100 boxes of dynamite and four cartons of explosives had been seized from an ammunition depot at Jiwon-dong. As was revealed later, demonstrators were flocking back toward downtown Kwangju with weapons they had acquired in such places as Jangsong, Naju, Hwasun, and Damyang.

Police Chief Yun Hyon Yong of Kwangju City and his staff met to discuss what to do. The army had already taken away all the weapons from the Provincial Hall, from police stations, and from police strong points the day before. The police debated whether there was a compromise solution between withdrawing from the city and asking the government to despatch more forces. One of the officers told us: "We cannot guarantee your safety, so please hide."

Weapons fire was going on all the time. We left the police station. As we did so, we encountered jeeps full of young people brandishing carbines. Jeeps and trucks were moving around in the streets and alleys.

From that afternoon the citizens organized themselves. They created a "Citizens' Army." A light machine gun placed on the roof of the building of Chonnam National University Medical School began firing—some said, but others denied—in the direction of the Provincial Hall. We heard that six men who tried to raid the Kwangju Penitentiary were killed.

The soldiers and police in the Provincial Hall evacuated the building from 5.30 P.M. Silence ruled in the city for some time from 7:50 P.M. By 8 P.M. the whole building was taken over by the citizen army.

We hid in the D Motel in Dongmyong-dong. We got in there at about 8 P.M. Ten minutes later the lights went off. The landlord switched them off, saying that big buildings stood out and were dangerous.

Noises continued outside until midnight. There was the sound of vehicles driven by the demonstrators and the wailing of sirens. At night Kwangju was scary, dark and full of the sounds of gunfire.

That was the night of May 21, 1980.

May 22: The Buzzing of Flies on the Sidewalk

At 5:20 A.M. a jeep with a loudspeaker, accompanied by buses and trucks loaded with armed demonstrators made a tour around the residential areas, calling on everyone "to rally in front of Provincial Hall at 7 A.M." Leaflets—headed *Fighters' Bulletin*—were distributed saying: "The cry of the citizens for an uprising was heard, and, as a result, a considerable number of weapons were gathered in from Jangsong, Hwasun and Naju." Crowds headed for the Provincial Hall from about 7 A.M. By 8 A.M. the fountain area and the square in front of the building was jammed with people.

The city was in ruins, following the battle. Burned trucks, buses, and taxis lay about abandoned. Debris was scattered all over the streets—broken glass, smashed street flowerpots, burned or fallen wayside trees, shattered phone booths, and so on. The two-and-a-half kilometers of sidewalk along Gumnam-ro was stained with blood. At the back of our branch office, there was still liquid blood on the cement. Swarms of flies buzzed. There were bullet-marks on the windows. Shoes were scattered everywhere.

However, there was no crime. No instances of robbery or theft were reported during the maelstrom. Jewelry shops and other places with high-priced items were not damaged at all. This was evidence of the high standard of behavior of the citizens.

Back to Peaceful Protests

Armed demonstrators raced around the city in vehicles, back and forth. Some of the demonstrators kept watch from the roofs of buildings around the Provincial Hall. Most were armed by that time.

The main entrance of the Jonil Building, which contained the offices of the *Chonnam Ilbo*, the local daily, and the Jonil Broadcasting Company, had been partly crushed by a truck. Armed demonstrators were there too. Speakers at meetings held in front of the Provincial Hall and the Jonil Building called, again and again, for "an end to martial law." Meanwhile, unverifiable rumors spread among the citizens. "Hundreds of people died" according to one such story. "Two thousand students came down from Seoul," was another tale. Students were raising funds for the injured. There were appeals for blood donations.

Foreign correspondents appeared on the spot.

I dropped by Chonnam National University at about 9 A.M. Demonstrators guarded the main entrance, but it was no problem to enter. The entrance to the morgue was blocked by a crowd of sobbing people and onlookers. There were eighteen bodies, of which only ten had been identified. The eight unidentified bodies were covered with cotton cloths, so they could be viewed.

"It May Be My Son"

Some people sighed with relief after checking the faces under the cloths. One lady in her fifties who found her son there fainted on the spot. People wailed over their boys, looking up to the skies and calling their names. It was as if people at the time of the Korean War had been looking for the bodies of their families among those who had been massacred.

The count of the dead confirmed during the morning was: 18 at the Chonnam National University Hospital; 14 at the Kwangju Christian Hospital; 21 at the Red Cross Hospital; 2 at St. John's Hospital; 3 at downtown clinics; and 4 at Chosun University Hospital. Overall, 62 dead and 150 injured. These numbers, in fact, were incredible.

Around noon the streets of Gumnam were packed with tens of thousands of people. The rally held in front of the Provincial Hall had finished at about 10:50 A.M. But not one participant left the place. Past noon, we managed to enter the Provincial Hall, with the help of a college student guarding the entranceway. We were given free passes to the building, to go to the general affairs section of the demonstrators' headquarters on the first floor. Getting in and out was relatively easy once we had the passes, though they were nothing more than pieces of paper with stamps on them. Guards stood at the doors into the building as well as at the main entrance gates.

Seeing how messy and disarranged the offices were, we could tell how suddenly the people working there had abandoned their desks. Meanwhile, the Settlement Committee of the Kwangju uprising was holding a meeting in the deputy governor's office. The committee was composed of notables in the city, from various walks of life. They elected lawyer Lee Jong Gi as their chairman, and Kim Chang Gil, twenty-five, a student at Chonnam National University, as the student chairman for the Settlement Committee. However, this committee was a wrecked ship from the outset. The two parties mainly involved—the notables and the students—had different opinions from the outset. A long, troublesome discussion ensued. In the end they reached agreement on eight resolutions, including "the prohibition of the armed forces from returning to downtown Kwangju." Their next move was to visit the local Martial Law Command headquarters, to negotiate.

At 5 P.M. the Settlement Committee members announced to the public that their eight principles agreed with the local Martial Law Command HQ. They made the announcement from a stage set up by the fountain in the middle of the square facing the Provincial Hall. As the eight principles were announced one by one, the citizens gathered there applauded and welcomed them. However, the younger generation seemed dissatisfied. . . .

A group of demonstrators then appeared with eighteen coffins carried on five jeeps and trucks. The people made a full circle around the fountain, laying the dead on the grass near the fountain. The bereaved families burned incense by the coffins with their loved ones and mourned their deaths. A memorial ceremony began at 6:30 P.M. A solemn mood prevailed for some time. Then, as the young people viewed the bodies, some grabbed the microphone and shouted: "Let's realize the true meaning of these deaths."

At 7 P.M. it began to get dark. The citizens started to break up. There was a rumor that the army might return at any time. Thus they retreated from Gumnam-ro, as the sun went down. The people looked exhausted. But they were also enraged, having seen the dead carried out before them.

By the time it was 8 P.M., according to my watch, hardly anyone was left in the square. The bodies had been moved to the front yard of the Provincial Hall. Some bereaved family members stood there. Once more, demonstrators came out into the streets. Vehicles raced up and down the streets. From that night the army and citizen demonstrators faced each other throughout the night at five locations at a distance of 500 to 600 meters apart, as between the two sides. The locations I refer to were at roadblocks on major roads connecting Kwangju and other towns— Hwajong-dong Industrial Complex, highway ramps, Baegun-dong on the way to Mokpo, Jiwon-dong on the way to Hwasun and Moodeung High School, near the Kwangju Penitentiary on the way to Damyang.

By 9 P.M. the city seemed dead. There was nobody on the streets. In downtown Kwangju the demonstrators checked passers-by. The night was relatively calm, though sporadic shots were heard.

May 23: A Dreadful Silence Dominates the City

The streets were gradually being put to rights. During the night there was a clatter of machine guns and rifles from time to time. However, from 5 A.M. the demonstrators came out appealing to the citizens to help clean up the streets. A number of people, including students, responded to the appeal. The mess was completely cleaned up.

The people gathered each morning automatically at 7 A.M. at the square in front of the Provincial Hall, as if they had actual appointments. From this day onward vehicles could enter the Provincial Hall only if they had passes issued by a student committee. With students playing the key roles, a number of matters were resolved. People started to return weapons. These arms were stored in the basement of the Provincial Hall.

This day the signature "Citizens' Army" appeared for the first time on posters put up in front of the Jonil Building—the item was a list of Principles of Democratic Citizens in four articles. From that point on people began to use the term "Citizens' Army."

At 10.30 A.M. approximately 100 high school students paraded with placards, to make their protest. They were escorting the body of Lee Sung Kui, sixteen, a second-year Kwangju High School boy. He had been killed on the mountain behind Chonnam National University. The body was moved to the Provincial Hall, and for a while thereafter a tense atmosphere prevailed.

Meanwhile, the Settlement Committee met but achieved little. It had agreed upon the eight principles adopted on May 22. Thereafter, there was no specific outcome.

At 4 P.M. a big rally was held, at which point a helicopter from the

Martial Law Command flew overhead, dropping leaflets. These contained a warning from the head of the local Martial Law Command. Once again that day there were rumors that the army might come back into the city. Citizens went home hastily, accordingly. A dreadful silence covered the city when night came.

Gunshots decreased in frequency. The number of cars racing pointlessly around the city decreased remarkably, notably in the residential areas. This was a quiet night. However, during the day a sense of disappointment and insecurity was beginning to make itself felt among the citizens. What lay ahead?

May 24: Standing Face-to-Face, Building a "Second Panmunjom"

Rain had fallen on the previous day. It became heavier and continued until about 10 A.M. The rain made the city look a whole lot cleaner.

That day Kwangu KBS, which had resumed broadcasting at 6 P.M. on the previous evening, broadcast an appeal by the local martial-army commander, General So Jun Ryul, calling on: "the Kwangju citizens who possess arms to return to the Joint Hospital of the National Army." People in other areas, he announced, should "return (their weapons) to nearby military bases or police stations."

When the rain stopped, a great number of people gathered in front of Provincial Hall as before. Meanwhile, the city was being put back in order. Shops on major streets reopened. Burned vehicles were dragged away. Superficially, the city looked calm and the citizens happy.

But on the outskirts the "Citizens' Army" and the regular army confronted each other in a highly tense situation—the two sides were separated by a mere 500 to 600 meters. At the Industrial Complex of Hwajong-dong, the citizens' side, facing toward soldiers gathered near the Joint Hospital of the National Army, constructed a barricade with 150 logs, some burned buses, some jeeps, and some broken trucks. The people called this "the second Panmunjom Truce Village" (in an allusion to the village of Panmunjom, north of Seoul, where North Korean and South Korean meetings have been taking place, with U.S. officers also participating on the South Korean side, since the armistice of 1953 that ended the Korean War).

Local residents brought food to the militias on the barricades on the Kwangju City side. The task of feeding them was assigned mainly to people living in the Samik apartment blocks. Meanwhile, downtown Kwangju hospitals were desperately short of oxygen supplies and medicines. The South Cholla Doctors' Association put out a strong appeal to the Korean Society of Medical Science and the Red Cross for help.

The biggest problem for reporters was finding a way to send our articles to our head offices. Once the phones were disconnected in the early hours of May 21, we had to come up with bright ideas to send our stories.

At 1 P.M. our team visited the office of the chief of provincial police, Ahn Byung Ha, to send our reports to Seoul. We read the article quickly, using an emergency phone. Suddenly two armed men in their twenties leaped into the room, shouting: "Who the hell are you?" Our Kwangju-resident reporter, Cho Gwang Heum, immediately responded: "I also am from Kwangju." He produced his press ID and his resident's card. That move ended the crisis. The two men glared at us. We didn't blame them. It was a time when just surviving was hard.

At 3 P.M. that afternoon we met Kim Dae Jung, our news editor from Seoul with responsibility for provincial news, at the office of the Joint Hospital for the National Army. He had flown down from Seoul, with the heads of various media organizations, on a visit arranged by the Ministry of National Defense. It was only a week since I had left Seoul. But I welcomed him as if we had been separated for years. Our meeting took place on a lawn near the main entrance to the hospital and lasted for twenty minutes.

I left Kim Dae Jung and returned to downtown Kwangju, passing through the barricades.

Meanwhile, members of the Citizens Committee had visited the points on the edge of the city where the two sides engaged in their stand-off. The committee, which included the Reverend Chang U Sok, persuaded the citizen militias to tone things down a bit. From then on, nighttime face-offs came to an end. Night patrols continued, however.

On this day a rally at the Provincial Hall that had started at 4 P.M. ended finally at 7 P.M.

That night President Choi Gyu Ha made a general statement on KBS. This made some citizens feel secure. They thought the statement was a prelude to a settlement. Not that that would be so easily achieved. That night the bodies of those who had been identified were moved to Sangmu gymnasium, just opposite the Provincial Hall. Many people visited there to burn incense before the coffins.

May 25: Gunfire Once More after the
Poisoned-Needle Incident

May 25 was a Sunday. Still, the square in front of the Provincial Hall
was full of people from the early morning onward. The citizens were in
a tense mood. The Provincial Hall was now closed even to reporters
with passes. This was the day when the so-called poisoned-needle incident occurred—a singular instance of harassing tactics used by the government against the citizens.

The Settlement Committee announced this day that two men who
had been hospitalized, having been pricked by poisoned needles—
wielded by North Korean agents, the two men claimed—were in fact
"spies" or agents provocateurs, sent in by the military. They were
Chang Gye Byom, twenty-one, from Hwanggum-dong, Kwangju, and
Chong Han Gyu, twenty-three, from Hampyong-gun, South Cholla.
Following this incident (it had showed how easily the city could be
penetrated by army agents) Kim Chang Gil, who was chairman of
the Students' Settlement Committee, and others canceled a plan to
hold a ceremony marking the return of weapons, to have been held in
the square outside the Provincial Hall at 3 P.M. that day. The settlement effort—attempts to bring about a peaceful settlement with the
military—was pushed all the way back to the starting point by radical elements on the committee.

At 4 P.M. there was a rally—"the third rally for protecting democracy." It commenced in the square by the fountain. Afterward the citizens staged a peaceful demonstration, walking six kilometers along
Gumnam-ro to Kwangju Station, then to the MBC office and back to the
Provincial Hall. Other than that, things were not going well. The Settlement Committee all but collapsed. The chairman of the Student Settlement Committee, Kim Chang Gil, announced his resignation to reporters.
The committee members sat late, trying to discuss a way out, to avoid
confrontation. Radicals, however, vowed to fight to the death; they fired
blanks at about 9 P.M. that night. During the night, again gunshots rang
out. There was once more a racketing of cars to disturb people at night.

May 26: The Settlement Committee Did Their Best, But . . .

At 5 A.M. on May 26, the news spread that the Korean army was moving
back into town. People were extremely upset. Four or five Settlement

Committee members, including Pastor Chang, hastened to the Martial Law Command's local headquarters, to make an appeal.

"We're going to calm them down," these worthies promised. "So withdraw your troops to the previous positions."

The army people responded: "It was just an operation to secure suburban paths, not for penetrating (into the city)."

Here I would comment on the Settlement Committee's activities. They did not accomplish their goals during the uprising. But we could not but compliment them on their efforts. They tried their best. Pastor Chang and others stayed up all night, on occasion, trying to persuade the radicals to tone down their demands. They experienced a certain amount of abuse and humiliation. Patience, patience, they kept saying.

At 3 P.M. this day there was a meeting to arrange for a Citizens' Funeral, to bury the many dead. Eight representatives of the bereaved families met with the deputy governor, Chung Si Chae . . . to discuss the procedure. May 28 was fixed as the date for the funeral.

It looked as if the situation would not change, considering how things were on May 25–26. Our team sent an article to Seoul titled: "The Ill Prospect of a Settlement." The people of Kwangju looked exhausted. It was simply deplorable. On the other hand, this night was peaceful and calm. The people of Kwangju held their breath.

May 27: Praise Be to the Dignity of the Citizens

Bang! Bang!

This time the gunfire came in the middle of the night—distant, but approaching. I woke up with a jolt. I picked up a cigarette. As I lit up, the husky voice of a young woman boomed out over the whole city through the loudspeaker system.

"The army is coming into the city. We're distributing weapons. Come to the Provincial Hall. . . ." This voice went on for about ten minutes, then stopped.

Listening to the gunfire, I could tell the army was coming in. I opened the window. It was pitch dark. I could see nothing. The only thought in my head was that the damage—the loss of life—should be minimized. Memories came surging back: of the chairman of the student committee, Kim Chang Gil; of the young kids asking around for blood donations; of the youngsters in school uniform.

Gunfire continued. It was 4 A.M. KBS repeatedly urged citizens to surrender, informing them that the martial-law authorities had sent in the army. Between announcements, they played jolly marching tunes, "Bridge on the River Kwai," then "The Soldier Who Returned." Firing ceased at 5:25 A.M., but the music carried on.

Precisely at 5:25 A.M. the local Martial Law Command officer, General So Jun Ryul, made a first announcement.

> The military waited patiently ever since evacuating the city on May 21. We promised the citizens' representatives not to come back in, provided certain conditions were respected. They were not so respected. Coming back into the city became inevitable, because the scum of society and criminal elements organized a so-called "citizens' army." They broke the law. The army has completed its mission successfully. Citizens, come forward. Order has been restored.

At 6 A.M. there was another announcement. "Two dead, 207 arrests. No civilians were hurt."

At about 9:30 A.M. we managed to make our way to the fountain in the square outside the Provincial Hall. We did so with the help of two Kwangju-resident reporters, Park Rae Myong and Wi Jong Chol, acting as if they were government officials. The streets were quite different. Soldiers were stationed here and there throughout the downtown area. The streets were almost empty. Young people were being arrested all day.

We were forbidden to enter the Provincial Hall. At this we became weak and numb. Our group sprawled on the sidewalk in front of the building.

At about 3 P.M., a group of newsmen accredited to the Ministry of National Defense in Seoul arrived in Kwangju. With them came cameramen. The group was under military police escort. We were finally able to enter the building. I saw fifteen men who had been alive the day before laid out there, dead. They had been lined up next to ten unidentified bodies we had seen the previous day in the backyard of the building. Tears trickled down my face.

We decided to return to Seoul. We would take turns with another team from the head office which included our associate director, Cho Yon Hung. This was our ninth day in Kwangju. The sense of frustration was unbearable.

A democratic uprising against bayonets and guns had come to an end. The people had been savaged in their souls. I cursed myself, crying at what I had seen. I was confused: Had democracy been served by the blood of these victims? Or not? The Kwangju uprising left numerous injured behind, and many were killed during those ten days. The damage was enormous.

But I praise the citizens of Kwangju for their spirit. They dealt with the crisis . . . going to the end. Once more I hear the roar of gunfire, I see the messy streets, I hear the wailing of the bereaved, the shouts, I see the buildings on fire. I lament this gloomy episode in our history.

CHAPTER THIRTEEN

"MAYBE I WAS TOO YOUNG..."

Chang Jae Yol

The Union World 1

E very year, when May comes round, my hands become sweaty. When I recall the numerous bodies, I grimace. Is this because the shock was too great? Twenty years have passed and I have forgotten many things, but some images are still fixed in my mind's eye like letters—written characters—carved into the shell of a turtle. Based on these memories and on my records I have created my own interpretation of the events that took place in Kwangju in May 1980. My record consists not only of what I witnessed, but what other reporters and witnesses said they saw. I cannot assert with much confidence that my story fits the facts perfectly. However, despite what may pass for disorderliness in my approach, I would like to try to reflect on the meaning of the Kwangju uprising.

I am retracing these sad events long after they took place. Still, my views have not changed. I went into Kwangju when I was still too young to understand the world. I was looking for a dream—for romance; and I found myself at the center of modern history. I still believe that my hands that wrote articles were as pure as those of the young dead. I discovered the tragedy of our modern history not only with my eyes, but with my entire body.

Strange Symptoms That Started to Surface from May 15 Onward

It is well known now that when the month of May came, there were demonstrations in Kwangju almost every day, as a matter of routine.

On May 2, as the result of a clash between students of Chosun University and other universities, the president of Chosun University, Park Chul Ung, was forcibly confined by students. On May 6, following a visit by an educational investigation committee set up by the opposition New Democratic Party, students demonstrated almost every day, calling for democracy in Korea.

From May 14 the demonstrations picked up in frequency and scale. Some 5,000 students from Chonnam National University and Chosun University paraded through the streets of the Gumnam-ro section, and marched to the Provincial Hall on that day. By May 15 the number was so great that the police were unable to control them.

These student demonstrations reached a peak on May 16. On that day students, teachers, and citizens staged a prodemocracy rally that went on until 9:30 in the evening. They held a silent, candle-lit ceremony later that evening. The inability of the police to douse the flames of democracy was obvious.

In the midst of this turmoil, paratroop forces had started to move. This was noted on the night of May 15. About 200 students were gathering in the student union hall at Chonnam National University. That night, around 11:45 P.M. my notebook says, two army trucks exited from the east gate of the university and departed via the main entrance. Possibly the military were getting the lay of the land in advance of the declaration of martial law (two days later).

The demonstration on May 16 ended peacefully. The students and citizens looked fresh—they wore cheerful expressions—for all that they were putting on prodemocracy rallies almost every night. The demonstration broke up that night without any clashes. No one would have imagined that on the following day the junta would attempt to annihilate democracy in Korea. Students worried lest the nationwide demonstrations at the time might lead to closing of the universities, but that was the most that anyone anticipated.

The students resolved to attend classes regularly starting on May 19. And meanwhile they cleaned the streets. Park Gwan Hyun, the chairman of the general council of students at Chonnam National University, told students to keep things in order and watch out for any suspicious strangers. At their torch rally on the night of May 16 students decided to "send a message to the army" that students were ready to serve on the frontline against North Korea, if the nation's security was at stake. This was intended as a warning to North Korea not to manipulate calls for democracy in the South for their own political purposes. However, the newly formed army junta, blinded by its own power, committed a stupendous atrocity.

A First Article: "The Hunt Has Begun . . . "

May 18 was a Sunday. I, the youngest to join in the *Joongang Ilbo* team reporting in Kwangju, was at our office. I happened to be looking out of the window when a truck loaded with soldiers went by. I knew something was up. Thereafter, moving around downtown to follow the troops, I witnessed their wanton violence. The soldiers carried M-16 rifles with bayonets mounted. They also carried very heavy-looking riot-control sticks. Their modus operandi: a pair of paratroopers would jump out of the back of a truck and start beating any young male in sight. One such young man, who was being pounded on near the bridge close to Moodeung Stadium, driven to his wit's end, simply fell off the bridge. Many, who were close by, witnessed this event at first hand. Reporter that I was—supposedly in control of myself—I found the blood draining from my face. My legs trembled at what I had seen. It was very obvious that similar things must be happening all over the city.

From May 19 onward, the response to the military grew greatly in scale. Student demonstrations gave way to a widespread action on the part of the public at large. Even elderly men joined in the demonstrations, carrying little stumps instead of proper sticks. The citizens shouted: "Everyone from Cholla [from North and South provinces, they meant] is going to be murdered." Then they gathered in the Gumnam-ro section. Atrocities committed by the paratroopers on May 19 made that day (a Monday) a terrible one.

"The Hunt Has Begun" ran our proposed headline on a story we sent to the Seoul head office of our national daily on May 20. We knew that the heading would not be used—it would have been censored, but what could we do?

My notebook has these words scribbled in it: "Stick 'em with bayonets." "A woman, severely beaten, stripped of everything but her underwear." "Followed a person to his home and beat him brutally." "Hurled a knife at the demonstrators."

In the end this wanton violence by paratroopers roaming the streets of Kwangju sparked the uprising. The strategy the paratroopers used was too brutal to be a riot-control plan as applied to unarmed civilians.

On the afternoon of May 20, like others I gathered on Gumnam-ro. I raged as I watched the mercilessness of the paratroopers. People threw stones at them, seeking to attack them from a safe distance, but the paratroopers did not budge. However, when the moment came, they leaped out and clubbed the heads of those running away. They looked like beasts hunting prey. I ran away as fast as I could. I never ran like that before in my life.

Later I visited a hospital close by on Gumnam-ro. It was filled with people whose heads had been crushed in. Most of the injuries treated there were broken heads and bones. Even in warfare, who used a strategy to conquer along such lines as those used by the brutal paratroopers sent to Kwangju? The clashes between Israelis and Palestinians could not have been this bad.

Their massacres led to the citizens' spontaneous uprising. Kwangju was not, like Seoul, a giant city. People knew each other. On the other side of the bridge were your friends, or your relatives, or your schoolfriends. The death of a neighbor's son was as meaningful as the death of your own son.

This is why the strategy of "annihilation"—of extreme oppression at the beginning—that had worked in other places in the previous autumn—for example, at Masan, where Special Forces paratroopers were used—did not work in Kwangju. On the contrary, the strategy sparked off spectacular rage. A sense of desperation, of being unwilling to take it anymore, burst out among people in Kwangju and in the entire province of South Cholla surrounding the city.

I believe that the incredible actions of the Korean military stirred up rumors of all kinds. The irrational, merciless behavior of the paratroopers made anything seem possible.

Why did the junta send thousands of paratroopers into Kwangju, making these men enemies of the people? Were they not aware of the possible consequences of sending in forces who were trained, not to control crowds, but to kill?

By 1980 the absolute dictatorship of Park Chung Hee, ruler of South Korea for eighteen years, had suddenly crumbled, following his death in October 1979. But new elements within the military—a new army junta—had sprung into being instead. They resisted the historic forces within Korean society that favored democracy. People were disappointed. Young people especially raged against the withering of democratic hopes under martial law. For this reason one might have anticipated that a popular uprising would take place anywhere, not only in Kwangju.

The paratroopers' atrocities were akin to pouring oil on the subconscious flames of democracy in people's minds. There was another factor. Regional factors—the discrimination against the Cholla provinces during the time of Park Chung Hee, when other regions were given favored treatment and Cholla was ignored—played their part in making the Kwangju uprising a part of history.

The new military aimed to use the paratroopers to root out democratic hopes on the spot. The intention was to destroy second and third generation resistance (notably among students). However, the *minjung* or "people's consciousness" that allows people in Kwangju to shed tears over their neighbor's pains and to resist arrant dictators made it possible for many there to stand up with only their bare hands to confront men with guns.

During the uprising our reporting team got together to compare notes. This is what my record of that meeting shows:

May 18

Reporter A: At around 11 that morning paratroopers entered the reading room in front of Chonnam National University and beat high school students there who were studying for their college entrance exams. Those students who were beaten for no reason reacted by weeping.

Reporter B: Around 3:30 that afternoon I saw a paratrooper throw his bayonet at a demonstrator who was running away. Fortunately, he missed.

Reporter C: Paratroopers went into a coffee shop and dragged out a young man whose head was bleeding. They tied him with ropes, and threw him into an army truck. A woman who seemed to be his girlfriend screamed that he was not a student, but she was thrown to the ground.

May 19

Reporter A: The hunt seemed to get going from the morning on. The paratroopers went into a lecture hall at an institute and clubbed the students who were working there.

Reporter B: At around 11:05 in the morning an armored vehicle appeared. While citizens watched, they stripped a student and beat him.

Reporter C: From the night of May 19 onward, the attacks on the police stations began. The Im-dong police station was burned to the ground.

Reporter D: Around 4:30 that afternoon, in front of the Gyerim police station, a first bullet was fired. Someone shot from a broken-down armored vehicle. This was when the first casualty was caused by gunfire.

May 20

Reporter A: All journalists covering the provincial police gathered and reported on casualties. A first list of casualties was—the whole task proved impossible—prepared.

Reporter B: About 7:10 P.M. the citizens started using vehicles. Some were riding in a bus and were trying to get through a blockade line that way. They were arrested and taken away by the soldiers.

Reporter C: Casualties are rising. I was told that four police and two paratroopers have been killed.

May 21

Reporter A: There is tremendous suspicion of reporters out there. Citizens throw stones at us; calling out: "What is the press for?"

Reporter B: Around 11 A.M. an armored vehicle showed up on Gumnam-ro. I saw demonstrators with stones in their hands.

Reporter C: I saw, right in front of me, a person who was hiding behind a wall. He was shot in the neck and died on the spot. I think it was a direct shot.

Reporter D: Yes, the paratroopers are deliberately shooting people from rooftops. At 2 in the afternoon they started shooting at anything that moved. Not even a shadow moves around Provincial Hall right now.

This (relatively tame) record of a meeting between five reporters from *Joongang Ilbo* could not possibly have been published under martial-law guidelines. The reporters were torn between the people and the censorship.

"Let's Keep Order!"—A Civic Awareness That Lived On

To judge by the articles the censors passed and allowed to be printed, Kwangju was hit by disturbances much like those in Los Angeles in the early 1990s. These were "riots" and there was no place for law and order. At that time, to justify their actions, the newly installed army junta attempted to portray the situation in Kwangju as an extended riot caused by "hooligans."

However, on May 21, during an impromptu rally held at Gumnam-ro, a remark by one particular citizen made us all think. "Let's not use violence. Even if they use guns and swords on us, let's not throw stones at them." These words appear in my notebook. And again:

"There is only one democracy! A free democracy!"

The civic consciousness that was apparent during the uprising transformed the situation. This was a Kwangju *Minjung* (people's) Uprising. In truth, a desire for democracy defeated the distortions and the coverups routinely used. Here is a statement made by Park Chung Hun, the newly appointed prime minister at the time. If you read this, you can see how the authorities chose to distort the facts.

> A few impure elements in society attacked public property and set fire to
> it, stole weapons and fired the guns at the army. However, the military is
> not permitted to fire back. Such are government orders. The problem

mainly lay with those minority impure elements and rioters with weapons in their hands.

Most casualties occurred on May 21 after the soldiers opened fire. Yet the most powerful man in the cabinet made an announcement consisting of a pack of lies. Such distortions and cover-ups triggered rage and tears in Kwangju. When the Provincial Hall fell to the people, the first list of demands submitted to the military by the demonstrators sums up the situation very well:

1. Recognize the fact that the uprising took place as a result of the excessive force used by the military.
2. The government must be explicit about this and publish an apology in the media that will be acceptable to all citizens.
3. Free those, including students, who were arrested.
4. Compensate those who were injured and the families of those who were killed.
5. When everything has settled down, the authorities must conduct no vendetta.
6. Until law and order have been restored, the military will not reenter the city.
7. The uprising, in a just cause, will not be distorted as a "rebellion."
8. Refrain from making inflammatory remarks and do not publish false reports.

At the time the citizens of Kwangju were especially sensitive about being portrayed as rioters. They reacted against what they saw as government attempts to blame them for the uprising, inciting regional hostilities in the process.

An Endless Line of Blood Donors

Despite the paralysis of the administration of the city, such was the civic consciousness in Kwangju that anarchy did not ensue. At the time, living in Nongsung-dong, I had to walk home late at night. But I do not remember being afraid. The hospitals overflowed with the injured, but my diary states that, thanks to donations, blood supplies at hand were ample.

From May 24 onward, despite the intense fighting with the army that had taken place (and the continuing confrontation on the city's edges), the city itself recovered. Around 2:15 P.M. that day reports came into the operations control room at the Provincial Hall that helicopters were shooting at anything that moved in the suburb of Baegun-dong and that much damage was being done.

I saw many dedicated people at work there. I myself walked around the situation control room with a ribbon on, pretending to be a student working there. The people in charge were pleading with citizens to clean up the streets and reopen their shops. They also wanted city officials and the police to return to their jobs. My functions in the situation control room ended after two days, when someone heard my Seoul accent and I was pulled into a civilian militia room and given a rough time.

Early on the morning of May 25 a force of thirty garbage collectors came out and cleaned Gumnam-ro.

Starting on May 24, to accelerate the recovery, a drive had already begun to collect all weapons. What was uppermost in the minds of the Settlement Committee was the possibility that there would be more casualties when the paratroopers reentered the city.

At 8 A.M., May 25, a Sunday, the lawyer Hong Nam Sun and fifteen others talked with paratroopers on the street, telling everyone that their purpose was to halt the advance of army tanks into the city.

The military pretended to retreat a little.

The conciliation group continued their efforts during three days from May 24 to May 26. They made desperate efforts to avert a conflict and thereby to minimize the sacrifice of life.

Meanwhile, the military distributed leaflets. They read as follows: "The armed forces hoped that an appeal to patriotism would induce people to disband (the Citizens' Army) and to restore order in the city. However, the rioters still have arms in their hands. We, accordingly, find it necessary to shoot."

It was only too obvious that when the army came back into Kwangju, there would be more bloodshed. Thus, the Settlement Committee tried to collect weapons to avoid giving the armed forces an excuse to reenter the city. At the same time, some hardliners were saying that they would blow up the Provincial Hall if the army came back in again.

Another topic of debate was setting up funeral arrangements for the still unburied victims of the previous few days.

Inside the Provincial Hall, the Settlement Committee met with Governor Chang Hyung Tae and Deputy Governor Chung Si Chae to discuss possible solutions to the conflict. However, all these worthies would say was that they were keenly aware of their responsibilities. Power was in fact concentrated totally in the hands of Chun Doo Hwan. The governor was completely powerless.

"Soldiers Killed People!"—The Memory of a Primary School Student

The week that had started on Sunday, May 18 was a week of history in the making. However, time was now running short for the Kwangju uprising to elevate itself into history as a "movement for democracy." A foreign reporter present on the scene observed that it would be good if people could hold out until May 30. In that event, some good might come out of the situation! On the other hand, there was a rumor that, as of Sunday, May 25, one's best option was to escape from the city after 6 P.M. The thinking was that anything might happen during the night, the obvious time for an attack.

The to-ing and fro-ing continued in the Provincial Hall. The citizens' committee did its utmost to collect weapons. Members tried to expand their role to bring about an end to the whole affair with minimal loss of life. However, the hardliners around would have none of this. These students resisted strenuously.

People swung between the extremes of hope and fear. Monday, May 26 passed in discussions over the possibility that the army would finally force its way back into the city, however difficult that might or might not be. In any event, the military launched a surprise attack (that, still, many had anticipated) at 3:30 A.M. on May 27. As soon as 5:30 A.M. the radio broadcast an announcement by the army:

"Do not come out into the street, and do not give shelter to rioters— the Provincial Hall and Kwangju Park have been completely recovered by the army."

Later I was able to go outside. I entered the old YWCA building, by now severely damaged. Upstairs, on the second floor, I found a sofa with a pool of blood in it. Someone who had been hit had sat there. A metal filing cabinet had been used as a barricade. It had been plugged full of bullet holes. There was a long trail of blood across the floor where someone had been dragged out.

"This blood is still not dry at 12:50 A.M." I wrote in my notebook, I find today. What had this young man thought, fighting alone in the early morning, I wonder? What did the spilling of his blood signify?

I hung on in the city. On May 31 the primary schools of Kwangju reopened.

My superiors sent me to cover the event. "What do you want to tell your teacher?" I asked a second-grader.

"I want to tell them that the soldier-uncles killed people," the boy responded.

I was taken aback by his words. When I had been a boy myself, I had exchanged letters with soldiers. I so much appreciated what they were doing for their country. That is how I was brought up. How would one heal the wounds in this little boy's being?

The Bloodstains Have Still Not Dried

The Kwangju uprising has been distorted over a long period of time. Many Koreans still see it as just so much regional "hooliganism," to use the government's expression. Only a couple of years ago a Korean court found that, under our system of law, those who were in fact directly responsible for the crimes in Kwangju—two former presidents—somehow were "unpunishable."

Those two men held power for a long time, fourteen years in all. Under the newly installed dictatorship dating to May 1980, there were plenty of opportunities for them and their zealous toadies to systematically search out all Kwangju uprising-related documents and to destroy them. So far, we still lack the time to study and assess the actual nature and the historical significance of the events. To heal the wounds, we need to pin down all the details and refresh our memories. As time passes, memories will fade, and evidence—in the form of testimonies—will be no more available.

It is far too early, I believe, to consign these events to the dim and distant past. The bloodstains are still fresh. The true meaning of the Kwangju uprising will be known only when the pain of that child I met—now a man in his twenties or early thirties—has finally ended.

Let us beware of simplistic logic along the lines: "It's time to set aside the past and concentrate on the future." Should we forget the past, we are condemned to rouse up the ghosts of that era. Only by letting our minds dwell on what happened can we build a bright future.

I could not speak when I saw what happened. Nor could I write what I knew. What can I say now to those young men who held out to the last? As a reporter who could not report the Kwangju uprising truthfully, I offer my apologies to the citizens of Kwangju. No, I apologize to all who witnessed the events and therefore know what happened and what I should have written.

Twenty years have passed. My reporter's notebook of that era has turned yellow with age. However, I believe that the truth is contained in this notebook, stained with the sweat of the young man I was then.

CHAPTER FOURTEEN

A PHOTOGRAPHER'S CREDO

Hwang Jong Gon

Bulletin of Warriors 1

Koreans use this expression: "Hearing it 100 times is no better than seeing it once." In other words: "Seeing is believing," as Westerners say. People trust what they can see, whether in the East or the West, no?

Photography is a medium that goes to the eyes. The reason why photojournalism is trusted more than the written word is obvious. People believe that pictures tell the truth and only the truth. Those who are aware of the power of images, politicians included, act accordingly. Park Chung Hee, the late military dictator of South Korea, permitted articles about his rival Kim Dae Jung to be published in the papers, but not photos of him. Simple! Articles about North Korea were permitted, but no images of Kim Il Sung, the so-called Great Leader, could appear in the South Korean press.

What of Kwangju?

The Kwangju uprising—these days baptized the "Kwangju Democratization Movement" by the government—lasted for ten days, namely from May 18 to 27, 1980. Prior to this we had the seemingly impregnable dictatorship of President Park, which lasted for eighteen years until suddenly curtailed by a single gunshot, fired at him by one of his closest aides, Kim Jae Gyu, the head of the Korean Central Intelligence Agency (KCIA) on October 26, 1979. This wholly unexpected development led to events that have been amply treated elsewhere. I move forward to the morning of Sunday, May 18. It was a lovely, sunny day. Ordered to do so by my boss, the head of the photography department, I headed for Kwangju, taking my time. When I got there, however, at about 7 P.M. I sensed instantly that something was wrong. Call it a reporter's instinct. The mood in the city was dreadful, tense. A curfew was being enforced that night—no big deal in itself. But the next morning, out on the street, I saw soldiers stationed here and there. That was just the start.

To point my camera at anyone was tantamount to suicide. Both the army and the demonstrators hated reporters, I knew. The reasons were simple. The press had published not a line on events in Kwangju. Nor was there any word on martial law, in a meaningful sense, explaining how censorship was working . . . under the military. Newspaper photographers had to take their pictures from moving cars or from behind curtains, peeping out of windows. Kwangju people made difficulties about letting people stay anywhere in inns. Foreign correspondents were OK, because their newspapers printed their stuff. But not we.

I wanted to get the hell out of there. My pictures would never be printed, I knew. But sheer obstinacy kept me there. I knew I was witnessing history. Some day, perhaps, the pictures could be published, if not tomorrow. At daybreak on May 21, all phones were cut off. That led to an exodus of domestic reporters, on the grounds that they could no longer function. Actually, they couldn't function anyway, not under military censorship.

I continued my work. On that same day, May 21, the day the army retreated from Provincial Hall after three days of fierce clashes in the streets. I hit a personal low when I was captured by a group of citizens while taking pictures from a second-floor room in the Sangmu Hall, opposite Provincial Hall, and taken over to the hall. These people took me for a North Korean spy.

The college students at the gate there took one look at my press ID and withdrew all accusations, but not without a dig: "Why are you taking pictures? They will never be used." . . . They let me go, with a final caution to hide my cameras. I could understand the discontent of the people there. They had been dying, spilling their blood in the streets, and the Korean media aired beauty shows, soap operas, and other entertainment. The locals expressed their feelings by torching the buildings of the two TV network buildings, MBC and KBS. They were burned on May 20 and May 21 respectively.

My stock soared briefly when *Dong-A Ilbo,* my newspaper, published one picture from Kwangju on May 23. Suddenly, the locals were much more friendly. Alone among the Korean press we refrained from using the term "rioters," which the military censors considered obligatory.

No Choice but to Take Pictures

Working was not impossible. On May 23 the Citizens' Army people who occupied Provincial Hall gave us armbands, made out of bits of curtain. As reporters, we had a degree of freedom.

Everything that I saw was all but too miserable to shoot. The bodies of the dead, the weeping families in the open, next to Provincial Hall, people searching for their loved ones. It hurt but I took pictures, going into the hospitals to photograph the injured and into Provincial Hall where the bodies were laid out on May 23–24. The next day my colleague Kim Yong Man, with whom I later published a collection of photos in book form titled *Kwangju, That Day,* showed up. I didn't know how he could make it in there, the city was supposed to be sealed off from the outside. Anyway, he did. Our head office had sent him down to join me, not knowing what had happened to me. That's how rough the situation was. . . and so it continued until May 27, when the military came back in before dawn. I hurried to Provincial Hall. Bodies were scattered . . . Young men were being taken away, tied up, their heads bowed. I asked Kim Yong Man to take care of anything else and headed back to Seoul, bumming a ride in a foreign correspondent's car.

Those ten days were a nightmare. The thing I did right was to bring plenty of film. I had thirty rolls of thirty-six-frame film, plus two more cartons of film in reserve. My supposedly short trip was extended to ten days. Always bring plenty of film, that was what I confirmed, as a photographer. The other thing, elementary as it sounds, is to keep shooting. There were times when it became painful to reiterate: "This is for the record . . . this is for the record," when people asked why I was shooting pictures, knowing that the pictures could not be used. Yet in the end—I had to wait until April 1994, when our book was published with our photos—we got the pictures out—fourteen years later, but we got them out.

What I felt after covering the Kwangju democratization movement— the uprising—was that a reporter must be on the spot and work. This was a whirlpool event in Korean history. One had to be there . . . A newspaper photographer collects news materials to publish them in a newspaper. Taking this to its conclusion: a photographer should not forget that he is "writing" history, that he is a witness.

CHAPTER FIFTEEN

"NOT ONE LINE..."

Ryu Jong Hwan

Distribution of Arms

May 21, 1980. It was Buddha's Birthday, supposedly an auspicious day. I saw numerous lotus-shaped lamps and all manner of fully blossoming flowers as I drove along the Namhae Highway, heading to Kwangju. The radio was broadcasting something: a Miss Universe contest. If I looked around, it was simply impossible to believe that somewhere, not far away, there was bloodshed going on on a massive scale . . .

There was no news from Kwangju. Nothing in the papers. Nothing in the newscasts on TV or the radio. Nothing. All we had were rumors. We had had meeting after meeting at my newspaper company in Pusan, and they finally decided to send just me, with all kinds of reservations, given that there is or was supposed to be animosity toward people from other parts of the country, especially Kyongsang where I came from. The risks were considerable. I might not be able to get into the city in the first place. I would risk being pilloried by the locals given where I came from. My newspaper, the *Pusan Ilbo,* wouldn't be able to publish a line of what I wrote. There had been numerous counterarguments against sending me at all, even this late.

I was just supposed to skim the news and come back. On the way I changed my car, to one with local license plates. As I approached Kwangju, I stopped at a local police station to ask the way.

"Are you here to die?" the policeman asked me.

That was a fine way to start. At that moment a truck went speeding by, filled with young demonstrators. This was my first sight of them. Meanwhile, a barricade of logs blocked my way. I abandoned my car, and headed off on a trail through the mountains, hoping to find my way, only to be stopped by soldiers. They took one look at my ID card and sent me back. Making a pathetic story short, I reported back to my newspaper. At my head office, the decision was that we must be serious. A team of us would go. Besides me there was Ahn Gi Ho, another reporter, and Park Sang Ryung, a photographer. It was May 23 by the time we left, and after various adventures we arrived in Kwangju, walking the last part of the journey.

The first impressions were staggering. The city was devastated. The dead were laid out in coffins in Sangmu gymnasium, opposite the Provincial Hall. It was as if a war had just ended. Huge numbers of people were gathered on the square in front of the hall. There was a drizzling rain, but they still turned out. Many of those present were the bereaved, I gathered. They were calm for the most part . . . Next, we visited hospitals. The injured groaned, those who had lost family members wailed. Yet, there were long lines of people waiting to give blood. Nowhere that I saw was there chaos or disorder for that matter. Kwangju was not a city of "rioters," to use the obligatory expression mandated by the military. That astounded me.

Facing Two Carbines

That same day, I had some trouble in front of the Provincial Hall. Our reporter Park had brought with him a huge camera box. It was made of aluminium, and it shone brightly. You could see the damned thing a mile off. From the word go, this box put me off. However, I found myself looking after it, I, the team leader, while the other two went off to report. I waited miserably for them, trying to make myself as inconspicuous as possible.

It was the box that did it. I was suddenly being watched. Not long afterward two members of the Citizens' Army—students in fact—came up to me, their carbines at the ready. I half rose, raising my hands. A half circle formed around me.

"What is that box?"

"It's a camera box."

"What? What do you do?"

"I'm a reporter."

"Working for who?"

". . ."

Somehow, I could not blurt out "*Pusan Ilbo*," given what I understood to be the animosities toward anyone from there. I took out my ID and presented it to the two interrogators. Their faces turned white. They were embarrassed.

"Ah, you're a reporter, thanks for taking the trouble to come here." And again: "Why don't you come with us to our headquarters? Let's go."

I took the bothersome box with me and set off with them into the Provincial Hall. Thus I penetrated into the impenetrable fastness of the militants' sanctuary. Those two showed me every corner of the Provincial Hall. They couldn't do enough for this reporter who had come all the way from Pusan. In my confusion, I forgot to ask their names. I wonder what happened to them.

"No Line on Kwangju!"

We had great difficulty in sending out my copy from Kwangju, only for me to find on my return to Pusan—we chose May 26 to go back—that not a single line of what we had sent in was published as we had written it. In spite of that we spent all night writing, went home, and then learned that the army had reentered Kwangju, invalidating everything we had done.

How could such damage be inflicted by a people upon itself? Back in Pusan I returned to my old job as a reporter. But I couldn't work. I could no longer discern events and write pieces. For a good while, I could only idle. The word "Kwangju" was running in my mind, like an old film.

Even now, after twenty years, Kwangju comes back to me in May. I cannot help it. I tremble with remorse. I have not paid back the debts I owe to those people. It is too bad that I could not cover the events properly.

CHAPTER SIXTEEN

KWANGJU, THAT CHANGED MY DESTINY

Oh Hyo Jin

Citizens' Army on Mount Moodeung

The Kwangju uprising was a historic event for our country. It also happened to be a fatal event for me. I covered the uprising in tears, literally, as head of a team organized by Munhwa Broadcasting Company, a commercial TV network. I was with other reporters, as leader of a team. They were Lee Ig Ho, Kim Yong Chol, Chung Dong Yong, and Chon Pyong Guk. When I came back to Seoul, I conveyed to my senior staff, in tears, what I had witnessed in Kwangju, all the stuff we had censored.

No doubt my emotional involvement got me into trouble. I was taken into custody by the military on the charge of violating their rules; that is, spreading false rumors and preparing false documents with evil intent. I was fired by my company. Thereafter, I moved from one job to another over the years. Had there been no Kwangju, I dare say, I would have been conventionally successful in my profession of journalism.

On Being Mistaken for North Korean Spies

Our MBC team departed for Kwangju on May 20 (the day our branch in Kwangju was put to the torch by citizens enraged by the fact that we were not covering events there in any way).

We found the expressway to Kwangju was blocked at Changsong. I sent our car back to Seoul and walked toward the city with my colleagues. On the way we spent a night nearby in a farmer's house. That was where we ran into danger.

The skies over Kwangju were red that night (our branch was burning, which we did not know). Sleep was out of the question, with the locals roaring outside. What was going on? Young men carrying clubs came in and out of the front yard. Our host, it turned out, had reported our presence to others. A posse had surrounded the farm where we staying. The theory was that we might be North Korean spies!

With the press being censored and no means of getting reliable information on anything to do with Kwangju, wild rumors spread. We were not being willfully misunderstood, it was a genuine case of misunderstanding. We took out our press IDs. That, in turn, was a signal for a frontal attack.

"Are you press people doing your jobs?" "Are you reporting?" "Whose side are you on anyway?"

We extracted ourselves from this messy situation and asked for help. One of the young men agreed to act as a guide. The route he chose took us past Asia Motors, a company there, and over a river, the Gugrag River, and into Kwangju. Still, we had a problem. We looked out of place. We had pale, freshly shaved faces, our clothes were smart, our shoes were clean. We spoke standard Korean. These were things that had made us the object of suspicion, as spies.

We had to change our spots. I took off a jumper I was wearing that was altogether too smart. I ruffled my neatly combed hair. Thus transformed, I strode into a road we had come upon and flagged down a passing truck crammed with demonstrators. We all boarded this vehicle. We were promptly offered fruit and *gimbab*—rice rolled in seaweed. The fact was we were starving. The food was most welcome, and we accepted it gladly . . . In due course the truck arrived at the Provincial Hall, with the square and fountain in front of it. We were there! Out we went onto the square.

"Down with Chun Doo Hwan!" The shouting of slogans proceeded. We joined in, stretching our arms out wide.

Meeting the Spokesman

Downtown Kwangju was in far worse shape than we had expected. Power lines and poles were down. Shops were destroyed. Burnt cars were scattered around. The streets were devastated, as if there had been a battle. There had been. The penny dropped. In the meantime how were we to cover the story? There were foreign correspondents around. Very well, these TV reporters had freedom to work, they even had escorts, we saw. It was time to secure equal opportunity.

I went into the Provincial Hall—I talked my way in—and made tracks for the person in charge of public relations, a student. Not that this was easy to do, if one was a domestic reporter (unable to report in real life). One needed one's courage simply to enter Provincial Hall. To persuade the people in charge to take one seriously was even harder, I found.

My line was: "OK, as you say, we have done wrong so far but . . . ." I continued: "We could not report the facts, as the people of Kwangju and our own company would have wished. So where are we? I cannot promise that we will be able to mend our ways. I do not have that authority. I will do my best. In the meantime are you entitled to block the domestic media? It's humiliating for us. You allow the foreign media to proceed, and them alone? What we film may not be broadcast. But it can serve as historical data for generations to come."

It worked. The guy in charge gave us the green light. We were given passes, and we even got an escort car with sirens, to accompany our car with all the equipment in it.

Not that everything went well though. Chun Pyong Guk, one of my colleagues, took out his 16mm Canon camera and started filming the streets around Gumnam-ro from the top of a jeep. Then he disappeared. He got separated from the students we were supposed to be with. Another group of people appeared and tied him to a tree. They took away his camera, of course. This time, the charge was that he was a Japanese spy. (So much for the joys of Japanese consumer items.) Chun got free from the tree somehow and returned well after midnight.

Kim Yong Chol and Chung Dong Yong covered the hospitals and the outskirts of town. And I stayed close to Provincial Hall, anchoring the operation and getting film out. I quickly lost all pretense to objectivity. I forgot that I was a reporter. How could anyone, I thought, ignore the fact that these friendly people around me had a real grievance?

Let me skip the horror stories as they are well known by now. I would like to say a big thank you to Suh Gong Sok, a local MBC reporter, who gave me untold help at the time.

Sending Out Articles

As mentioned, we reached Kwangju on May 21. By that time the telephones had been cut off. What to do? There was one hope. I had covered the Ministry of Transportation in Seoul in my time. I knew how the railway communications system worked. The thing to do was to head for Kwangju Station. I set out on foot from Gumnam-ro. Arriving there, I found the station deserted. Bodies were strewn about the waiting room. The staff had disappeared.

I headed for the stationmaster's office. Sure enough, there was a phone, and it was alive. In a moment I was connected to the reporters' room at the ministry. There I found a Miss Yu on duty. She connected my line to her line into our head office. At the same time reporters for other organizations could hear our call. I blurted out everything, omitting no detail. This call became known to the authorities. From then on, I was a marked man.

We pressed on, however, to get communications going. The next step was to head for our burned-out MBC building in Kwangju. We had one useful piece of information. Radio broadcasts from Seoul were first transmitted to that branch and from there to the transmission tower. In other words there was a line. It was in a scorched state but we could use it. Connecting the line to our portable speakers, we could hear the voice of the announcer Ms. Im Gug Hee from Seoul MBC Radio. We then connected the line to a magnetic telephone, dialed, and in due course we got a response from Seoul.

That way, I sent in reports daily, while not broadcasting. Our staff received these reports up at head office. I was told later that some who listened wept. I also heard that the tapes were copied and got spread around. One of them finally came into the hands of "the information agency" (KCIA). After that, their hostility toward me increased by leaps and bounds.

But that was later.

I now come to the end: the last day, May 27. Again, I will skip the details known to everyone. I ran out onto the street, while gunfire continued . . . All I could do was to stand aside. Students were being led away, roped together by the soldiers. They hung their heads.

"I had thought you reporters were on our side," one of them told me, happening to run into me five years later. "But when we were taken away by the soldiers, why, you stood with the soldiers."

CHAPTER SEVENTEEN

KWANGJU IS NOT OVER YET

Kim Yang Woo

The Battle at Yangdong

Our team from the *Kukje Shinmun* (the Kukje Daily) covering Kwangju left from our Pusan head office at 6 A.M. on May 21. We were four: I, a general news reporter; Uhm Chol Min and Kang Yong Bom, also reporters; and Kim Tag Don, a photographer. The order to cover Kwangju came from Lee Chol Ho, our editor-in-chief. In our assigned Pony car, driven by someone called Lee, our driver for this occasion, we took the Namhae Expressway. Army men stopped us on a bridge over the Sumjin River. We therefore turned about and left the expressway. We passed by Hadong, sticking to highways 18 and 19, traveling via Gurye and Gogsong, to finally reach a highway ramp near Kwangju Penitentiary. A road junction there offered a choice of several destinations, but not Kwangju. Our Pony could go no further. Soldiers blocking the road there, I noted, were from Regiment 8004, one of five army reserve regiments under Division 31.

By this time it was 5 P.M. We had taken eleven hours to get from Pusan to the vicinity of Kwangju. Now we were stuck. There was no hole to bolt through into Kwangju. The army and the police had the city sealed off.

While we hesitated—should we return or not? An officer in uniform, a Captain Kim, came up to us with a suggestion: We would stay overnight in the vicinity, a place called Changpyong; the next morning, he would show us how to get through to Kwangju, using a military road. It was getting dark. We accepted the kind offer.

The same Captain Kim rented a room close by. He let us use it overnight, he himself being a bachelor. Meanwhile, he had mentioned a Major Chong, an officer commanding Regiment 8004. From Changpyong to Division 31 was about thirty kilometers and would take us no more than an hour, even driving slowly. We would have to pass through several military checkpoints, but they would let us through when we mentioned Major Chong's name. (Wherefore the positive attitude of these two officers, without whom we would have been stuck? They happened to come from the Pusan area; to help reporters from their hometown was natural.)

The next morning, an incident occurred, just as we were about to leave Captain Kim's lodgings. Two men appeared with carts, each bearing a wooden coffin. These were the coffins of dead from Kwangju, the first we saw. The two men were sweating as they toiled up a steep hill. We and Captain Kim thereupon helped them with the carts, pushing together as far as the foot of a mountain. A white wild rose had been placed on each of the two coffins. These dead came from Changpyong, we learned. But the local people didn't dare to turn out to help bury them. They feared revenge, according to Captain Kim. It was a taste of what lay ahead.

Setting off by car, we did as we had been told by Captain Kim. We followed the military road until we reached Regiment 8005 headquarters, just behind Division 31 headquarters. There, Major Chong was waiting for us by prearrangement. We left the Pony there and set out on foot for Kwangju—for the fountain square in front of the Provincial Hall, the natural rallying spot. The first of five successive daily Kwangju citizens' protest rallies—these took place as long as the Citizens' Army was in control—was in progress when we got there.

By that time we had learned a valuable lesson, walking the nine kilometers from Regiment 8005 to the Provincial Square. The rumors that the authorities put out about Kwangju, as circulated in Pusan, were mistaken. They were lies. Examples of the false reports circulating where we came from were: "Kwangju people will immediately kill anyone from Pusan or with Pusan number plates on their cars"; "If anyone from Pusan enters Cholla, he will be battered to death"; and again "Everything grew much worse because a paratrooper from Kyongsang cut off the breast of a girl demonstrator"; and once more "A bus from South Cholla was burned by Kyongsang people when it crossed the Sumjin River bridge." These were so many evil lies circulated by the authorities, to blur the reality of the Kwangju Incident.

"Tear the Murderer Chun Doo Hwan to Pieces!"

What was not in doubt was the animosity toward Chun Doo Hwan. The demonstrators gathered on the square in front of Provincial Hall numbered around 10,000. They shouted out slogans, their voices echoing to every corner of the square.

"Tear Chun Doo Hwan to Pieces!"

The demonstration finished at about 6 P.M. Then, despite a light drizzle, the people set out on a protest march from Gumnam-ro to Kwangju Station. They hoisted placards to carry as they marched.

"Tear the Murderer Chun Doo Hwan to Pieces!"

Wall newspapers and flyers carried the same message: "Tear the murderer . . . "

We had to find a place to stay. The Kwangju Tourist Hotel had been shut down for several days. Most inns thereabouts had been closed since May 20. We finally settled on the Sejong Inn. The manager there at first declined to let us stay, saying that there were no staff. He eventually allowed us to use only one room on the third floor, on condition that we provided our own food outside and only slept in the room. This was where we stayed for four nights and five days starting on the night of May 22. Thus room 305 at the Sejong Inn became the "headquarters" of the *Kukje Shinmun*'s special team covering the Kwangju uprising.

The entire staff of the inn had gone in the middle of the demonstrations. We found rice to eat on the first and second day we were in Kwangju. Thereafter we had to make do with *ramyon*, a kind of noodle. That inn, by the way, was located in the heart of Kwangju, about one kilometer, as the crow flies, from the Provincial Hall.

On our first morning in the city, May 23, we oriented ourselves. To our surprise, we were the only domestic newspaper reporters around. We saw correspondents from several Japanese papers. There was also a U.S. network team. But there were no Korean reporters from Seoul, let alone the local papers. Or none that we could see. In fact during the five days the Citizens' Army was in charge, the only Korean reporters covering Kwangju, to the best of our knowledge, were the members of our *Kukje Shinmun* team, up from Pusan.

Every day, the pattern was the same. About 10,000 to 15,000 people gathered for the Kwangju Citizens' Protest Rally, organized by the Citizens' Army. Of all the slogans they shouted, "Tear the Murderer Chun Doo Hwan to Pieces!" was the one that stirred people most powerfully. The citizens of Kwangju were all fully aware of who had caused the Kwangju uprising, namely the person who was in charge of national security, Chun Doo Hwan.

Each day, the Citizens' Army headquarters made announcements from a stage above the fountain in the square in front of the Provincial Hall. They had microphones and loudspeakers, which were kept going all the time. They reported as follows: They said 2,000 Kwangju citizens had died, 1,000 were injured, and another 2,000 were missing in the wake of the brutal massacres by the army. They also announced that they had 100 identified bodies out of those 2,000 dead. These were laid out in

Sangmu Hall. They urged the relatives to come and identify them. In addition, they requested that people come forward who knew of burials of unidentified dead. Finally, they wanted anyone who had done army reserve duty and had finished their service and thus knew how to handle guns, to volunteer and teach members of the Citizens' Army how to handle weapons.

We checked every one of the dead laid out in Sangmu gymnasium. The coffins, we saw, had been made in a hurry. Each was covered by the national flag, the *Taekukki*. A wild rose in bloom was laid on every coffin. These bodies were kept in that hall for almost a whole week up to May 27.

During that time the weather was exceptionally changeable. One day was a sticky summer's day and everyone sweated. The next day it drizzled and was even chilly. By May 26 the smell of decay wafted all over the Fountain Square. People had to cover their noses.

"Two Thousand Dead and Two Thousand Missing"

The Citizens' Army had a method for marking military trucks and jeeps they had commandeered. The number 44 signified a truck carrying dead bodies; the number 119 was for emergency messages; number 48 indicated food and vegetables being transported.

A strict curfew was declared by the Citizens' Army, running from 6 P.M. to 6 A.M. the next day. During the hours of curfew, when few were on the streets, we saw seventeen- or eighteen-year-old boys, wearing on their left arms red armbands that said "Patrol." They carried rifles and made rounds of the city in jeeps marked with the number 112 in red ink.

Throughout the five days when the citizens were in charge, there was no public transport. On the street, apart from the trucks and jeeps driven by the Citizens' Army, there were no vehicles moving—no buses and no cars. Some people had bicycles, others carts or wagons that were pulled by oxen or cows, for stuff that needed moving.

We sent a first consignment of news articles and photos off to Pusan on May 23. To do so, we went back to the military base where we had left our Pony car. I myself went as far as Namwon, where I made a call to the head office in Pusan. Then I returned to the army base and from there sneaked into Kwangju once more. I left our driver to carry on to Pusan by himself, carrying our articles plus 120 or so photographs. This man was stopped at a checkpoint at Gogsong. The military intelligence agents confiscated all the film. They made photocopies of our articles and returned them to the driver. The latter continued to Pusan and handed over our pieces to our editorial chief. The driver said nothing about having been stopped.

Our chief in Pusan believed that the articles were original, untampered reports from Kwangju. He had no idea that they had been censored. Strict censorship prevented a single line of any articles from Kwangju from being published at the time. Still in Pusan, our driver received money to bring to us for additional expenses for our coverage in Kwangju, and he returned. He left the car at the military base and walked into the city to rejoin us downtown.

The man said not a word of the fact that all the photos had been taken from him. We came to know of this only several years later, when Mr. Lee told us that he had been so terrified by the agents who stopped him that he did not dare to open his mouth on the subject, not for years.

There was, at the time, no TV broadcasting out of Kwangju. That did not mean there could be no broadcasting into the city. Suddenly it was announced that there would be a special broadcast by acting President Choi Gyu Ha. It would in fact be the last broadcast to the citizens from outside. Thereafter there would be nothing until after the army came back in.

The president, for the record, defined the Citizens' Army as "rioters" who had occupied Kwangju. He urged them to surrender their weapons and to give themselves up to the martial-law authorities voluntarily, throwing themselves on the mercy of the latter. . . The broadcast lasted for about half an hour. During that time the president let his eyes rest on a manuscript in front of him and read the text. He lifted his head to face the camera only three or four times during the whole program. Later, we learned that President Choi came down to the local martial-law HQ, close to Kwangju, and that the authorities aired the broadcast exclusively into Kwangju. Some Seoul-based reporters were supposed to have been with him. Our guess was that the army would come back into the city on the night of May 25. Very soon.

The opposing force was nothing. The Citizens' Army, occupying the Provincial Hall, numbered about 300 in all, as a core force. Only about 100 of these had guns; that is, only 100 knew how to handle a gun. Against this small number of "rioters" the martial army prepared to mount a full-scale operation code-named *Chungjong* (Loyalty). For this purpose they planned to use tanks, armored vehicles, and aircraft. Thus, the army was using a sword to swat at a mosquito. It was laughable.

I thought that the Sejong Inn, where we were staying, was too dangerous to stay in overnight, given its central location. We finally pulled out of there on the afternoon of May 26. We took up lodgings at an inn in front of the HQ of Division 31 instead. That was where we spent the night of May 26.

It rained. As early as 10 P.M. the sky over Kwangju began to light up, as operations began. Flares lit the dismally rainy skies. Helicopters, tanks, and armored cars were on the move, roaring through the night. Finally, things calmed down at about 5 A.M. Noises stopped.

We hurried out. We headed back to the Provincial Hall, a distance of nine kilometers. Sporadic firing could be heard. Some mopping-up was continuing, it seemed. Five large helicopters buzzed overhead, making announcements through powerful speakers.

"Citizens of Kwangju! Be at ease! The rioters have been rounded up! Government officials are asked to go to your offices immediately you hear this announcement."

We took backstreets. Finally we reached the Provincial Hall at about 7 A.M. It had taken us almost two hours.

Thousands of troops already occupied the Provincial Hall. They gathered in front of the building. The city itself was silent, once the firing stopped. However, loudspeakers roared out announcements in metallic tones. Bits of paper cascaded from the skies. Everything had to magnify the "triumph" of the armed forces.

Bound Men Murdered

A massacre among brothers—men of the same nation slaughtering each other—was now to be presented as something else. The official term used by the Martial Law Command was "brilliant triumph."

We approached the Provincial Hall. Soldiers were clearing away the bodies of members of the Citizens' Army. The army men teamed up in pairs. Each team dragged a body. The corpses were dumped into a four-ton truck waiting at the main entrance to the Provincial Hall. The soldiers dragged the bodies by the legs, thus the heads scraped along the sidewalks, lolling to either side, left, right. Some were still bleeding. They had apparently been dead for a short time.

We took pictures. A lieutenant saw us and shouted out. "Hey! Who told you to move them like that! Let another soldier join in and take the head!"

Then he turned to us. "Who are you? Who the hell are you to come into this place where an operation is still going on?"

He spoke rudely from the word go. He was enraged because reporters were there.

Suddenly, there was a shrieking behind us. "You bastards! Kill us quickly! You coward soldiers! You dirty bastards, you bind us as captives and beat us to death." It was a young man. He was one of a group bound and laid on the ground. There were six of them, laid out on the cemented ground. We had paid no attention to them, believing them to be dead.

"Even on the battlefield, they do not kill captives. You swine!"

The group of youths had been laid face down on the concrete. Their wrists and ankles were bound together behind their backs. The rope went round their necks. The soldiers had trussed them up so tightly that their feet and faces were off the ground. Their bodies were stretched tight like bows. Four of them had been bound with a single length of electrical wire. They were strung together like fish.

Of the four youths bound by a single wire, the two at each end were already dead. Their heads drooped down far toward the concrete. Right next to one of those four were two more bound together and already dead. All these six young men wore long-sleeved shirts, without ties, and light-weight trousers. Their wrists had watch-marks on them, lighter patches of skin. Their watches must have been taken away at some point in the operation. Most of them lacked shoes. Some of the dead had no socks on either, and some had only one sock left. For sure, these youths fought with guns to the end against the marauding army, were captured, bound with wire, and beaten to death. They were all strongly built. Four of them seemed above 180 centimeters in height. One of the two bound and lying in the center seemed to be still just alive. He moved a trace. But he was almost gone. He did not lift his head. He did not spit out a word or a curse. The one who had shouted looked about twenty years old. Our first glimpse of him told us that he must be a college student. He still glared.

How could he bear the pain? I have never seen clearer and purer eyes than his. Sometimes, I see those glaring eyes in my dreams. They are so vivid then. If he was right, the Martial Command soldiers killed the captured members of the Citizens' Army with their hands, legs, and necks bound together.

At that moment an army specialist and two privates appeared. "Hey you little runt! Still alive! Don't worry. We'll take care of you. We will kill you soon enough!"

The soldiers trampled on the young man with their boots. They beat his face with the butts of their rifles. The young man was soon covered in blood. His head drooped helplessly. They were about to trample to death the last of the group still living.

This was too much to bear.

"Excuse us, soldiers! How could you do that to a living person? Isn't that too much?"

The specialist turned toward us. "Hey, who the hell let these civilians in here? Come, who was it? Who let you in? What are you doing here? Get them outta here!"

We were pushed back, prodded with rifle barrels, and ejected from the Provincial Hall premises.

I have no information as to what became of the young man. Presumably he was killed. We have no way to identify him. We had neither his last name, nor his first name. The young man, who had been so calm, must have shouted out suddenly, seeing us there, expecting us to help— we who did not look like soldiers. He used his last ounce of strength to shout out that the soldiers were killing bound captives. We had no chance to ask his name, nor anything else about him. We were chased away at gunpoint. How devastated that young man must have been. Had he survived that occasion, by some total piece of luck, he would have blamed us, no doubt. (Reading this through today, even now, I am ready to choke.)

I have never suffered more than at that time. I was totally helpless. I was unable to mount a protest, to save that dying young man. What was this? Human beings binding other human beings like fish and trampling them to death? And that in the presence of others?

We were thrust out at gunpoint, with our eyes still on the young man!

It took me sixteen years to recount this event for the first time.

This is human weakness. *This* is something I feared to remember.

The March of the Triumphant Generals

We went back outside the Provincial Hall. There were three or four police buses, big buses. We counted tens of captured Citizens' Army members, hunched on their knees on the cement ground. Hands on their heads, they were waiting to board the buses.

Trucks came. They carried coffins by the tens. My impression was that the Martial Law Command was moving out the coffins that had been in the Sangmu gymnasium nearby for five days. They were hauling them off to some unknown destination, I sensed. We were not allowed to come near. We could not count them, nor could we confirm how many had died in the latest action—the army's reentry and recapture of the Provincial Hall.

There was a buzz in the skies. Pretty soon, two helicopters came whirring in and landed right in the center of the square with its fountain in front of the Provincial Hall.

We watched while something like forty officers and men lined up, including those who had been carrying away the dead bodies. They lined up and saluted as one body to the person who got off the first helicopter.

It was the defense minister, Chu Young Bok. He wore an army uniform. With the minister, we saw, was a two-star general. Behind him came two brigadier generals—one star each. So that was four stars so far. Then came the second helicopter. Out of that came first a two-star general, then a brigadier general. Altogether seven stars had come down from the sky onto the square with its fountain.

A colonel briefed the minister. Standing rigidly at attention, he recounted what action was being taken. He mentioned the clearing away of the corpses. While this briefing continued, the generals stood by. They held their hands at their waists and grinned, continually looking around. They seemed, to my eyes, to be on the verge of bursting into speeches of self-congratulation. It was a triumph.

The defense minister now pointed with a baton at the provincial officials and police officers of South Cholla lining up at the main entrance of the Provincial Hall.

"Who are they?"

"Yessir!" responded the colonel. "They are the officials from the Provincial Hall and the Provincial Police Department."

"So, what are they doing now?"

"They arrived ten minutes ago. They responded to the announcement to return to their offices. We let them in after identifying them."

The defense minister nodded his head.

One of the generals who had accompanied the minister then stepped toward the men on duty. He spoke in a loud voice. It was clear that he wanted everyone to hear what he said.

"Look you men! You had to protect your place of work with your lives, no? You ran away instead and hid yourselves for days at a time. Now you appear, once the army recovered the Provincial Hall for you, risking their lives. How could you act like that? We are all fed by the same nation. One of us fights and bleeds. The other takes a rest at home."

"Is that all right with you?"

Some fifty or sixty people had to hear that condemnation, spoken out loud. Nobody talked back. The officials stood in silence and hung their heads, as if they had committed a deadly crime.

Yes, martial law prevailed at the time. Still, the attitude of the army men who accompanied the minister was unbearable. Just onlookers, we were angered. But the general kept right on talking, glaring fiercely. "The director of police should be somewhere. And how about the governor? Are they here yet?"

"We don't know."

"They are not taking responsibility. That is how they lost the Provincial Hall to just a handful of rioters! Watch out for them! Bring them to me when they arrive. I need to see their faces!"

"You Are the Director of Police?"

A tall man at the end of the line stepped forward.

"I am the director of the South Cholla provincial police department. I humbly offer my respects and beg for your consideration."

We wheeled about. This was the chief of police for the province. Another general turned sharply toward the police chief and stared at him.

"Ah! You are the police department chief? How did this situation come about? You lost the Provincial Hall in its entirety! So where have you been up to now?"

The general plunged on, speaking as brusquely as before.

The police chief rubbed his hands together, stumped for a reply.

"I'm awfully sorry. The demonstrators were so strong. Our police force could not keep control of the situation. It is rather fortunate that things have returned to normal at this point."

"Isn't it because the police could not cope, that we had to step in," cut in the general. "OK, now return to wherever you were."

The general added a word of ridicule at the departing back of the police director, as he headed for the main entrance of the Provincial Hall. "Hey! There goes the police department director. Check his ID!"

The arrogance of the generals did not stop there. People had started to gather in the square. The officers shouted out toward them. "Hey! Don't let those people gather in the square around the fountain there! Block all entries into the square immediately!"

Armored vehicles and tanks already blocked one side of the square.

A few army trucks were moving triumphantly into the open space.

Meanwhile, the police director was exiting from the scene. He oiled his hair, I noticed. He combed it back neatly and oiled it. He was a tall, handsome man. It was a little annoying that such a fine-looking person had to beg the generals for mercy, I thought. He gave the impression of being a well-mannered person. He looked to me a trace noble to be involved in an emergency. He wore a suit, but no tie. I looked again at his coiffure. His hair shone. We could watch the police chief, as he made a dignified exit, and entered the Provincial Hall by the main entrance.

At this moment one of the two-star generals motioned to an MP colonel to come over. He gave an order to the colonel. The latter walked to the main entrance and issued an order to a lieutenant there. Ten minutes later an MP jeep came hurtling out from inside the Provincial Hall, exiting through the main entrance. In the back sat two MP's, one on either side of the police department chief.

I was taken aback. I asked a lieutenant who was close at hand: "Wait a moment! Isn't that the police department head, who just entered the Provincial Hall a moment ago? What's going on?"

The lieutenant said not a word. He pretended not to hear us.

We asked again, "What's going on?"

The lieutenant spat out a word or two, obviously reluctantly. "Don't you see? The MPs are taking him away."

"Why did the MPs arrest the provincial chief of police? What has he done wrong?"

The lieutenant looked very annoyed. He was walking away from us. As he did so, he threw a remark back at us.

"We do not know what he has done wrong. Go and ask the generals over there!"

But we hardly dared do that. Who had access to the generals? They were surrounded at that point by young officers, who seemed to be their staff. All were in high spirits. They talked to one another and laughed out loud. If we walked up to them at this point and asked questions, we could be driven away at gunpoint, instead of getting an answer.

We were only about fifteen meters away. Still we almost had to shout.

"General! We are reporters. Why did the MPs arrest the chief of police? What is the charge against him?"

The two-star general, the one who had given the order to the MP colonel, ignored us. He spoke finally. "Oh! The director! We cannot let you know at this point. We will make an announcement through our spokesman. Can't you wait until then?"

He did not wait further, but yelled at his men. "Hey! What's going on here? How come the security got so loose? Keep unnecessary people from approaching here. What are you waiting for? Move!"

A group of officers and privates rushed toward us. We had to get out of there.

EPILOGUE

Henry Scott-Stokes and Lee Jae Eui

Onlookers

We would like to keep these remarks short and to limit them to comments on the texts—or the gaps in the texts—present in this book. Few will have the impression on reading these pieces that more than partial justice has been done to the truth. The press could not be everywhere. Perhaps 99 percent of the action in the side streets and alleys, the suburbs and outskirts of Kwangju was not covered by the media. Kim Yang Woo, up from Pusan, wrote that he and his team were the *only* Korean reporters on the spot in the last few days of the uprising. He was incorrect, but, yes, there were very few journalists around, whether Western or Korean, even in the heart of the city at the height of the battles there. Crucial facts were unknown and unknowable even years after the uprising. As we have seen, it took Brad Martin until the mid-1990s to establish the name of the "spokesman" for the students' and the citizens' army in Kwangju. It took fifteen years for interested parties to learn basic facts. Kim Yang Woo did not make public what he saw on May 27—see the end of Part Three—for sixteen years. We called him, to ask why he kept what he saw to himself.

"I was scared," he said. "I would be arrested, tortured . . ."

Lest We Forget

The facts are only now beginning to come out. Thus we felt this book had its place. Lee Jai Eui's *Kwangju Diary* is the comprehensive account of the Kwangju uprising. It doesn't take one far into people's innermost beings, however, as does Kim Chung Keun of *Dong-A Ilbo*, with his description of sleeping with two corpses and being too tired to get up and sleep somewhere else. Not, to repeat the point, that we have the facts at our fingertips. What, for example, was the name of the courageous boy who stood up on an armored personnel carrier—commandeered by the locals on May 21, as that light armored vehicle careered toward Provincial Hall—waving the national flag, bare-chested, with a bandana round his head, until he was shot down? We don't know. We do know the name of the young woman who uttered that gigantic cry—that scream for freedom—into the night in the early hours of May 27. She was Park Yong Sun, twenty-one, a student at Songwon Polytechnic College . . . But there are many unknowns. For example—and this is a key question having to do with the fighting around Provincial Hall on May 21—were the light machine guns set up on the roof of Chonnam University Hospital nearby, pointing at the Provincial Hall, ever fired? Some say yes, but very possibly no. Hundreds of people, no, thousands, were in a position to know. Still, we can't confirm what happened, not even with the resources available today, not even with the passage of time.

We support an idea put forward by Gebhard Hielscher of *Suddeutsche Zeitung*. He suggests in his piece that a Truth and Reconciliation Commission should be set up—along the lines of the South African body of that name—to determine what happened at Kwangju, who did what, when. The originator of the mass crime, Chun Doo Hwan, is not going to be brought to justice—President Kim Dae Jung amnestied him from prison where he was held on other charges. Thus, in fairness, there is no way to prosecute the lesser criminals. Very well, let other means be sought of getting at the truth. In probing into the events under apartheid, the South Africans made a rule: No one could be prosecuted for what he or she revealed. The idea was not to bring people to the bar of justice. It was to heal. That is what this book was for, at least in part. Almost all the contributors, to a greater or lesser degree, were wounded by the experience of covering Kwangju. Consider what Terry Anderson of the Associated Press had to say in his piece: "It left me with emotional and psychological scars that took years to heal." What, then, of the people of Kwangju? What scars remain there?

What Was Left Out

We would like to cite here two passages from *Kwangju Diary*, which describe the last day—the evening of May 26—before the military forced their way back into the city. One passage describes a scene in the big open square in front of the Provincial Hall; it confirms that the big underlying aspiration at Kwangju, quite as much as democracy—a value system with no deep historic roots—was the reunification of Korea, a nation that was divided by the Americans and the Soviets at the end of World War II, for no other reason than victors' arrogance:

> Darkness fell. In one corner of the square, a high school girl began to sing in a pure voice,
> *Our Wish is National Reunification.*
> *Our wish is national reunification*

Even in our dreams. Our wish is reunification
With whole dedication, reunification
Let's fulfill reunification.

The girl's voice flowed into the crowd. Finally the song echoed throughout the square.

Reunification that revives this nation
Reunification that revives this country
Reunification, come true soon
Reunification, come true.

This was just hours before the military reentered the city. That night:

In the darkness, the stench of rotting corpses wafted over the front of the
Provincial Hall and mixed with the spiced scent of the incense the militia
were burning. . . . Every light in the building was extinguished . . . At 2:30
A.M. the entire Provincial Hall went on red alert. Those who had been
nodding off to sleep quickly assumed their stations. The leaders—Yun
Sang Won, Kim Yong Chol, and Lee Yang Hyun—held each other's hands
in farewell. "We will see each other again in the next world," they said
before returning to their positions. (*KD*, pp. 163-166)

Those young fighters expected to die.

Yet—with the exception of Yun Sang Won, who was killed by a grenade in the auditorium of the Provincial Hall—no outstanding member
of the key group of student and worker leaders was killed. The last battle
for the Provincial Hall ended in about "ten to thirty minutes," according
to Lee Yang Hyun and others who were there, interviewed by Lee Jai
Eui. The students were no match for professionals. Called upon to surrender by soldiers who had taken up positions within the corridors of the
Provincial Hall, the students and other young activists immediately complied. Lee Yang Hyun has described the last moments of Yun Sang Won's
life. He and Yun were both in the auditorium, which is a large second-
floor room in the rambling Provincial Hall. They could see nothing out
of its windows in the dark. They discharged their rifles—the students
had M-1s—but they couldn't actually see anyone to shoot at. It was a
token effort. Neither used up a clip—a magazine—in the course of this
random firing. It was a haphazard effort. Mostly the students took refuge behind filing cabinets and desks, and when the moment came and
they faced a choice between surrender or being shot, they preferred to
come out with their hands up.

There was, in effect, no last battle. This is not the only aspect of the Kwangju uprising in its final phase that has escaped public attention. There are other unknowns. How many students and militants were in reality killed on that last night? Who were they? And how about casualties on the government side? How many soldiers were killed and wounded? Where? There is no official account, no record that we know of. What is clear, is that the incoming military—whatever their faults—did not seize the opportunity to round up everyone in sight and kill them. That such needless killings did occur, when people had surrendered, is not to be doubted in view of Kim Yang Woo's salutary report. But the overall view is that brutality and wanton murder was not the pattern in the early hours of May 27. So it seems. This does nothing to qualify the fact that such a pattern existed in the earlier phases of the Kwangju uprising, indeed provoked the rising for precisely those reasons. But once additional troops were involved—they came from the 20th Division, which was brought in for the job; and from the 31st Division, which was locally based—the initial shock-troop tactics used by the Special Forces sent into the city during the night of May 17–18 were in effect disavowed.

Yet another point that has been widely overlooked is that the local martial-law commander, the general in charge, was replaced on May 21, the day the government forces withdrew from the city. Instead of General Yun Heung Jung a new man, General So Jun Ryul, was put in overall command. General Yun—so he told Lee Jai Eui in a 1989 interview—was compelled to quit his post after he expressed reservations about the brutality of the troops under his command between May 18 and May 21 and made it clear to his superiors that he aimed to control the troops. It would be an error, we feel, always to attribute to the Korean military the heinous attributes that apply to the Special Forces' actions in their first days of horror in the city. To say this is to excuse nothing, but to suggest that it will be more fruitful to seek to understand than to condemn everyone in blanket fashion. All the more reason for a Truth and Reconciliation Commission to be set up and to hold its hearings, preferably within the five-year term of President Kim Dae Jung, which began in 1998 and ends in 2003.

Such a commission would do well, we believe, to be given the broadest terms of reference. It is customary to dismiss as irrelevant Chun Doo Hwan's claims that he declared full martial law because there were sudden, unspecified threats from North Korea. We do not know anyone who has found evidence to support that contention, which Chun used to try to excuse himself at his trial in 1996. Still, it would be absurd and mistaken to overlook and take no account of the fact that North Korea existed and has a record second to none in Asia as a belligerent power, over a period of nearly half a century since the Korean War ended in 1953. No other regime in Asia that we can think of has used the weapon of terrorism outside its own borders, as did Kim Il Sung's people, when they bombed a meeting in Rangoon, Myanmar in 1983, during a visit there by Chun—killing several of his ministers, including three known to us personally, Kim Jae Ik, Ham Pyong Choon, Lee Boum Sok—the first an economist, the second an ambassador, the third serving as foreign minister. We have ruled out North Korea as beyond the terms of this work, wishing to concentrate on events in Kwangju. But a commission to look into the Kwangju uprising would need to have terms of reference extending to the whole peninsula, not just to the south.

It seems that there was no threat from the north in the 1979–80 period or none that drew special attention from the United States. Those years were, despite events in Seoul and in Kwangju, a period of marked relaxation in the absolutely frosty relations between the United States and North Korea. In June 1980, one month after Kwangju, a U.S. congressman, Steve Solarz, visited Pyongyang, with three reporters in tow (Henry Scott-Stokes of the *New York Times*, Richard Bernstein of *Time* magazine, and David Tharp, a freelancer). Solarz was the first U.S. lawmaker to visit North Korea since the Korean War. Scott-Stokes was the third *New York Times* reporter to enter the north during that period (the two others were Harrison Salisbury and John Lee, who visited in 1971). With the benefit of hindsight one can see that this visit was part of a policy of gradual easing by the north, in granting Americans access to their country. Events were moving slowly in exactly the opposite direction to that predicated by Chun in fact. Not increased and sudden hostility but the opposite—a tentative, wary extending of invitations to Americans and, soon, South Koreans— was the pattern observed, for all that the end of the Cold War was still a half dozen years away. So Chun's actions in Kwangju look all the more awful. But *was* it always he who gave the orders? Or was it someone close to him trying to please the boss? Where *is* the evidence on these matters? There are still scores of officers alive, including Chun himself, who know the truth but have so far not chosen to speak.

Not that such an inquiry should consider personal issues alone: Who did what, when, and why. We feel it should spread into the realm of politics. Essentially, what value system raised its head that such terrible crimes were committed? There is a need to understand the values of Chun and his group. They were driven by extreme instincts of a kind we have seen before in history, for example in the mid-twentieth century in Europe. A left-wing leader of that era in Britain, Aneurin Bevan, had this to say about the extreme right:

> The divorce of parliamentary discussion from action brings discussion itself into contempt. If the deed lags too far behind the word then the word itself turns sour. This is the psychological basis of Fascism. Fascism is not a new social order in the strict sense of the term. It is the future refusing to be born. It is the fruit of an aborted democracy.

This quotation is taken from a 1999 publication, *The Penguin Book of Twentieth Century Protest*, edited by Brian MacArthur, associate editor of *The Times* of London. Isn't "aborted democracy" a fitting term for South Korea in the spring of 1980? A new constitution was to be approved, a president was to be elected by a direct vote of the people, and all of a sudden Chun Doo Hwan stepped forward and, in the words of one of our contributors, Sam Jameson, "then Chun Doo Hwan smashed it all" by dissolving the National Assembly, grabbing control of the media, and shutting down the universities, using paratroopers. Here was a case of extreme right-wing violence. To understand it, one has to probe a bit.

The Heirs of Park Chung Hee

There seem to have been three or four sources of the confusion that entered the minds of the military junta that suddenly emerged in December 1979 following Park's murder.

First, the fellows who came out on top after their putsch in Seoul on December 12 all owed their promotions to Park Chung Hee, South Korea's ruler for eighteen years. Park, who was a "father" to ambitious officers rising in the chain of command in South Korea, had served in the Japanese imperial army in his early youth, spoke Japanese fluently and had right-wing Japanese friends. He had imbibed ultranationalist Japanese thinking of the pre-World War II era, as was apparent from his creation of a new constitution in 1972, the infamous Yushin Constitution, that all but made him "emperor" for life in South Korea. At the same time Park had no truck with democracy—the values that were espoused by his great rival for power, Kim Dae Jung. Park was a mentor to ambitious Korean army men, notably Chun, a favorite of his. Thus a younger generation picked up his absolutist notions—for example, that army officers somehow incarnated virtue and had a responsibility to intervene in politics if corrupt politicians overstepped the mark, breaking the law if necessary, as Park himself had done, when he seized power in 1961 by staging a military coup d'état. The coup of December 12, 1979—for which Chun was sentenced to death in 1996 only for the sentence to be commuted to life in prison and then to a pardon—was an act of mutiny in the eyes of the law; it was also almost a photocopy of the type of military coup that young army officers staged repeatedly in Japan in the 1930s, brushing aside the chain of command. Faithful to such ideas, Chun and his fellows shoved out of the way scores of officers senior to them to grab power at the end of 1979. That they broke the law meant little to them, as they were serving the nation, in their own eyes.

Another influence on Chun and his fellows was Vietnam, where many of them served under U.S. command. Their contempt of civilians as people who just got in the way was learned in part in the field in South Vietnam, where the Koreans—some 50,000 soldiers served in South Vietnam—earned a reputation as by far the toughest troops on the U.S. side, not to be compared with the Americans. The Koreans would go into a village and break it apart, without the slightest compunction. They were trained to act that way. No Korean officer was ever prosecuted for crimes such as those committed by Lieutenant Calley at My Lai in South Vietnam. How did they feel, these men who returned from the mayhem of South Vietnam and then spent not just months but years biding their time in South Korean army camps on low pay, with nothing to do? They were informed that deadly enemies had taken up position in Kwangju, a city riddled with North Korean spies. They had to go in and clean up the place, just as if they were on one of those hamlet missions in South Vietnam where there were *supposed* to be no survivors. This was "zapping the gooks" of the type beloved by certain types of American military commanders in South Vietnam, or it was a Korean near equivalent given regional animosities fired up by Kyongsang-born commanders and soldiers against Cholla natives regarded as vermin who had to be cleared away. That was the spirit in which Special Forces paratroopers who came into Kwangju during the night of May 17–18, 1980, acted when they came to grips with old men and women who sought to protect youngsters. They smashed their heads in without compunction. But mainly they smashed the skulls of youngsters. We have terrible photos of the victims of these crimes against humanity, pictures which we have not published here. These techniques had been honed in Vietnam under U.S. command, overall command, to be sure, but nonetheless American command. The actions in Kwangju, including those at the outset—the very actions that triggered the uprising—were all but an extension of their field duties in Vietnam to some of the officers and men involved. They, Korean auxiliaries, had been on the losing side in Vietnam. It wouldn't happen *this time*, not in their own country. They were going to stick it to the commies this time around.

An Agent Behind Every Tree

A third influence on Chun's generation was their thinking on North Korea. They were convinced—or they professed to be convinced—that Kwangju was infested by "spies"—agents—from the North. Were there in fact any North Korean agents in Kwangju? We have no record of any, not even one. However, there was an episode up in Seoul at the time of the uprising that bears on this matter. All of a sudden, in the middle of the uprising, the South Korean press—at that time under the control of the military—broke the news that a spy had been arrested in Seoul. The newspapers, with *Chosun Ilbo* leading the way, reported on May 24 that a North Korean agent had been apprehended the day before at Seoul Station. This person, Lee Chang Yon, had been sent down from the North to foment the troubles in Kwangju, *Chosun Ilbo* and other newspapers reported on their front pages along with news stories on the "rioters" in Kwangju.

What had really happened? Like much else to do with Kwangju it has taken decades for the truth to come out. For many years no one could track down Lee. Then finally a Seoul monthly called *Mahl* (Word) carried a piece by Oh Yeon Ho in its August 1998 issue. Oh, the piece disclosed, had made repeated attempts over the years to contact "agent Lee." These efforts had finally come to fruition after the reporter struck a deal with prosecutors in Seoul under which "Lee" would not be pursued by them for anything he disclosed. He could not incriminate himself. Thereupon Lee, somewhat reassured, finally met his pursuer. He told reporter Oh the following story. He had indeed been a North Korean agent. He had come down to the South by boat, landing in South Korea on May 18. Almost immediately, he had been arrested. His real name was Hong Chon Sul. For years, he worked with the South Korean authorities, helping them to handle the cases of others from North Korea and staying out of sight. Hong said—and finally South Koreans got the truth—that his own original mission had nothing to do with Kwangju. The North Korean authorities, when they sent someone to the South, infiltrated them according to plans laid down at least three months in advance or as much as a year ahead. No one anywhere had known anything about the Kwangju uprising that far in advance. There was absolutely no connection, in short, between Hong and Kwangju. The story was a government—KCIA or army intelligence—concoction, picked up by the dutiful *Chosun Ilbo* and others in the Seoul press, but still a fabrication.

We have told the story at some length partly because it helps to illustrate the extreme difficulty that the authorities in Seoul had, even with all the massive resources at their command, in demonstrating any connection between the uprising in Kwangju and North Korea. In the end the military fell back on a trumped-up story which those responsible thereafter spent not just years but decades concealing from the public they were supposed to serve. Yet those close to Chun, and the man himself, perhaps sincerely believed that North Korean agents were a threat to the security of South Korea. Some who met him had the impression that Chun—he granted two interviews to Henry Scott-Stokes as *New York Times* correspondent—honestly suspected that behind every tree in Kwangju there must be a North Korean agent or at least a communist sympathizer in league with Kim Dae Jung. To meet in the flesh Chun came across as no arch-villain capable of living up to the stereotype of those in Kwangju who wanted to "tear Chun Doo Hwan to pieces"—in the words of the slogan used in Kwangju. He just seemed not very bright and not well informed. A joke that was current in Seoul at the time of his rise to power—not a remark that it would have been wise to shout out in public—had it that "if you put Chun Doo Hwan up against a wall the whole of the back of his head would touch the wall." There was nothing in his head or no room for brains. Not that being stupid makes a tyrant any less dangerous; quite to the contrary. Chun's lack of brains was surely one of the keys to the tragedy of Kwangju. Sending Special Forces paratroopers trained to kill with their bare hands into Kim Dae Jung's political stronghold—with orders to fix bayonets and charge student demonstrators—was crazy.

There is one final strand in these military men's world—still referring to the small group or junta that seized power in December 1979 in Seoul. To a degree, they were attracted by the same telltale chic of right-wing martial behavior seen elsewhere in modern times. We think of

Goering's heavy overcoat; of Mussolini's bulky uniforms and his love of black; and of the South American military man's attraction to braid as in the C-in-C's hat that Pinochet of Chile wore. The junta of Chun's generation were more restrained. They zipped about in fast, unmarked black cars with smoky-dark back windows. They favored a Spartan style in their offices and command posts, as we saw visiting Roh, Chun, and others in their group, all classmates from the military academy. But they were vain—the bald-headed, stocky Chun perhaps least of all—and self-conscious. The intelligent Roh all but strutted in those glory days when the new men came out in public for the first time—at a ceremony held close to the DMZ in August 1980, to mark Chun's retirement from the armed forces, attended by foreign correspondents. These men's jokey, brash style is described by Kim Yang Woo in his piece at the end of Part Three. The generals surrounded themselves with lackeys and subordinates to whom they showed smiling faces while they barked out cheerful orders that meant torture or death.

How out of touch they were, these men who dreamed up a little exercise in Kwangju that they named "Fascinating Vacations." They could not prevail. They could not hold onto office for more than half a dozen years as a junta. What went wrong for them? Surely Kwangju was the crux. Chun broke norms of civilization. Norman Thorpe, one of our contributors, wrote in his piece as follows: "A government's foremost duty is to protect its citizens. To kill them is an atrocity, and to deny the deaths is an even greater injustice."

A Weight of Responsibility

Where does ultimate responsibility for what happened at Kwangju reside? We know now, though the truth was kept hidden for ten years, how the incoming Reagan administration made a deal with Chun Doo Hwan in late 1980, according to which the new Korean president agreed to spare the life of Kim Dae Jung in return for an invitation to Washington, D.C., in early 1981 as President Reagan's state guest. That was a thoughtful move by the Reagan entourage in the main, but also by officials from the outgoing Carter administration.

We return to the question of the responsibility for the Kwangju uprising itself. As to the first phase, the onset of brutalities in the street on Sunday, May 18, culminating in the open shootings of civilians on the night of Tuesday, May 20 around Kwangju Station and in front of Provincial Hall on Wednesday, May 21, the blame lies on those—presumably Chun Doo Hwan and those around him—who took the decision to send in the Special Forces, trained in a particular way for the occasion. How this happened and who precisely took what decisions is still a bit of a mystery, hence that need for what we are calling a Korean Truth and Reconciliation Commission.

As to the second phase, the attack on the city on the early morning of Tuesday, May 27 the responsibility—the ultimate responsibility we should say—appears to lie primarily with the United States government, essentially the Pentagon, rather than the Korean martial-law authorities, to judge by the contents of a letter printed by the *New York Times* on July 22, 1982. It was written by Ambassador William H. Gleysteen, who was of course the U.S. envoy to South Korea at the time of the Kwangju uprising, and it read in part:

> Although national security interests properly dominated our actions during the turmoil of 1979–80, most informed Koreans, including opposition elements, appreciated the role the U.S. played in trying, initially, to achieve a more broadly based government in Seoul and, later, to counter political repression.
>
> These efforts were constrained by our lack of overwhelming influence in Korean domestic affairs and by the fact that we were dealing with sovereign authorities, not colonial subjects. Nor were we helped by the impatience of certain dissident elements, whose lack of restraint played a tragic role in the political crackdown of May 17, 1980. To acknowledge, as I do, that the result of U.S. efforts was in many ways disappointing is not to say they were wasted or amounted to strengthening authoritarian forces. Throughout, the U.S. played a moderating role, resented only by extremists.
>
> Mr. Cumings's comments [Ed: he refers to a July 6 Op-Ed article, "The Devil to Pay in Seoul," published by the *New York Times* and written by Professor Bruce Cumings] about General Wickham are misleading. *The general, with my concurrence, permitted transfer of well-trained troops of the twentieth R.O.K.A. Division from martial-law duty in Seoul to Kwangju because law and order had to be restored in a situation that had run amok following outrageous behavior of the Korean Special Forces, which had never been under General Wickham's command.* (Editors' italics)
>
> We were appalled by events in Kwangju, we encouraged cooperation with church groups, which at one point seemed close to negotiating a peaceful compromise, and we contributed significantly to the humane way order was restored in the city.

The map supplied by Lee Jai Eui (page xxvii) shows which units were engaged in the task of taking Kwangju by storm. Was the action "humane"? Was "the situation amok" within the city at the time? We would like readers of the contributions printed here, including our own, to draw their conclusions. The Special Forces units that had perpetrated the original horrors, we note, came back into the city, vengeance in their hearts, with the 20th Division. See the arrows in the map. This was a Tiananmen Incident rounded off by a decision by the United States—a foreign power that had the honesty to be open, if not to apologize.

Twenty years later, what can we say? There are no means to restore the dead to life. Lee Jai Eui has in his possession another map, not printed here, showing the spots, here and there around the city of Kwangju, in the environs, in hedges and ditches and obscure places, where unmarked graves have been found, victims of the atrocities in Kwangju whose fates remain unknown to this day. These lost souls were dumped and abandoned like so many stuck pigs or quarantined carcasses. Only a Dante could do justice to them—here is how the poet Dante Alighieri (1265–1321) greeted those abandoned spirits for whom there must yet still be hope in his *Divine Comedy, Purgatorio xxxiii: 145*. The poet considered that they were still:

> *Puro e disposto a salire alle stelle.*
> *Pure and made apt for mounting to the stars.*

INDEX

ABOUT THE EDITORS

Henry Scott Stokes was born in the United Kingdom on June 15, 1938. He was educated at Winchester College and at New College, Oxford. He served the British press in Tokyo (*The Financial Times*, *The Times*) and Seoul, and later *The New York Times* as Tokyo and Seoul Bureau Chief from 1978 to 1983. He is a journalist and writer living in Tokyo. He has 30 years of experience of covering Korea.

Lee Jai Eui is currently the foreign investment manager for Kwangju City. He participated in the May 1980 uprising at the age of twenty-five while a third-year student at Chonnam University, for which he served a ten-month prison sentence for violating martial law. He is the author of *Kwangju Diary* (1999), and does volunteer work as director of International Affairs at Kwangju Citizens' Solidarity.